FINANCIAL FITNESS FOR LIVING TOGETHER

FINANCIAL FITNESS FOR LIVING TOGETHER

Elizabeth S. Lewin, CFP

Facts On File, Inc.

Financial Fitness for Living Together

Facts On File, Inc.
11 Penn Plaza
New York NY 10001

Library of Congress Cataloging-in-Publication Data
Lewin, Elizabeth
Financial fitness for living together / by Elizabeth S. Lewin.
p. cm.
Includes index.
ISBN 0-8160-3281-5
1. Unmarried couples—Finance, Personal. I. Title
HG179.L473 1996 96-5792
332.024'0652—dc20

Facts On File books are available at special discounts when purchased in bulk quantities for businesses, associations, institutions or sales promotions. Please call our Special Sales Department in New York at (212) 967-8800 or (800) 322-8755.

Cover design by Semadar Megged
Printed in the United States of America

VB FOF 10 9 8 7 6 5 4 3 2 1

This book is printed on acid-free paper.

For two very young friends, Joshua and Sarah, and for five happy seniors, Annie, Bob, Frank, Marie, and Ruth—all of whom I had the pleasure of meeting while researching this book and all of whom you will meet in its pages.

ACKNOWLEDGMENTS

My special appreciation to Bernard Ryan, Jr., whose contributions over the years have made this all possible; Seymour Goldberg, C.P.A., M.B.A., J.D., Ingber & Goldberg P.C., Garden City, N.Y., who read and reread chapters on pensions and estate planning; Virginia and Henry Bright, retired actuaries formerly with Watson Wyatt Worldwide; and to Budd S. Schwartz, who checked and rechecked all the numbers and whose knowledge and suggestions were greatly appreciated.

I would also like to thank Terry Boggis, Center Kids Administrator, Lesbian and Gay Community Services Center; Attorney Margaret Cassella, Cassella & Rothchild P.C., Hartford, Conn.; Mark Doyle and Suzanne Gingerich, Social Security Administration; Marjorie Marlin, Executive Director, Community Housing Corporation, Raritan, N.J.; and last but certainly not least all the people who shared their lives with me.

CONTENTS

CHAPTER ONE

WHY THIS BOOK?

This book is a guide to financial fitness for unmarried people who are living together—a guide for your financial and estate planning. It is not a substitute for legal advice. In its pages, you will meet a variety of people who live together and you will find out how they have arranged their financial lives.

Probably the chief reason why I have written this book is because unmarried couples do not have many of the financial advantages and legal protections that married couples enjoy. To put it simply, the law provides for married couples. If one dies or becomes incapacitated or if the relationship ends in divorce, the law is ready to help. Corporations, as employers, have long provided benefits to the spouses and children of their workers, in the forms of health insurance, life insurance, and pension benefits. Most companies do not make these benefits available to couples who live together without specific legal documentation or recognition of their relationship. As a result of this difference in their situation, those who live together as partners must create their own safety nets, prepare pertinent legal documents, and enter into independent financial and estate planning.

To demonstrate some of the need, think about how we handle divorce. If one party starts selling off assets and pocketing the profits, restraining orders roll off the judge's bench with scarcely a ripple. In many states, the court starts the proceedings with the assumption that no matter how much each spouse contributed to the union in terms of financial resources or property, the split must be made generally "equitable."

But look at what happens if two people who are living together decide to break up. It can quickly become a nightmare. No divorce court exists to handle the case. No uniform rules apply. No assumption of fairness is made. Each case is different, handled by the participants themselves or by lawyers who entirely lack legal guidelines.

Or think about benefits. Some municipal governments and some corporations have extended benefits to the domestic partners of employees. Health insurance is the most important. But in the vast majority of situations, each partner must buy health insurance, which is a big expense.

Another example is what happens when a death occurs. A live-together partner has no automatic legal rights to an inheritance. Unless a will carefully provides for the partner, he or she can end up with nothing while the deceased partner's next of kin lays claim to—and is awarded—the estate. And, by the same token, one whose partner is hospitalized may find himself or herself excluded from decision-making authority and even from visiting privileges if a medical power of attorney is lacking.

All of this means that financial planning is essential for anyone who lives with another person outside the bonds of matrimony. And, if you own a home together or share property or debt, agreements and contracts—in addition to financial planning—are important to protect each of you. They become vital the moment you split up or either of you dies, for you have no other legal protection.

Who are live-togethers?

According to the U.S. Census Bureau, well over 4 million households can be identified as those of unrelated adults. Who are these people who are living together? Unmarried male-female couples number some 3.6 million. The balance are same-sex couples.

Some observations:

- Gays and lesbians comprise many same-sex households, and many are long-established. Often they include children from a former marriage, other biological children of one of the partners, or adopted children. None is able to get Social Security benefits when a partner is disabled or dies. Usually no pension benefits are available. Without proper estate planning, no inheritance is forthcoming.
- Couples who have been through divorce or widowhood are among the heterosexual group. They do not remarry because, until they reach certain ages, they may lose the pension benefits left by a deceased spouse, Social Security benefits, alimony from a divorced spouse, or a civil service or military pension.
- Couples who have figured out their tax situation and realize that live-togethers who earn approximately equal incomes are each permitted to earn higher incomes, before their Social Security benefits are taxed, than those who are married and file joint returns. The so-called "marriage penalty" deprives those who are legally married of this advantage. In addition, individual retirees are permitted to have more earned income, before their Social Security benefits are considered taxable, than retired married couples are permitted.
- Couples who want to protect their estates for the children of former marriages. Even if they must lose the unlimited marital deduction that can reduce or avoid federal estate taxes, many widows, widowers, and divorced people keep their financial affairs separate from their partners' lest they muddy the waters. They also simply want to avoid antagonizing children from previous marriages who may resent a stepparent's gaining assets that the children feel belong to them. If there is real hostility toward a live-together situation, trusts should be set up carefully to protect such offspring.
- Others over age 65 may be receiving Supplemental Security Income (SSI) and will lose this benefit if they remarry and, as a result, their incomes exceed certain limits. In 1996, the SSI pays up to $470/month for an individual and $705/month for a couple. In addition, for those eligible, most states add money to the basic federal rate.
- Couples do not marry because each owns a home and each may take the one-time $125,000 capital-gains exclusion on the profit from the sale of a residence. As a married couple, they would get only one exclusion.
- Many unrelated Americans who are single find it more affordable and congenial to live together in shared housing. Such "alternative housing" has been on the rise since the 1980s. About 75 percent of Americans over age 65 own their own homes and seek ways to maintain them.

These nontraditional living arrangements can be a boon to both young and old. A large platter of choices for living can mean better housing for less money, income from existing housing, opportunities for companionship, freedom from isolation, improved security, and a useful exchange of services among parties. Alternatives to the "normal" household thus make it possible for more people to gain, or to continue, the enjoyment of independence, privacy, and other rewards that come with having a place of one's own.

Experts on the elderly say that 25–30 percent of those who now live in nursing homes could live independent lives if shared housing was available to them. Two types of services can help:

1. *Match-up programs.* These help the home owner who has space available find a compatible "home seeker" who can pay rent or provide some services, such as housekeeping and/or cooking, in exchange for a reduction in rent.

2. *Group shared residences.* In these a number of people who are not otherwise related live cooperatively in a single large dwelling. Usually they share the cooking, laundry, housekeeping, and maintenance, but in some homes these are provided.

In recent years, the proportion of the adult population that is currently married has gone down. The proportion of unmarrieds—those who never married or are widowed, or divorced—has gone up. Now with the aging of the baby boomers and the increased longevity of all Americans, we are likely to see far more older single people as we near and enter the 21st century than in any preceding generation. In addition, the fact that the baby boomers have had greater experience with group living arrangements may also produce more non-traditional households than in the past. The women of the baby-boomer generation, in particular—because their ranks account for more divorces, fewer offspring, increased longevity, and iffy retirement incomes—are likely to find that alternative living arrangements play a greater role in the middle and later years.

Introducing several live-togethers

To help illustrate many of the points made in these pages, a number of live-together couples are introduced. With varied backgrounds and lifestyles, their financial situations and experiences are typical of many found all across America. Say hello to them now.

○ ○ ○

DAVE AND DICK

They live in a New England village, population 1,242, near a town of 10,000 and 40 minutes from a major city. During the first five years of their 42 years together, both worked for an insurance company, Dave as a physician and Dick in the back office. In the late 1950s, they bought a home for $17,500. Dave, who was making at least three times Dick's salary, paid most of the bills, while Dick bought the groceries and covered his personal expenses for clothing and gifts.

In 1960, Dave became a "country doctor" in private practice in their village. He converted an abandoned one-room schoolhouse into his office, practicing there for 28 years as a board-certified internist and treating patients from obstetrics to geriatrics. Within four years after starting his practice, he had paid off the mortgages on both the house and his office.

Dave and Dick never formalized any division of expenses until they retired. They simply maintained separate checking accounts. Some years back, Dick found a small seaside home on a section of rugged coastline. It was reasonably priced at $17,000. Not wanting to borrow from Dave, he borrowed from a friend. Sixteen years later, he sold the house for $115,000, and invested the proceeds through a stockbroker.

At that time, Dave and Dick decided to merge their savings and checking into joint accounts—including the brokerage account. They kept only their retirement accounts separate.

In their village, Dave's office was only half a mile from their home. His mother moved in with them in her senior years, then was diagnosed as an Alzheimer's sufferer. For her last six years, as the disease progressed and she had to use a wheelchair, Dave tended her in the morning, stopped in again after his hospital rounds, and returned home for lunch. When help was needed, he hired it. If he was called out by an emergency in the late afternoon or evening, Dick took over after coming home from work, feeding Dave's mother, helping her in the bathroom, getting her ready for bed. "I never asked him to do that," says Dave. "He just did it." After she died in 1976, Dave and Dick built a new home on four and a half acres just at the edge of the village. By including a den, bedroom, and bath served by a walk-out basement door, it meets their only concern—long-term care—for it could house a nurse-caretaker comfortably.

When it came to personal possessions, Dave and Dick simply enjoyed what they had. If Dave wanted to buy an expensive item—say, new stereo equipment—he never asked Dick to pay half. He knew he was in the better position to pay for it. His attitude was, "It's something we'll enjoy, and I want it—in fact, we both want it—so I'll get it."

Both men have been active in their town. Dick is currently the town treasurer—a job without a computer and with minimum pay, but he does it to keep busy. Dave served as town health officer for many years, and continues to work part-time in an emergency facility.

○ ○ ○

BOB AND EVAN

Evan and Bob met nine years ago. Both are now in their late thirties. Evan owned a condominium in New York City. Bob moved in, and they shared all expenses. At first, each maintained a separate checking account, and they set up an "us" account to pay for entertainment. Now they operate the household on a single joint checking account, but maintain separate savings and investment accounts. Evan has sold the condo, and they now rent an apartment with the lease in both names; the law permits one unrelated person to co-sign a lease.

Although their incomes are not the same (Bob earns almost double what Evan earns), they collect artwork together, charging it on a joint credit card so as to get airline frequent-flier mileage, and paying for it out of the joint checking account. Bob often moves money into the joint account from his money-market account to help pay for the art, and they do formal bookkeeping on a computer program.

○ ○ ○

BOBBIE AND JACK

Bobbie is in her late 60s. Jack is over 70. They have lived together for several years.

Bobbie found herself divorced after 30 years of marriage to a man who had risen through management to become a senior executive of a large corporation. They lived in Scarsdale, a posh New York City suburb in the heart of Westchester County. In the divorce settlement, fixated on getting the large, four-bedroom house, Bobbie took it in exchange for her rights to part of her ex-husband's large corporate pension plan.

Jack was widowed 10 years ago. He has three grown children and is a successful real estate developer, still actively managing his investments in real estate.

○ ○ ○

MAUREEN AND CINDY

Now both 38 years old, they met in high school, then went to college together. They have lived together since right after college, in 1980. Initially, they rented apartments, then a house. They bought a house together in 1989.

Cindy has worked for eight years in the computer information and technology department of a prestigious Ivy League college. Before that, she and Maureen both worked for the same company, but Cindy wanted out of the stressful corporate life after her father died when he was 52 and she was diagnosed with thyroid cancer.

Cindy and Maureen wanted to bring up a child. They considered adoption. Then, after careful thought, they made the decision to try artificial insemination. Who would be the mother? Careful planning brought them to the decision that one of them would stay at home with the child after birth. But the one to have the child would have to be the one who worked, because the one who had a job could get health insurance, under the employer's group plan, that would cover the child. Since Cindy was earning more than Maureen, they decided that Cindy would have the child. Joshua was born in November 1992. Since then, the university has extended coverage to same-sex partners and Maureen also decided to have a child. Sarah has now joined the family.

❍ ❍ ❍

THE GOLDEN GIRLS AND GUYS—MARIE, FRANK, BOB, ANNIE, AND RUTH

Ranging in age from 64 to 88, these five are unrelated, except for the fact that they live together in a shared home in New Jersey. All five live on Social Security and with the addition of a small pension in some cases.

The home was built through the efforts of the Cooperative Housing Corporation, an entirely volunteer, not-for-profit organization that was founded in 1987 to provide affordable housing alternatives for older people who are on low or moderate incomes. The house was the first to be designed and built for this purpose. It provides each of them with a spacious bedroom and a private bathroom, which they furnish. Each room has its own small refrigerator—important not only for snacks and soft drinks but for storing medications without mix-up. The shared space includes a large living room, dining room, kitchen, laundry room, powder room, and a large deck. Furnishings in the shared space belong to the house.

Using funds paid in equal shares by the group, the Cooperative Housing Corporation pays a part-time housekeeper, Nancy, who comes in five days a week for three hours (see chapter 5: Your Cash Flow and Your Spending Plan). She also stays longer on Thursday, as she does the food shopping for the house.

The residents take turns making dinner five nights a week. Frank cooks on Monday, Marie on Tuesday, etc. On weekends, they fend for themselves. All have family in the area so some spend the weekends away from "their home."

The Golden Girls and Guys plan their menus a month in advance. If Marie wants to make her meatloaf, she must tell Nancy, the housekeeper, about it the week before, ordering precisely the ingredients she will need.

"They are eating better," says Marjorie Marlin, executive director of the Cooperative Housing Corporation, "than they would if each was living alone. Many older people, living alone, are on what I call the 'tea and toast syndrome.' When a friend or adult child calls, they say "'I'm fine today, I'm just having tea and toast.'"

The Golden Guys and Gals, on the other hand, have become so proficient and creative in their cooking that they are thinking of putting together a "shared housing" cookbook.

The newest member is Ruth. She moved in from a nursing home where she lived for four years, and where the cost to Medicaid was $45,000 a year. Now the cost to the taxpayers is $4,500—and Ruth will tell you, in no uncertain terms, that she moved from "hell to heaven."

Cooking is not the only responsibility. Each member of the household is also responsible for light chores and for sharing communal furniture and appliances. They have no set regimen and live quite independently as individuals. Annie spends four days at the senior center. Bob volunteers at a local food bank and also handles the basic exterior maintenance—anything that does not require a ladder or heavy lifting. Frank has undertaken the pleasant chore of baking bread. He also helped Bob design and build a set of exterior stairs.

All five are physically active and mentally alert. They insist on their independence and each has plenty to look forward to on getting up each morning.

Finally, as Marjorie Marlin points out, a home such as this can be multigenerational, including a broad range of ages (see chapter 11: Housing—What Kind of Roof Is over Your Heads?). Or it can be set up for the disabled. Shared homes have been created for those with AIDS, cerebral palsy, the mentally retarded, etc.

❍ ❍ ❍

CHAPTER TWO

SETTING GOALS FOR YOUR FINANCIAL FITNESS PROGRAM

A new house?
Retirement and travel during "the golden years"?
Who knows?

Only you and your live-together partner know where you want your financial fitness program to take you. And only you two can put your goals on paper, designing your program so it does indeed reach the goals you are dreaming of.

Putting your goals down on paper is important. It helps you to articulate, scrutinize, weigh, and judge them. It enables you to:

- Examine your values with your partner, and clarify them, so you can put priorities in order.
- View money as more than something to have and use here and now. Most people have very little concept of money for the future, for the lengthy trip through Europe next year or the year after, for the new car that's sure to be needed to replace the present car, for the retirement that always seems so far in the distance. Most will think of such things next year—or the year after. But then it will be too late.
- Establish a framework for financial stability. The basic framework involves not only a steady source of income but seeing that it increases each year to keep up with inflation and with your needs and desires. In addition, it must include money set aside for such minor emergencies as getting the car repaired or such major demands as an unexpected medical emergency. And it must incorporate some form of protection in case of disability or death.
- Utilize your income to the best advantage. It helps you to devise ways to use your available resources toward maximum saving, so you can achieve your desired goals. Remember that you are working and you want your money working for you as well.
- Take control of your money and your life by putting *you* in charge.
- Accept the reality of your particular situation, so you can learn not to spend against an impossible dream.

How do you establish your own goals?

Start by asking yourselves, What is important to us? Your goals reflect your value system—usually the attitudes you were raised with. For most of us, values are based on what is desirable and worthy. And, for most of us, value systems aren't usually very flexible.

Values are closely tied to ego fulfillment. And ego fulfillment is tied closely to money. Money, in turn, is a major measure of success. And success brings the circle around to fulfillment.

The fulfillment of one's ego, and one's involvement in his or her success, may often leave little room for recognition of what's going on with a partner's success—or lack of it. Often success and ego fulfillment are communicated through material signs—a Mercedes-Benz automobile, Gucci shoes, a Louis Vuitton bag, a Hermes scarf, or a ski chalet in Aspen. They demonstrate that one is successful in society, for one can afford all the trappings. People who have all the trappings may not talk about such signs very much, but they are expressing their values through them.

Within the framework of goals, based on your values and attitudes, you will have priorities—goals that are most important.

Values dictate behavior

Now comes the catch. How do you actually behave when it comes to finances? If your behavior is not consistent with your values, attitudes, and goals, you are off base.

Say you've been raised with a value system that holds that owning a house is of prime importance: Home ownership is a must. Such a goal may dictate that you save $200 a month toward that goal. But say your behavior is not consistent with your goal: You decide you cannot afford to save $200 a month for the house. Or you put some other goal first. Your behavior reveals that your goal of buying a house is not your top priority, after all.

Because their desires often exceed their resources, most people need to establish priorities among their financial goals. To do that, you must take a good, hard look at your goals and at your behavior. Is your behavior helping you to achieve your goals, or hindering you? Are you faced with a conflict? Any individual, or pair of individuals, may have two goals that cannot both be satisfied because achieving one prevents achieving the other.

Important: Don't try to do it alone. Get your partner into the act. If you have just begun a relationship, talking about the future, and the goals you each have in mind, is vital. Each of you has come into the relationship with your own set of values and patterns of saving—or not saving—for the future.

Short-, mid-, and long-range goals

What is a short-range goal? Something you want to do within the next year. Pay off a loan, maybe, or plan Christmas shopping money in advance, rather than paying off bills through the winter and spring. Or buy a vacation in advance, so you can really enjoy it instead of moaning as the Visa and MasterCard charges mount up.

A mid-range goal? Something you want to do in three to five years. Get a better car, perhaps. Buy a weekend or vacation home. Take a trip abroad.

Long-range? The big-ticket items that spread out over the years. Education. Retirement.

Agreement on goals

Time is one dimension of goals. Commitment is another. Certainly you and your partner must talk freely, openly, and at length about goals. If you each communicate your individual financial objectives and reach an understanding about them, you can avoid many arguments and financial crises. Many, many misunderstandings about money develop simply because people haven't let their goals be known.

Remember that the primary objective of a viable financial plan is the accumulation of money or capital. Everything else in your plan is directed to achieving this goal.

Saving to meet goals—especially long-term goals—requires a knowledge of saving and investing. You will find it invaluable to seek saving and investing vehicles that match your individual goals. That means that you must carefully consider the time frame for your goals and build your plans to meet it (see chapter 7).

You must not only define your goals and align your saving and investing with the time frame you set for achieving them, but you must also follow through on details. Is buying a home a top goal? Take the time now to estimate what it will cost. Use today's dollars, then update the figure once a year, just as you update your spending plan—right down to the weekly expenditure for groceries—to meet inflation.

What you are trying to avoid, of course, is waking up one day to find that you have to borrow to meet a goal such as retirement. Make such an avoidance one of your primary goals.

Life is change, and goals and needs keep changing, too. Check them every year. Never feel that you must stay locked into a specific goal. But, by the same token, never use the money set aside for a medium- or long-term goal to pay for something you want now.

List your goals. Give each a dollar amount and a time frame.

Worksheet I:
SAVING FOR A SPECIFIC GOAL

A. GOAL	____________
B. DATE NEEDED	____________
C. NUMBER OF YEARS TILL GOAL	____________
D. AMOUNT NEEDED	____________
E. MONEY ALREADY SET ASIDE	____________
F. AMOUNT MONEY SET ASIDE WILL GROW TO AT ______% (see Exhibit 2)	____________
G. AMOUNT STILL NEEDED	____________
H. AMOUNT TO BE SAVED PER YEAR AT ______% INTEREST (see Exhibit 3)	____________

Exhibit 1
INFLATION FACTOR TABLE

YEARS BEFORE GOAL IS MET	3% INFLATION	5% INFLATION	7% INFLATION
1	1.03	1.05	1.07
2	1.06	1.10	1.14
3	1.09	1.16	1.23
4	1.13	1.22	1.31
5	1.16	1.28	1.40
6	1.19	1.30	1.50
7	1.23	1.41	1.61
8	1.27	1.48	1.72
9	1.30	1.55	1.84
10	1.34	1.63	1.97
11	1.38	1.71	2.10
12	1.43	1.80	2.25
13	1.47	1.89	2.40
14	1.51	1.98	2.58
15	1.56	2.08	2.76

Exhibit 2
ASSUMED RATES OF RETURN
(less estimated inflation)

ESTIMATED RATE OF RETURN LESS INFLATION	Years to Goal 5	8	10	12	15	20	25
2%	1.10	1.17	1.22	1.27	1.35	1.49	1.63
3%	1.16	1.27	1.34	1.43	1.56	1.81	2.10
4%	1.22	1.37	1.48	1.60	1.80	2.19	2.66
5%	1.28	1.48	1.63	1.80	2.08	2.65	3.39
6%	1.34	1.59	1.79	2.01	2.40	3.21	4.30

Exhibit 3
ASSUMED DISCOUNT FACTOR

DISCOUNT RATE FACTOR	Years to Goal 5	8	10	12	15	20	25
2%	.192	.116	.091	.074	.057	.041	.031
3%	.188	.112	.087	.070	.053	.037	.027
4%	.184	.108	.083	.066	.049	.033	.023
5%	.180	.104	.079	.062	.046	.030	.020
6%	.177	.101	.075	.059	.042	.027	.018

CHAPTER THREE

KEEPING RECORDS: THE FOUNDATION OF YOUR FINANCIAL FITNESS

○ ○ ○ ○

Where are your life insurance policies?
Where is the certificate of title to your automobile?
Where is your health-care power of attorney?

○ ○ ○

Do you know the answers to basic questions like these? You do if you have a good record-keeping system in place. It is an important part of your financial fitness program, providing a paper trail that can help you, your partner, and your legal and financial advisers to locate all the people and all the documents that together make up your financial life.

Live-togethers are not protected by the same laws that apply to married couples. That means the location of important documents can make a tremendous difference. What if no one knows where to look for a will that names a partner as guardian of a child? What if your partner is seriously ill in the hospital and a health-care power of attorney cannot be located? You could find yourself unable to make medical decisions for your partner. You might even find that you were excluded from visiting your partner in the hospital. That has happened in more than one case.

Financial fitness means being able to prove what you spent, where you spent it, what you spent it for, and how it improved or failed to improve your financial situation. To prove all this, you need records—not a mountain of paper, but a practical system for keeping track of financial matters, and important papers related to them, over a long time.

Your record-keeping should begin with your first job and continue through your retirement. Record-keeping can be a simple file system containing various papers, some permanent, some semi-permanent, some temporary. For instance, obviously you keep a life insurance policy as long as it is in force. You keep automobile papers as long as you own the car. You keep home-improvement receipts until you sell the house and want to prove how much extra capital you have put into it over the years. You keep income-tax records for at least three years, until the statute of limitations runs out (an audit by the Internal Revenue Service [IRS] may go back no more than three years; however, you should keep your final IRS return for each year in a permanent file; it makes an excellent financial history).

A costly failing

Not having a good system of record-keeping can be embarrassing. It can also be costly. Some examples:

- A misplaced, and unfindable, life insurance policy can mean that a beneficiary waits months to receive the proceeds on thc policy.
- An inactive bank account can be taken over by the state. Banks regularly run local newspaper advertisements listing the names and last known addresses of thousands of customers whose accounts have been inactive for a specified period. If an account is entirely inactive for a certain number of years (the period varies from state to state), and if the bank is unable to locate the owner after placing advertising that lists the last known address, the state gets the unclaimed money. Billions of dollars are held in state treasuries simply because no one can trace the assets to their rightful owners.
- A city or town is legally entitled to seize property on which taxes have not been paid. If you own property, move away, and forget to tell the tax assessor where you have moved to, and then fail to pay the taxes (every year, an astonishing number of people do just that), the town may auction your property to the highest bidder and keep the proceeds.
- A state that levies a personal-property tax can refuse to license a car or boat on which the tax has not been paid. One of my clients sold his boat but did not save the bill of sale. Months later, the state demanded the personal-property tax due on the boat. To prove it had been sold and he owed no tax, my client had to trace the boat dealer to Florida and get another receipt.
- You can find yourself trying to reconstruct the history of an illness a year or more after you recuperated. Most doctors' offices now ask for payment at the time of your visit. They leave it up to you to handle major medical and other insurance claims. Make a habit of getting a photocopy of all receipts and claim forms and filing all claims promptly, then filing copies carefully.
- Records can be replaced, but it takes time, effort, and postage to replace them. Take stock certificates: If you own more than one or two, you should maintain an accurate list by name, number of shares, purchase price, and date of purchase. Compiling such a list after your certificates have been lost, stolen, or destroyed can be a horrendous task, and you may end up with incomplete results. Just one aspect of the headache is the fact that, before any company will issue a replacement certificate, you must sign an affidavit that the certificate was destroyed. You must also put up a surety bond, which may cost as much as 3 percent of the current market price.

> **DON'T DILLY-DALLY ON PAYING**
>
> If you did not pay your doctor or laboratory or hospital at the time of your visit and your insurance company reimburses you, it is important that you pay the doctor, lab, or hospital as soon as the insurance company pays you. If you spend the insurance money, saying, "Oh, I'll pay those bills later," you are playing with fire.

What goes to the bank, what stays home

Where should you keep important papers and records? Some belong in a safe deposit box in a bank. Others should be at home in a safe and sensible file.

Into the safe deposit box go all those papers that you would have a tough time replacing, including:

Birth certificates
Stock certificates
Citizenship papers
Bonds
Automobile's certificate of title
Real estate deeds
Copies of wills (but not originals)
Divorce decrees
Death certificates
Passports
Discharge papers from military service
Veterans Administration papers
Adoption papers
Contracts and agreements with partner
Household inventory (with photos for appraisal purposes)
Detailed list of who owns what in the house (with photos)

Why not put your life insurance policies and the original copies of your wills in the safe deposit box? Because, in most states, when the owner or joint owner of a safe deposit box dies, the bank is required to seal the box until all tax and legal matters have been taken care of. The bank grants access only when it receives legal permission, and then in the presence of an authorized person—usually a bank officer or official. But a life insurance company will not pay a claim until its policy is surrendered, or turned in. And the probation of a will cannot begin until the most recent will is presented in probate court. So, if legal permission must be obtained to open the safe deposit box and get out these important papers, everything gets held up.

The best place to keep your life insurance policies is at home. The best place to keep your wills is in the files of the attorney or attorneys who drew them up. You might also want to have your attorney keep all contracts and agreements, with copies in your safe deposit box.

Each partner in a live-together situation should fill out the worksheets at the end of this chapter on Personal Information (II), Personal Contacts (III), Recordkeeping (IV), and Locations of Other Important Papers (V). Don't be afraid to write down plenty of detail; better to jot down too much than too little.

Some of these details may seem obvious. Getting hold of some of them may seem like a nuisance. Just remember that they will not seem obvious to anyone who must track down all this information if you are not around to supply it. And lawyers can tell you how much they are paid to take care of nuisance details their clients could easily have had ready in their files.

When you have these sheets filled in, get duplicates made. Give a set to someone else to keep for you—your partner, your attorney, a trusted friend . . . someone who will understand the method of your madness. Update the sheets every year, or whenever a significant change occurs in your finances.

File and throw out

What counts is not what your filing system looks like but how well you have organized it. It can be in an elaborate, decorated file cabinet or in a collection of shoe boxes. The key to keeping it effective is to get into the habit of filing those papers that are important and throwing out those that are not. Take receipts on purchases, for example. Keeping such records of who paid for what (especially expensive items) will help you remember who owns what. It won't hurt to store receipts along with a detailed list.

> **SEPARATE FINANCES, SEPARATE FILES**
>
> Bobbie and Jack, who keep their finances entirely separate, carefully maintain their own filing systems. In their home office, each knows where the other's important papers can be found.

Materials you are keeping permanently at home, or paperwork describing them, should be filed under such headings as:

- Annuities
- Automobile insurance policies
- Bankbooks and statements
- Children's records
- Credit histories
- Disability insurance policies
- Educational records
- Employment histories
- Federal income-tax returns
- 401(k) plans
- Gifts
- Gift-tax returns
- Health insurance policies
- Health records
- Home improvement records
- Homeowner's insurance policy
- Household inventory (with receipts and appraisals)
- Inheritances
- Insurance policies (if not filed under subject headings, such as auto, medical, etc.)
- IRA (individual retirement account)
- Keogh plan
- Life insurance policies
- List of important advisers
- Loan applications
- Loans
- Medical insurance
- Medicare
- Money-market funds
- Mutual funds
- Paid bills
- Pension and profit-sharing plans
- Property-tax bills and receipts
- Real estate investments
- Social Security earnings records
- Social Security numbers
- State income-tax returns
- Stock and bond record book
- Stock options
- Warranties and guarantees
- Wills (signed originals filed with attorney)

Good records for tax purposes

One of the most valuable departments in your record system covers stock and bond transactions and home improvements. Why? Because you will want to use this information in your income-tax returns. You need to know when you bought a particular stock or bond, and at what price, because when you sell it you will have to figure out your gain or loss on the sale. Many years may have passed between buying and selling, and the Internal Revenue Service, as well as your state (in most cases) will tax you on any profit.

Keeping track of profit or loss is also important when it comes to your house or condominium. When you sell, you must pay a tax on your profit (i.e., the difference between the original purchase price and the sale price). But you may deduct from that profit every permanent improvement you have made over the years. That includes landscaping, converting a garage to an additional room, installing insulation and other energy-saving devices, putting in a swimming pool, adding a room or a wing, a deck or patio—or doing anything else that added value to the house. You must be able to prove what you spent, so an accurate record of bills paid and checks canceled will be invaluable when you sell the house.

If and when you sell, take pictures in and around the house before you move out. When you are preparing tax returns, they will help jog your memories. You'll be surprised at how many deductible improvements you will see in those photographs.

Colored pencils come in handy. Use one color to write down what you pay when you buy securities or make other investments, a second color for what you get when you sell them. That makes it easy for your eye to spot the sales when you are doing your income taxes. On your personal computer, try one of the money-handling programs—Managing Your Money or Quicken. Or, if you are computer-literate, set up your own program on Lotus or Excel. You can then print out spreadsheets that show your sales with gains and loses, all ready to turn over to your CPA or whoever does your taxes, to be attached to Schedule D.

○ ○ ○

SUPPOSE CHRIS DECIDES TO SELL HER HOUSE . . .

Chris and her late husband bought their home in 1980. She finds that with appreciation over the years (mostly due to inflation) since they bought it, the split-level purchased for $75,000 can be sold for more than $220,000. If Chris sells it for $220,000 before she is 55 years old, she must pay a capital-gains tax on $145,000 of the price. (If she were over 55, she could benefit from a once-in-a-lifetime exemption of $125,000 when selling.) But Chris's well-kept records can cut down the tax bite:

Permanent improvements:		
Landscaping	$3,000	
Insulation	1,000	
New bathroom	5,500	
Kitchen	12,000	
New driveway	4,000	
Total	$25,500	25,500
Original purchase price		75,000
Original purchase price plus cost of improvements		$100,500
Selling price		$220,000
Less original purchase price plus cost of improvements		$100,500
Capital gains tax is calculated on		$119,500

○ ○ ○

If the Internal Revenue Service decides to audit your return, the burden of proof will be on you, so a continuing file is vital from the tax standpoint. But it can help you, too. For example, an accordion file of canceled checks, organized by categories, will help you with planning your cash flow as well as preparing your tax returns. Include such categories as:

Automobile expenses
Bills from specific stores
Charitable contributions
Children's expenses
Clothing
Education
Entertainment and recreation
Household maintenance
Household purchases (major)
Insurance premiums
Medical, dental, and prescription drug expenses
Mortgage payments
Taxes (real estate and personal property)
Utilities (telephone, gas, electricity, water)

With this file, you can tackle a new year's spending plan and your end-of-year tax returns with confidence in your accuracy. Then you can throw out many bills (yes, this is worth repeating, because it is so hard to get people to realize that "throw out" means what it says). Save only the bills you need as evidence for tax purposes.

If the IRS audits you

Cardinal rule: Always remember that the IRS does not understand the words "I can't find it." If you want to prove you made an expenditure, you must show up with the proof in your hand.

The fact is, the IRS considers you guilty until you prove yourself innocent. The law permits it to audit you any time within three years after the date you file a return. For example, if your 1995 return was filed on April 15, 1996, you may be audited on it at any time until April 15, 1999, but no later. (Exception: The IRS is legally entitled to audit you at a later date if it expects to charge you with fraud or gross negligence.) Once the three years have passed, you should throw out most of your canceled checks and other documentation. Keep only those items that have to do with possible future capital gains tax information, such as home improvements or purchase of collectibles and stocks and bonds.

It's not root canal

In most people's minds, a summons for an IRS audit evokes horror equivalent to the feeling produced by the words "root canal" in the dentist's office. What can you do?

The answer is: Be prepared. Your notice from the IRS will indicate the sections of your tax return that it wants to check on. The letter will tell you to call for an appointment, probably at the nearest IRS office. If your return was prepared by an accountant, contact him or her and see if the accountant will go in your place. Be sure to check on whether you will have to pay your accountant an additional fee for this service. If you decide to make an appearance yourself, take with you all the bills and canceled checks relating to the particular items the IRS has said it wants to check on.

Important: In an IRS meeting, keep your eyes and ears open and your mouth closed as much as possible. Answer only the questions you are asked. Do not chitchat. Control the natural tendency to babble in nervous situations. Concentrate on counting the holes in the ceiling tiles, if you must, but fight the urge to blurt out something you may regret. Let out your primal scream when you get out of the office.

Record-keeping has its emotional aspects. Being able to put your hands on the right piece of paper, at the moment when you need it, is the greatest relief ever devised for an anxiety attack. If you have taken the precaution of letting someone else in on the secret of your method, you will be in much better shape during an unexpected period of transition or emotional turmoil.

How to gather data

Your financial plan is only as good as the data you accumulate for it. Gathering data takes time, thought, and care. But it is important that you gather accurate financial data, as erroneous financial information can lead to disastrous financial decisions. Some suggestions:

- *Don't try to do it in an hour.* Or even a single session. Or even over a single weekend. Divide the data gathering into "do-able" sessions with a realistic time frame for completing the job. Maybe decide to do it for an hour each weekend over the next several months. You can probably determine fixed expenses easily in one sitting. But flexible expenses are not so easy. You might take one category each weekend.
- *Don't be too ambitious.* Tough guidelines are no good. They will make you self-destruct before you are finished.
- *Don't be dictatorial.* Gathering data has to be done by agreement, not by decree. You and your partner must work on it together. Otherwise, expect sabotage.
- *Don't overdo the paperwork.* Elaborate bookkeeping appeals to some—but not to many. Round cents up or down to the nearest dollar. Don't be surprised that some expenses just aren't 100 percent accurate.
- *Focus on essentials.* Don't let small details bog you down. Make it easy to do the minimum amount of essential reporting.
- *Stick to it.* Give yourself enough time so you can walk away from it if it gets to be too much. Then come back another day. The papers will still be there.

Worksheet II: Partner 1
RECORD-KEEPING
personal information

Yourself:

1. Name__________ Address__________
   City/State__________ Telephone Number__________
   Place of Birth__________ Date of Birth__________
   Social Security #__________ Marital Status__________

2. Partner's Name__________ Address__________
   City/State__________ Telephone #__________
   Place of Birth__________ Date of Birth__________
   Social Security #__________

3. Children:

Name	1	2	3	4
Address				
City/State				
Telephone				
Place of Birth				
Date of Birth				
Social Security #				
Marital Status				

4. Parents
   Name__________ Address__________
   City/State__________ Telephone #__________
   Place of Birth__________ Date of Birth__________
   Mother's maiden name__________

5. Partner's Parents
   Names__________ Address__________
   City/State__________ Telephone__________
   Place of Birth__________ Date of Birth__________
   Mother's Maiden Name__________

   Next of Kin:
   Name__________ Relationship__________
   Address__________ Telephone #__________

   Neighbor or Close Friend
   Name__________ Address__________
   City/State__________ Telephone__________

Worksheet II: Partner 2
RECORD-KEEPING
personal information

Yourself:

1. Name________ Address________
   City/State________ Telephone Number________
   Place of Birth________ Date of Birth________
   Social Security #________ Marital Status________

2. Partner's Name________ Address________
   City/State________ Telephone #________
   Place of Birth________ Date of Birth________
   Social Security #________

3. Children:

Name	1	2	3	4
Address				
City/State				
Telephone				
Place of Birth				
Date of Birth				
Social Security #				
Marital Status				

4. Parents
   Name________ Address________
   City/State________ Telephone #________
   Place of Birth________ Date of Birth________
   Mother's maiden name________

5. Partner's Parents
   Names________ Address________
   City/State________ Telephone________
   Place of Birth________ Date of Birth________
   Mother's Maiden Name________

Next of Kin:
Name________ Relationship________
Address________ Telephone #________

Neighbor or Close Friend
Name________ Address________
City/State________ Telephone________

Worksheet III: Partner 1
RECORD-KEEPING
personal contacts

NAME	ADDRESS	TELEPHONE NUMBER
Attorney		
Accountant		
Clergyman		
Stockbroker		
Physician		
Trust Officer		
Banker		
Life Insurance Agent		
Other Insurance Agents		
Homeowner		
Automobile		
Medical		
Disability		
Executor of Estate		
Financial Planner		
Others		

Worksheet III: Partner 2
RECORD-KEEPING
personal contacts

NAME	ADDRESS	TELEPHONE NUMBER
Attorney		
Accountant		
Clergyman		
Stockbroker		
Physician		
Trust Officer		
Banker		
Life Insurance Agent		
Other Insurance Agents		
Homeowner		
Automobile		
Medical		
Disability		
Executor of Estate		
Financial Planner		
Others		

Worksheet IV: Partner 1
RECORD-KEEPING

1. CHECKING ACCOUNTS, SAVINGS ACCOUNTS, CREDIT UNION ACCOUNTS, OTHER CASH ACCOUNTS

Name of Institution	Type and # of Account	Interest Rate	Current Balance	Owned By	Location of Checkbook or Passbooks

2. MONEY MARKET FUNDS, CERTIFICATES OF DEPOSIT, TREASURY BILLS AND NOTES

Name of Institution	Type and # of Account	Maturity Date	Amount Invested	Interest Rate	Owned by	Location of Passbooks
		TOTAL				

3. SECURITIES

Stocks & Mutual Funds:

Number of Shares	Company	Date Purchased	Total Cost	Current Market Value	Owned By	Location of Stock Certificate	Annual Income
				TOTAL:			

Bonds: Corporate & Municipal

Face Amount	Company	Purchase Date	Maturity Date	Total Cost	Interest Rate	Current Market Value	Owned by	Location of Book	Annual Income

4. REAL ESTATE (RESIDENCE, RECREATIONAL, INCOME PROPERTY)

Location:	1.	2.	3.
Date Purchased			
Cost			
Current Market Value			

5. LIFE INSURANCE

	1.	2.	3.	4.
Insured				
Company				
Type of Policy				
Number of Policy				
Face Amount				
Owner				
Beneficiary				
Case Value				
Amount Borrowed Out				
Location of Policy				

6. ANNUITIES, PENSIONS, PROFIT SHARING PLANS, INDIVIDUAL RETIREMENT ACCOUNTS

Description	Participant	Company or Institution	Benefits	Present Value

7. BUSINESS INTERESTS

Company Name	Type of Business	Percentage of Ownership	Value of Your Interest

8. CREDIT OBLIGATIONS

Real Estate (Residence, Recreational, Income Property)

	1.	2.	3.
Mortgage Holder			
Mortgage Balance			
Interest Rate			
Monthly Payment			

Other Debt Obligations (automobile loans, education loans, life insurance loans, home improvement loans, etc.)

Lender	Type of Loan	Interest Rate	Balance Due	Monthly Payment	Co-signer

Credit Cards

Name of Card	Number of card	Balance Due

Worksheet V: Partner 1
LOCATION OF OTHER IMPORTANT PAPERS

Homeowner's Insurance __________

Name of Company __________ Policy Number __________

Automobile Insurance __________

Name of Company __________ Policy Number __________

Medical Insurance __________

Name of Company __________ Policy Number __________

Type of Policy __________

Location of card __________ Group Number __________

Disability Insurance __________

Name of Company __________ Policy Number __________

Last Will __________

Codicils __________

Birth Certificates __________

Mortgage Papers or Lease __________

Deeds to Real Estate __________

Titles to Automobiles __________

Military Discharge Papers __________

Citizenship Papers __________

Divorce Decree __________

Social Security Cards __________

Income Tax Returns __________

Power of Attorney __________

Living Will __________

Worksheet IV: Partner 2
RECORD-KEEPING

1. CHECKING ACCOUNTS, SAVINGS ACCOUNTS, CREDIT UNION ACCOUNTS, OTHER CASH ACCOUNTS

Name of Institution	Type and # of Account	Interest Rate	Current Balance	Owned By	Location of Checkbook or Passbooks

2. MONEY MARKET FUNDS, CERTIFICATES OF DEPOSIT, TREASURY BILLS AND NOTES

Name of Institution	Type and # of Account	Maturity Date	Amount Invested	Interest Rate	Owned by	Location of Passbooks
			TOTAL			

3. SECURITIES

Stocks & Mutual Funds:

Number of Shares	Company	Date Purchased	Total Cost	Current Market Value	Owned By	Location of Stock Certificate	Annual Income
				TOTAL:			

Bonds: Corporate & Municipal

Face Amount	Company	Purchase Date	Maturity Date	Total Cost	Interest Rate	Current Market Value	Owned by	Location of Book	Annual Income

4. REAL ESTATE (RESIDENCE, RECREATIONAL, INCOME PROPERTY)

Location:	1.	2.	3.
Date Purchased			
Cost			
Current Market Value			

5. LIFE INSURANCE

	1.	2.	3.	4.
Insured				
Company				
Type of Policy				
Number of Policy				
Face Amount				
Owner				
Beneficiary				
Case Value				
Amount Borrowed Out				
Location of Policy				

6. ANNUITIES, PENSIONS, PROFIT SHARING PLANS, INDIVIDUAL RETIREMENT ACCOUNTS

Description	Participant	Company or Institution	Benefits	Present Value

7. BUSINESS INTERESTS

Company Name	Type of Business	Percentage of Ownership	Value of Your Interest

8. CREDIT OBLIGATIONS

Real Estate (Residence, Recreational, Income Property)

	1.	2.	3.
Mortgage Holder			
Mortgage Balance			
Interest Rate			
Monthly Payment			

Other Debt Obligations (automobile loans, education loans, life insurance loans, home improvement loans, etc.)

Lender	Type of Loan	Interest Rate	Balance Due	Monthly Payment	Co-signer

Credit Cards

Name of Card	Number of card	Balance Due

Worksheet V: Partner 2
LOCATION OF OTHER IMPORTANT PAPERS

Homeowner's Insurance__________
Name of Company__________ Policy Number__________
Automobile Insurance__________
Name of Company__________ Policy Number__________
Medical Insurance__________
Name of Company__________ Policy Number__________
Type of Policy__________
Location of card__________ Group Number__________
Disability Insurance__________
Name of Company__________ Policy Number__________
Last Will__________
Codicils__________
Birth Certificates__________
Mortgage Papers or Lease__________
Deeds to Real Estate__________
Titles to Automobiles__________
Military Discharge Papers__________
Citizenship Papers__________
Divorce Decree__________
Social Security Cards__________
Income Tax Returns__________
Power of Attorney__________
Living Will__________

CHAPTER FOUR

WHAT IS YOUR NET WORTH —SEPARATELY AND TOGETHER?

When two of you decide to live together, you each bring more than yourself to the relationship. You each bring your personal property. You each bring your financial assets. And you each bring your financial liabilities, or debts. You must look at all three sensibly and realistically, so you each know where you stand.

How do you accomplish this? By each working up a **Net Worth Statement**. *Each* is the key word here. Whether you should also work up a *joint* Net Worth Statement together depends on how you are handling property, assets, and debts—pooled together? Half-and-half? Entirely separately? Unequal ownership?

Take a look now at the Net Worth Statement Worksheet on page 26. Just for starters, as you look at it, ask yourself some tough questions:

- How much will I have to pass on to my live-together, or to my children, if any?
- Will what I leave them produce income enough for them to survive?
- Am I accumulating enough assets to help support myself during my retirement years?
- Should my investments be producing income now, or in the future, or both?
- Am I carrying too much debt?
- How about inflation? Am I keeping ahead of it? Am I even keeping up with it?

Just what is net worth?

Net worth is the difference between your assets, or everything you own that has monetary value, and your debts, or everything you owe to someone else. It is an inventory, an indicator of where you stand financially at any given point in time. Think of it as kind of like weighing and measuring yourself at the start of a physical fitness program or at any time during the program.

Why go to all the trouble of calculating your net worth? Because, broadly speaking, knowing your net worth can give you and your partner a sense of security both now and in the future. And because if you don't know your net worth you cannot do any sensible retirement planning or estate planning, nor can you develop a sound investment strategy.

Mandatory for estate planning

One of the most important aspects of financial planning for people who live together without the legal status of matrimony is estate planning. The vital first step in setting up an estate plan is to know your net worth and who owns what.

Worksheet VI:
NET WORTH STATEMENT
Date________________

When filling out this form, refer back to Chapter 3, Record-keeping, Worksheet IV.

ASSETS	MONETARY VALUE	OWNER OF ASSET		
		Self	Partner	Joint
Current Assets (see 1. Current Balance, 2, Amount Invested)				
Checking Account				
Savings Account				
Credit Union Accounts				
Money Market Funds				
CDs				
Treasury Bills				
Treasury Notes				
Securities (see 3. Current Market Values)				
Stocks				
Bonds				
Mutual Funds				
Real Estate (see 4. Current Market Value)				
Residence				
Recreational Property				
Income Property				
Long Term (see 5. Cash Value, 6. Present Value, 7. Value of Your Interest)				
Insurance				
Annuities				
Pensions				
Profit Sharing Plans				
401(k)				
401(k)				
Individual Retirement Accounts				
Business Interests				

The laws that govern what happens to your assets if you die without a legally binding plan in place are called *intestate succession* laws. Their objective is to pass your assets to blood relatives. If one partner in a live-together relationship dies without a will or other legal mechanism in place, the surviving partner inherits nothing. If you want to make sure that your friend or companion will inherit any tangible or intangible property—i.e., *any* asset of yours—you must arrange the transfer of such an asset or assets through a proper legal device: a will, a trust, or some other expedient. You will find more detail on this subject in chapter 14 on estate planning.

PERSONAL PROPERTY	MONETARY VALUE	OWNER OF ASSET		
		Self	Partner	Joint
Home Furnishings				
Automobiles				
Clothing & Furs				
Jewelry				
Antiques				
Stamp Collection				
Coins				
Fine Art				
Other				
TOTAL ASSETS				

LIABILITIES OR CREDIT OBLIGATIONS

CURRENT LIABILITIES:	AMOUNT DUE	OBLIGATOR		
Medical & Dental				
Current Bills				
Charge Accounts				
Unpaid Taxes				
Capital Gains				
Federal				
State				
Local				
Real Estate (see 8).				
Residence				
Recreational				
Income Property				
Other Debt or Installment Debt (see 8.)				
Automobile Loans				
Home Improvement Loans				
Education Loans				
Life Insurance Loans				
Margin Accounts				
Bank Loans				
Credit Cards				
TOTAL ASSETS				
TOTAL LIABILITIES				
NET WORTH				

Essential for investment planning

The Net Worth Statement is equally valuable for investment planning, for you must know just how liquid your assets are before you start investing. In other words, how easily can you cash in some of your assets if an emergency occurs? Liquid assets are defined as whatever money you have in the bank—except certificates of deposit (CDs), which may carry penalties if you cash them in early—or in a money-market mutual fund account. You can, of course, convert stocks, bonds, or mutual funds to cash in a hurry if you have to. But because they go up and down in value, you risk selling them at a lower price than you bought them for if you must cash them in quickly.

How much should you have in liquid assets? Enough, in savings and money-market accounts, to cover your current bills and an emergency fund. The emergency fund should be large enough to cover from three to six months of living expenses. The exact amount depends on your age, your health, and whether your household includes more than one wage earner.

Your Net Worth Statement, then, will help to tell you whether you are short of liquid assets and need to build them up before you begin investing. Or, on the other hand, it may reveal that you have more money in the bank or money-market account than you need to keep there—and that now may well be the time to start a long-term investment program.

Vital for retirement planning

You must think today about your retirement, and knowing your net worth will be increasingly important for that planning. Why? Because American businesses, by and large, have stopped providing attractive pension plans. Rather, they want *you* to pay for the plan and manage it. They have been glad to see the corporate pension plan replaced by the individual 401(k) plan, which demands that you put in your own money and that you decide how it is to be invested. Knowing your net worth is basic to your planning and decisions.

Three ways of owning assets

Whether you are buying a house, stocks, or bonds—and even when you establish a bank account—you have a choice among three kinds of ownership:

1. *Separate.* You alone own it. Full ownership is in your name only. When you die, it passes to another owner or owners by the terms of your will, or, if you leave no will, by the intestate laws of the state in which you reside.

2. *Joint tenancy with right of survivorship.* Here, two or more people hold title and ownership. When any one of the joint tenants dies, that person's entire interest in the property passes automatically to the survivor or survivors. No will is needed to make this happen. It is instant and self-fulfilling. *Warning:* Joint tenancy does not work in every situation. Two of you may buy a house on a 50–50 basis. That's okay. Three of you may each own one-third of a house. That's all right, too. But if, for example, one of you is putting in 75 percent and the other is buying 25 percent, you cannot establish joint tenancy with right of survivorship. Ownership must be equal.

3. *Tenants in common.* Here is where you are permitted to have unequal ownership. Two or more tenants may be involved. Each may sell or give his or her share to someone else or dispose of it in a will. It does not automatically pass to the others.

> **PUT IT IN WRITING**
>
> If you decide to own property jointly, put it in writing. Draw up an agreement that outlines the details—how the property is to be paid for, what happens if you and your partner separate, who is to get the share of a partner who dies. This is especially important if you buy a house together. Sensible written agreements can increase trust between two people and provide a tremendous sense of security, for you are living without the laws that protect married couples. They simply do not apply to live-togethers.

In most cases, people who decide to live together simply retain sole ownership of whatever property they owned beforehand. But what if you acquire property *after* you get together? The cleanest way to handle your financial affairs is to keep them separate. But that is not always easy to do. Suppose, for instance, you buy expensive items that you intend to own and use jointly? What about sharing household expenses?

Joint checking and savings accounts can make it easy to share expenses. But remember—you are each responsible for all checks drawn on the account, and live-togethers have been known to clean out an account and take off for places unknown. So, regardless of how much trust you have in each other, use your hardheaded business sense. Set up a joint account that requires the signatures of both of you for any withdrawal. From that account, pay all household expenses—heat, light, insurance, mortgage, real estate taxes, even groceries. Then, each of you maintain a separate account and, by agreement, regularly pay from your individual account into the joint account whatever is your fair share of the balance that is needed monthly.

How much are things worth?

Now it's time to be objective. As accurately as possible, write down the actual market value of your property, be it your home, your great-aunt's heirloom diamonds, your automobile. Not what you think your property might be worth, but what it would actually fetch if you were putting it up for sale.

How do you figure out what things are worth? Your best bet is to get in touch with a dealer or appraiser who knows houses, diamonds, automobiles, rare coins, antique dolls, or whatever else you own that is of real value. Ask the dealer to make a professional estimate or appraisal. Talk with a real estate broker or two about the current market value of your home. Check your local newspaper for advertisements for comparable houses.

Getting accurate values on personal property can be tough. Clothing, furniture, and other household furnishings may have depreciated since you bought them. Silver, gold, stamps, antiques, and coins have probably gained in value since you acquired or inherited them. In some cases, such as coins or antiques, a reputable specialized magazine may include listings you can depend on.

To compile your list, go back to your record-keeping worksheets for guidance. Start with cash on hand, in savings or checking accounts. Then itemize all certificates of deposit (CDs) due within the coming year, money market funds, stocks, and bonds. Your newspaper's daily listing will tell you today's market value of stocks, bonds, and mutual funds.

Then there are hidden assets. Don't forget:

- Your pension or profit-sharing plan. Be sure to list only that portion of its present value (that is fully vested in your name). *Note:* Do not include any pension plan that you can receive only as an annuity.
- Life insurance. Include the cash values of whole life policies.
- Business partnership or similar venture. Specify the amount you would receive if you sold your share today (for many people, the largest asset and the most difficult to appraise).

How much do you owe?

Here you list all your liabilities. Start with current bills—every amount you have been billed but have not yet paid (it helps to include a notation on just what item the bill is for, unless it is obvious in the name of the store or business firm that is billing you). List all unpaid taxes, including all that have not been deducted from your paycheck, such as estimated federal or state income tax—or balances due—capital gains tax, real estate taxes, and personal property taxes.

The unpaid balance on the mortgage on your home or condominium or vacation house goes on the list. Next: installment debts—everything you owe to MasterCard, Visa, American Express, Diners Club, any rotating charge accounts, and your own cash reserve in use on your checking account. Don't forget any unpaid balance on a car loan, home improvement loan, education loan, or life insurance loan.

Got the form filled out? Check it again. Anything you forgot to list under assets? Any missing liabilities?

Total each column. Now subtract your liabilities from your assets. The result is your net worth as of right now.

What if your liabilities turn out to be greater than your assets? You have a *negative net worth.* Not good news, but it proves the exercise has been doubly worthwhile for you: it has drawn your attention to a precarious situation that needs immediate attention.

Assets and liabilities change continually, of course—almost on a daily basis. You do not need to redo your Net Worth Statement weekly or even monthly to reflect fluctuations. But it will be important to keep an eye on your net worth because, as your major needs and situations change, the emphasis on assets and liabilities is sure to vary.

When to revise your net worth statement

What kinds of major needs and situations are important enough to make you revise the statement? I'd say these are: buying a larger house, inheriting stocks and bonds, becoming vested in an employee profit-sharing plan, signing for a loan for a car or boat or second home or Steinway concert grand piano.

Definitely review your Net Worth Statement once a year, even if you think not much has changed. And think of the statement positively as a barometer of your financial situation. When you are weighing needs or pondering a major purchase decision or a job change, some quiet consultation with your net worth—letting your assets and your liabilities do their share of the talking—can be more helpful than you may have dreamed possible.

Overall, if your Net Worth Statement reveals some negatives, if your net worth is not growing, if you have taken on more debt than you can handle, if your investments have not kept up with inflation, you can analyze what is going on and be prepared to do something about it. Financial needs do change. Your Net Worth Statement can help you to see just what are the hurdles, imposed by change, that you must leap over.

○ ○ ○

DAVE AND DICK'S NET WORTH

Dick's net worth has been building up since the day 15 years ago when he was paid $115,000 for that small house he had bought 16 years earlier. He invested the proceeds through a stockbroker, setting up a joint account with Dave.

Dave, the physician, with earnings almost triple his partner's, set up an account—also joint—with the same broker. Their only separate accounts are their retirement funds. As a self-employed person, he has about $200,000 in his Keogh plan, with Dick named as beneficiary. Dick has rolled over $400,000 from his pension into an IRA, naming Dave as beneficiary. Neither has any liabilities.

Their real estate adds to their net worth. The tenant farmhouse they renovated as a rental property is worth $100,000 on today's market. Their home is worth $250,000.

○ ○ ○

BOBBIE AND JACK'S NET WORTH

In her divorce agreement, Bobbie settled for a small share—only 25 percent—of her husband's $200,000 portfolio of stocks and bonds in exchange for full rights to their substantial home in affluent Scarsdale, a New York City suburb. The house's current market value is $575,000. These are her only assets.

Jack's hard work as a real estate developer has brought him a net worth of more than $3.5 million, of which one million is in stocks and bonds. He and Bobbie own no joint assets. His Cadillac and her Chrysler Town and Country are in their own names. When Jack moved in with Bobbie, he brought along several treasured pieces of antique furniture and a collection of art, all of which are left to his children in his will. Together they have compiled a complete household inventory that specifies exactly who owns what and estimates the value of each item. Keeping up with the times, they have even made a videotape of the interior of the house.

○ ○ ○

CINDY AND MAUREEN'S NET WORTH

Working over their net worth statement, Cindy and Maureen are careful to include even the small balances that each carries on her credit cards. They note that their house is owned jointly, with the mortgage in both their names, and that their checking and savings accounts are also joint. While Cindy knows that she will be coming into an inheritance when her mother's estate is settled, they both know that it would be unwise to list that money as an asset. "When you're adding up net worth," says Cindy, "you can't count your chickens before they're hatched." They are careful about how they list their cars, too: Cindy's is paid for, so its current book value is listed. Maureen still has a loan on hers, so she listed the current book value as an asset. The loan balance is then shown as a liability. And they still have some unpaid balances on their credit cards.

○ ○ ○

CHAPTER FIVE

YOUR CASH FLOW AND YOUR SPENDING PLAN

Let's forget that bugaboo word *budget*. Everybody hates it, including me. Instead, think of two important annual documents. The first is your **Cash Flow Statement**. It is oriented strictly to the past: where your money came from, and where it went, over the past year. The second is your **Spending Plan**. It looks at where you are spending your money now and how you want to spend it in the future. Incidentally, there is nothing magic in thinking one year at a time, but it is a real convenience because that's how calendars and date books and (that terrible word) budget books are organized. If it suits you, you can just as well do six-month or 18-month Cash Flow Statements and Spending Plans. Those in the teaching profession, for instance, often find it convenient and practical to think in terms of 10-month and two-month plans (i.e., September–June, and July–August) because their lifestyles in the two different periods have different repercussions on their cash flow and spending.

Think of your Spending Plan as headlights in night driving: It shows where you are going, so your daily spending can stay on course.

> *Warning:* Before you get into developing your Cash Flow Statement and projecting your Spending Plan, talk together about parking your emotions somewhere far away while you are discussing money. *Any*—repeat, *any*—discussion of money seems to ignite emotions. And if either one of you feels that he or she is being financially exploited, you can bet there will be a lot of resentment lurking in the background, if not right out in the foreground.

Many people think that talking about money is crass. But a written agreement covering such major items as household expenses is an essential element if you are going to live together successfully. Literally put down on paper who is going to be responsible for what. By putting the facts of your financial life on paper, you each become aware of who is responsible for what. You head off endless discussions—monthly debates, probably —about who paid for what and who didn't, or should have or should not have, or should or shouldn't in the future.

What to include in cash flow

Before two people move in together, the smartest thing they can do is sit down and look at one another's Cash

Flow Statements. To do that, you must each have such a statement in the first place. If neither of you has one, try to assemble as much information as you can, covering the past year if possible, or at least the last six months. See Worksheet VIIA: Cash Flow on this page. This will give you a sensible framework within which to discuss how you plan to manage a joint household and come up with a spending plan.

Every Cash Flow Statement has two sides. One covers revenue, or what is coming in. The other covers expenses, or what goes out. These two sides, income and outgo, are basic to every plan ever created, whether it is that of a single person or a giant corporation with worldwide production, employees, and sales.

Money coming in

Write down all income. Include your gross wages or salary, plus any income from other sources: dividends from investments, pay for freelance or overtime work, interest from savings, Social Security or other pension payments, payments from disability or unemployment insurance, tax refunds.

Important: Be honest with yourself. Don't count any unhatched chickens. Expecting a raise? Don't list it as income until you see it in your paycheck. Your spending plan tells what is happening right now, never what might be.

Then list deductions for Social Security, Federal and state taxes, benefits, and pre-tax savings programs.

Money going out

There are two kinds of expenditures: fixed and flexible. Gather figures on what you paid out for all your fixed expenses, such as rent or mortgage payments, utilities, taxes, insurance, household maintenance and repairs, installment loans or credit-card debt—everything it took to sleep, eat, and live somewhere.

Next, put down what you have spent for flexible expenses—food and household supplies, clothing, telephone, and such nonessentials as entertainment, gifts, dining out, pets, books and magazines, laundry and cleaning, travel and vacation, doctors and dentists, charities and savings. For each of you, add up the totals to see your individual Cash Flow Statement. What you are getting is the pictures of two lifestyles—how you have lived, the goods and services you have spent your money on.

Your Cash Flow Statement can talk to you. It can tell you if you have overspent in any one area (or more than one). It can tell you exactly where you have spent your money. It can advise you on whether you can safely afford to carry any more credit. It can tip you off if you are buying before you can afford to buy, for it shows you just what is the risk when you want to take on a new credit obligation and answers the question: Can we really afford the payments?

> *Note*: Two complete fixed and flexible expense worksheets for your Cash Flow are included, so you can each use one. If living together is something you are both thinking about but have not

Worksheet VIIA: CASH FLOW STATEMENT
SOURCES OF INCOME

EARNED INCOME	PARTNER 1	PARTNER 2	JOINT	TOTAL	MONTHLY
Wages/Salary					
Self-Employment Income					
Bonus					
INVESTMENT INCOME					
Interest/Savings					
Interest/Bonds					
Capital Gains					
Dividends					
Rental Income					
Trust Income					

EARNED INCOME	PARTNER 1	PARTNER 2	JOINT	TOTAL	MONTHLY
RETIREMENT INCOME					
Social Security					
Employer's Pension					
Private Pension					
Other					
OTHER INCOME					
Family Contributions					
Gifts					
Unemployment, Disability Insurance					
Alimony/Child Support					
GROSS INCOME					

DEDUCTIONS	PARTNER 1	PARTNER 2	JOINT	TOTAL	MONTHLY
Social Security					
Federal Taxes					
State Taxes					
Local Taxes					
Benefits					
401(k) Contributions					
Other					
TOTAL DEDUCTIONS					
NET INCOME					

undertaken, separate worksheets should help you toward making the decision. If you are working up a single worksheet together, it will help to make things clear if you use colored pencils—red for one of you, blue for the other, and green for all joint items.

Looking ahead: What to include in your spending plan

Committed to paper, your Spending Plan actually does double duty. First, it shows how you will handle the day-in day-out expenses that must be covered to keep your household running smoothly. Second, it sets up goals—specific major expenses you want to plan for, such as a vacation trip or a large one-time purchase that, in terms of your planning and thinking, you fund over a long period, or areas you want to cut down on.

Your Spending Plan is to Your Financial Fitness Program what your diet or exercise is to your physical fitness program. It has no fixed rules. One man's hamburger is another man's steak. Some put their money into cars while their homes fall apart. Some eat well but wear threadbare clothes. Some achieve a nice balance among home, cars, clothing, and food. The variations

Worksheet VIIB: Partner 1
CASH FLOW STATEMENT

	FIXED EXPENSES	JAN	FEB	MAR	APR	MAY	JUNE	JULY	AUG	SEPT	OCT	NOV	DEC	TOTAL
1	Rent/Mortgage													
2	Fuel													
3	Electricity													
4	Telephone													
5	Water													
6	Homeowner's Insurance													
7	Automobile Insurance													
8	Disability Insurance													
9	Life Insurance													
10	Personal Property Tax													
11	Real Estate Tax													
12	Estimated Income Tax													
13	Automobile Loan													
14	Loan Repayment													
15	Loan Repayment													
16	Other Debt													
17	Emergency Fund													
18	Savings/Investing (IRAs)													
19	Other													
20														
21	TOTAL FIXED EXPENSES													
22	MONTHLY AVERAGE													
23	DIFFERENCE													

Worksheet VIIB: Partner 1
CASH FLOW STATEMENT

	FLEXIBLE EXPENSES	JAN	FEB	MAR	APR	MAY	JUNE	JULY	AUG	SEPT	OCT	NOV	DEC	TOTAL
1	**Food**													
2	Food/Beverages													
3	Take-Home Food													
4	Dining Out													
5	Lunches at Work													
6														
7	**Clothing**													
8	Clothing/Shoes													
9	Laundry/Dry Cleaning													
10	Alterations													
11														
12	**Gifts**													
13	**Animals**													
14	**Personal Care/Toiletries**													
15	**Periodicals/Books**													
16														
17	**Entertainment**													
18	Recreation													
19	Travel/Vacations													
20	Movies/Theater Tickets													
21	Sporting Events													
22														
23	**Household Expenses**													
24	Lawn/Snow Removal													
25	Maid													
26	Garbage													
27	Repairs													
28	Home Furnishings													
29	Major Appliances													
30														
31	**Transportation**													
32	Gas/Oil													
33	Repairs													
34	Licenses/Registration													
35	Commutation, Parking													
36														
37	**Children's Expenses**													
38	Allowances													
39	Lessons													
40	Camp													
41	Babysitting/Child Care													
42	Recreation/Sports													

Worksheet VIIB: Partner 1
CASH FLOW STATEMENT

		JAN	FEB	MAR	APR	MAY	JUNE	JULY	AUG	SEPT	OCT	NOV	DEC	TOTAL
1	**Education**													
2	Tuition													
3	Room/Board													
4	Books/Supplies													
5	Travel													
6														
7	**Medical Expenses**													
8	Doctor													
9	Dentist													
10	Drugs													
11														
12	**Contributions**													
13	Church/Synagogue													
14	Other Charity													
15														
16														
17														
18	**TOTAL FLEXIBLE EXPENSES**													
19	**TOTAL FIXED EXPENSES**													
20	**TOTAL EXPENSES**													
21	**NET INCOME**													
22	**PROFIT (LOSS)**													
23														
24														

Worksheet VIIB: Partner 2
CASH FLOW STATEMENT

	FIXED EXPENSES	JAN	FEB	MAR	APR	MAY	JUNE	JULY	AUG	SEPT	OCT	NOV	DEC	TOTAL
1	Rent/Mortgage													
2	Fuel													
3	Electricity													
4	Telephone													
5	Water													
6	Homeowner's Insurance													
7	Automobile Insurance													
8	Disability Insurance													
9	Life Insurance													
10	Personal Property Tax													
11	Real Estate Tax													
12	Estimated Income Tax													
13	Automobile Loan													
14	Loan Repayment													
15	Loan Repayment													
16	Other Debt													
17	Emergency Fund													
18	Savings/Investing (IRAs)													
19	Other													
20														
21	TOTAL FIXED EXPENSES													
22	MONTHLY AVERAGE													
23	DIFFERENCE													

Worksheet VIIB: Partner 2
CASH FLOW STATEMENT

	FLEXIBLE EXPENSES	JAN	FEB	MAR	APR	MAY	JUNE	JULY	AUG	SEPT	OCT	NOV	DEC	TOTAL
1	**Food**													
2	Food/Beverages													
3	Take-Home Food													
4	Dining Out													
5	Lunches at Work													
6														
7	**Clothing**													
8	Clothing/Shoes													
9	Laundry/Dry Cleaning													
10	Alterations													
11														
12	**Gifts**													
13	**Animals**													
14	**Personal Care/Toiletries**													
15	**Periodicals/Books**													
16														
17	**Entertainment**													
18	Recreation													
19	Travel/Vacations													
20	Movies/Theater Tickets													
21	Sporting Events													
22														
23	**Household Expenses**													
24	Lawn/Snow Removal													
25	Maid													
26	Garbage													
27	Repairs													
28	Home Furnishings													
29	Major Appliances													
30														
31	**Transportation**													
32	Gas/Oil													
33	Repairs													
34	Licenses/Registration													
35	Commutation, Parking													
36														
37	**Children's Expenses**													
38	Allowances													
39	Lessons													
40	Camp													
41	Babysitting/Child Care													
42	Recreation/Sports													

Worksheet VIIB: Partner 2
CASH FLOW STATEMENT

		JAN	FEB	MAR	APR	MAY	JUNE	JULY	AUG	SEPT	OCT	NOV	DEC	TOTAL
1	**Education**													
2	Tuition													
3	Room/Board													
4	Books/Supplies													
5	Travel													
6														
7	**Medical Expenses**													
8	Doctor													
9	Dentist													
10	Drugs													
11														
12	**Contributions**													
13	Church/Synagogue													
14	Other Charity													
15														
16														
17														
18	**TOTAL FLEXIBLE EXPENSES**													
19	**TOTAL FIXED EXPENSES**													
20	**TOTAL EXPENSES**													
21	**NET INCOME**													
22	**PROFIT (LOSS)**													
23														
24														

are endless, for no one can tell anyone else how to spend his or her money. Each of us must decide for ourselves just what our priorities are.

Consider your Spending Plan a road map. Its purpose is to show you where you are going and how to get there. But like any road map, it can also show you where you can sensibly get off the road, and then get safely back on again without losing direction or missing your destination. That is important. Sometimes you do have to change your route in order to cope with an emergency or a change in plans that may delay your reaching your destination. There's nothing wrong with that if you have your map to guide you and remind you of your goal and the route you structured to reach it.

The Spending Plan includes the same fixed and flexible expenses that are in the Cash Flow Statement. In fact, your best guide to how much you will need each month to meet expenses is your Cash Flow Statement from last year. That's why it is important, if you have not kept either individual or joint records, to start keeping records today. Not tomorrow. Today.

But let's stop and think a moment. We're talking about a Spending Plan for live-togethers. And probably your household has two incomes. If you really want to keep things straight, shouldn't you think of *three* Spending Plans—one for partner A, a second for partner B, and a third that is a joint plan? Sounds complex, but it is actually the cleanest and simplest way to go about it.

Consider that word "joint." You must be ready to differentiate between expenses that are joint and those that are not—i.e., expenses that you two agree to share, whether you are sharing them equally or unequally. That raises a practical question: Should you set up a joint checking account?

What is your other most important fixed expense each month? Payment to your own emergency fund. This is not the same as a fixed-expenses account. Your emergency fund should contain the equivalent of the net income you get regularly for a period of three to six months. If you and your partner are young and both working, if car and appliances and house are new and not likely to cry for major repairs soon, it is safe to keep a minimum of three months' income stashed away. If you are older, or have many obligations (or both), you will find yourself feeling a lot more comfortable when you have built up *and maintained* a cushion for emergencies that matches six months' income.

> *Important:* Use this cash reserve or emergency fund only for real emergencies such as a major medical expense that insurance does not cover or for a stretch of unemployment—the kinds of emergencies that can, if you do not have reserves ready to meet them, send you off to sign for a loan (which may be tough to get if you're between jobs). Don't forget that a loan would also add to your monthly obligations at just the wrong time, giving you more to pay, more to worry about, and less to have for flexible expenses and discretionary spending.

Where to keep your emergency fund? Depends on your own self-discipline. If you are the type who can keep track of it within your own separate fixed-expenses account, by doing good bookkeeping, that's fine. But even better is to put it in a separate savings account. Another important point: Don't even think about an investment program until you have established your emergency fund. It's the first order of business.

Depending on your particular situation and how you have set up your checking and savings accounts, you may each do a separate plan or you may do a joint plan.

Adding it all up

Now add all the columns. Are your total expenditures greater than your income? If so, don't be discouraged. Overspending can prod you into making a cash flow analysis the way being overweight can force you to diet, or at least challenge you to do so. Ask yourself some questions:

- Do we need all these magazines we subscribe to? Are we reading them all?
- Why are we eating out so frequently?
- Does our dog (or cat, or bird) really need gourmet food?
- Can't we buy in larger quantities, storing extra supplies of nonperishables that we buy on sale or at a discount, so we reduce the unit costs?
- How much can we save by cutting back on recreation and entertainment?

The ultimate question, always, is the one the experts call "purchase analysis": Do we *really* need it? If you answer that question with honesty to yourself and your partner, you will tend to put a clamp on impulse buying. You will find yourself distinguishing between buying for pleasure and buying for need. Unless you make this distinction every time you make a significant expenditure (and only you know what is significant for you) you are not financially fit.

Here's a good way to test whether you really need to buy something. Rather than buying it when the impulse seizes you, first write out a check to yourself for the item's purchase price. Look at the check. Do you need that amount in order to buy groceries or pay a department-store bill? If you do, you don't need the item you're thinking about.

Maybe you can make up that amount by skipping several trips to the movies, by putting off buying some special book or item of clothing, by postponing a trip. Better to do so than to find that you cannot pay for basic flexible expenses or, worse still, that you are dipping into money that belongs to the fixed-expenses spending plan (not so likely to happen if you have set up a fixed-expenses account and are keeping that checkbook locked in your desk when you go shopping).

Other cut-down-the-spending tips: On your next vacation, rent not your usual luxury auto but an economy car. Get in the habit of shopping for clothes at off-season sales. Join a warehouse club and buy staples in bulk. Such small incremental changes in your spending can make a real difference. And once you have made adjustments—by starting with small changes and working up to big ones—you will realize how the savings can add up. And always remember: Your spending plan is not set in concrete. You may find some valuable changes in your lifestyle.

Think cost-effectiveness

Whatever you are buying, whether goods or services, figure out its cost-effectiveness. Going to use an item only rarely? You don't need to buy it. Rent it. Almost any appliance, furniture, special clothing, camping gear, ski equipment, party dishes and tableware can be rented. Smart grandparents whose even smarter grandchildren (aren't they all?) live too far away to visit more often than a few times a year are better off renting a crib or high chair when they are needed. Smart couples think twice about owning two cars. If you think about the cost of gasoline today, not to mention insurance and maintenance, you may well find that carpooling, riding public transportation, or renting a second car only when needed can make excellent sense.

Thinking cost-effectiveness and controlling expenditures carefully can actually help you increase the amount of money you have available to invest for intermediate and long-range objectives. View it as profit: the difference between income and the cost of doing business.

You will not find yourself dreading the Spending Plan if you let yourself think positively and practically about your lifestyle—what you want to be and how you want to live and how much money you have available to provide that lifestyle. Keep these key points in mind:

- Recognize that you can achieve financial fitness only by tracking your spending habits and knowing where your money goes.
- Formulate judgments about what is important and how you may not only need to but *want* to shift your priorities.
- Create your own road map that shows you how you are going to reach your destination, and stick to it unless you have good reason for a detour.

One detour you sometimes have to make is to pick up assistance in the form of credit. Credit is a pleasant, friendly word. But one of its synonyms is debt—a dreaded word. The next chapter will tell you about debt and how to get into it and out again safely and successfully.

Bank accounts—how many?

One of the first decisions you must make is how to set up checking and savings accounts. As soon as you move in together, questions come up about pooling money—not to mention the property, large or small, you buy with that money—or keeping everything separate. Living with someone does not necessarily mean you have to live a single financial life. *Recommendation:* Each of you have your own checking account. Use it to pay for those items that are not joint, such as clothing, lunch money on the job, car expenses, certain individual insurance premiums, any financial obligations to a previous mate or family, or any joint expenses for which you have agreed to take sole responsibility.

If you combine your bank accounts, you are each responsible for the activity in the account. That includes bounced checks and bank charges. One of you can easily clean out the account. And if each of you is writing checks and withdrawing cash from the ATM, the record-keeping can be a pain in the neck. Or elsewhere.

Many couples do open joint accounts to pay the joint bills, with each contributing according to his or her income. The joint checking account should be used only to handle those items in your Spending Plan that you are truly paying jointly—rent or mortgage, homeowner's insurance, real estate taxes, car payments (if you are joint owners rather than owning cars individually) and motor vehicle licenses. Since some of these are paid monthly, some quarterly, and some annually, you must run up a total for each category of payment and divide by 12 to get a monthly average. Each of you must put half of that amount (if you are sharing equally) into the joint checking account each month. Payment to this account is—*for each of you*—one of your two most important fixed expenses every month . . . month in, month out. (Incidentally, your joint account should be an interest-bearing account, as you will be storing money there for future use.) That's a tough habit to form, at first, but once you have set the habit it will be easy to maintain, and your joint account will always have enough in it to pay the tax bill or the insurance premium when it comes due.

Important: expenses to be paid from this account are clearly defined. Make sure that, before you decide who puts how much into a joint account, you go over your incomes and expenses, both joint and individual, together. Only then will you know how much each should contribute.

Some live-togethers keep everything separate. Each partner is responsible for her or his own support, buying everything—including food—on an individual basis. Others maintain separate buying only for what is truly separate, while they pool their funds through their joint account to buy food and pay for household maintenance, entertainment, vacations, and the fixed expenses such as the mortgage or the fuel bill. Some go so far as to set up joint accounts for each of several distinct funds: the vacation fund, the house-renovation fund, or whatever.

Warning: Don't let any such arrangements go to extremes. One partner's nickel-and-diming can lead to the other partner's sabotage of any good Spending Plan. If your Spending Plan gets too cumbersome or detail-oriented, stand back—it is likely to self-destruct.

How do you pay for things?

Cash cards, anyone? The cash card is here. It is your ATM card. With it, you can now shop in millions of stores and restaurants in the United States and around the world. Originally, you will recall, the ATM card gave you access to your checking and savings accounts only at machines owned by your own bank or credit union. Then came regional networks. Next you discovered access to your accounts from any machine anywhere—at home or abroad.

Now the ATM card has been enhanced so you can shop with it at all kinds of participating merchants, from supermarkets to gas stations, from high-class department stores to mass-market discount outlets. When you buy with the card, your purchase amount is immediately deducted from your account. The seller is paid then and there.

How does it work?

1. You slide your card through a slot that reads the information contained on the magnetic strip on the back of your card.
2. The cashier enters the amount of your purchase.
3. On a keyboard, you punch in your Personal Identification Number (PIN) or secret code. You may (or may not) be asked to sign for the purchase, as you do with a regular credit card.
4. The cashier presses a key that initiates an automatic phone call to your bank or credit union, to confirm that your account has enough money available.
5. Your bank or credit card then automatically deducts the amount from your account, just as when it processes a check.
6. You receive a receipt of the transaction.

The cash card works more easily than writing a check, and is safer than carrying cash. You don't need to show various forms of identification. A store will accept it more readily than an out-of-town check. But be cautioned: Be sure to keep your records straight, recording your purchases immediately in your checkbook. This makes sure you always know how much money is in your account and prevents you from overdrawing.

Cash Then there are the more traditional ways of paying. Cash is nice, but it moves fast. If you cannot break the habit of carrying cash, try to control the habit of spending it. Keep a pocket notebook. Jot down every expenditure, so you can enter accurate figures in your Spending Plan.

Check Paying by check is better than paying cash. Just about any store will take your check if you provide identification—most just want to see your driver's license; some want a look at your MasterCard or Visa card, too. Writing checks gives you accurate records, if you are careful to keep the stubs legibly filled in (always write the stub first).

Credit cards Credit cards are here to stay, at least until the cash card becomes so universal it puts them out of business. Collect your credit-card receipts and use them to verify your monthly billing from the credit-card company and to keep your spending plan on track. But watch the monthly statement so you don't mix actual purchases, as noted on your Spending Plan, with installment payments on earlier purchases.

Computer If your computer has a modem and if it is on line with such an online service as CompuServe, you can probably pay many bills—telephone, utilities, credit cards, and stores—via your keyboard, telling your bank how much to pay to whom without human hands touching cash or checks, envelopes or stamps. You will need a program like Microsoft's Money or Intuit's Quicken. If you maintain a sufficient balance, which can include your IRAs and CDs, there should be no cost involved.

Phone An easy way to pay many bills even if you do not have a computer is by telephone. Most banks, utilities, major stores, and credit cards are networked so you can call your bank and tell them whom to pay, how much, and when.

Receipts are valuable. Always get one, whether you are paying cash or by cash card or check or credit card. If you cannot get a receipt or a cash-register tape, make your own note of the date, item, and amount. Stick receipts on a spindle or in a large envelope, filed chronologically. Make sure checkbook stubs note what the purchase was, and for whom. The spindle or envelope method is especially useful if you have used your own account to pay for something that should have come out of the joint account.

> *Tip:* Keep an eye on installment payments. Each month, categorize on the record of your charge accounts any new charges, but not the amount of your monthly installment payment.

Tax angle? You bet.

Many live-togethers pay less in federal income tax than married couples pay. Generally speaking, a working couple whose incomes are about equal will find a tax advantage in not getting married. If your incomes are quite disparate, however, you may gain some savings if you are married. Keep getting up-to-date advice: tax laws are constantly changing.

How about dependents? As a taxpayer, you may claim a partner or his or her children even if they are not related to you, if they meet certain requirements:

- The dependent must be a United States citizen.
- The dependent's gross annual income may not exceed $2,300.
- The dependent must live in your residence.
- You must provide at least 50 percent of the dependent's total support for the year. This may include food, shelter, clothing, education, and medical and dental care.
- The relationship may not be in violation of local law. This is a matter you must check out carefully.

Many employers have extended benefits to cover an employee's domestic partner. But the IRS does not recognize domestic partners as dependents except in certain specific situations, so it considers the cost of such benefits as taxable income to the employee.

❍ ❍ ❍

CINDY'S HEALTH PLAN

Cindy's health insurance, for example, as provided by her employers, covers Maureen and the two children. Because she claims Maureen as a dependent, she does not have to pay tax on that part of the premium that covers

Exhibit 4
TAX RATE SCHEDULES FOR 1996

SCHEDULE X: Single Individuals

Taxable Income Over		But Not Over	Pay +	% on Excess	of the Amount Over
$0	—	$24,000	$0	15%	$0
24,000	—	58,150	3,600	28	24,000
58,150	—	121,300	13,162	31	58,150
121,300	—	263,750	32,738.50	36	121,300
263,750	—	....	84,020.50	39.6	263,750

SCHEDULE Y-1: Married Individuals Filing Jointly and Surviving Spouses

Taxable Income Over		But Not Over	Pay +	% on Excess	of the Amount Over
$0	—	$40,100	$0	15%	$0
40,100	—	96,900	6,015	28	40,100
96,900	—	147,700	21,919	31	96,900
147,700	—	263,750	37,667	36	147,700
263,750	—	....	79,445	39.6	263,750

Maureen. If Maureen were not a dependent, Cindy would have to include that money in her taxable income.

○ ○ ○

What about deductions? The law says your employer must take money out of your pay and put it into Social Security and Medicare, and your employer must match the amount you put in. In 1996, you and the company each pay in 7.65 percent of your gross salary, until your pay for the year reaches $62,700. If you are self-employed, you put in 15.3 percent of your taxable income until you reach $62,700 for the year. You continue to pay into Medicare after you get to that limit. (The Medicare portion of your Social Security payment is 1.45 percent for employees and employers, or 2.9 percent if you are self-employed.)

Your paycheck will also be reduced by deductions your employer must take for federal, state, and local taxes. Then, on your income-tax returns, you may deduct several items from your gross income, including alimony payments, and contributions to an Individual Retirement Account (IRA) if allowable. If you are self-employed, a portion of your health insurance, retirement contributions, and one half of self-employment tax is deductible from your gross income. These deductions bring you to your Adjusted Gross Income (AGI).

If you are not itemizing deductions, you subtract a standard deduction from your AGI. For a single taxpayer, the standard deduction in 1996 is $3,800. A married couple can take a $6,350 standard deduction. That means that two unmarried people living together and filing single returns can take a total of $7,600 in standard deductions—a distinct advantage of being unmarried.

Tax rates are based on your filing status (See exhibit 4).

Note that these are called "marginal tax rates." The rate for your tax bracket applies only to income that exceeds the limits for the lower bracket. For example, if you are a single taxpayer and your income is $34,000, you will be taxed at the 15-percent rate on the first $24,000 and at the 28-percent rate on the balance above that figure.

Important: If you double that $24,000, you realize that two people with equal incomes can earn up to $48,000 but, filing separate returns, each stays in the 15-percent bracket. But a married couple who earn more than $40,100 move into the 28-percent bracket. Two singles, *each* with taxable income of $25,000, will pay about $1,027 less in taxes than if they were married and filed a joint return with taxable income of $50,000. If each has taxable income of $50,000, they pay about $1,110 less. If the incomes are quite disparate, however, the two will pay more in federal income taxes than if they were married. That's because if one partner is the principal wage earner, the tax code helps those in the "traditional" married family.

Married couples have a number of advantages: They may deduct a spouse's business or investment losses against that person's income, claim one another's dependents, and combine one another's itemized deductions (e.g., excess medical expenses, mortgage interest expenses, state and local taxes, property taxes, and charitable contributions). Live-togethers suffer from the disadvantage that the person who has the higher income is not allowed to use deductions that belong to his or her partner. If one is the owner of their home, for example, only that one may deduct the interest and property expenses. Of course, if they both own the house, they may each take deductions in proportion to the amount each has contributed for mortgage interest and real estate taxes.

○ ○ ○

ETHEL AND BILL'S SEPARATE ACCOUNTS

Bill moved into Ethel's home. Every month, he gives her a check for half of the mortgage payment and half of the gas and electric bills. They maintain separate phone lines, so each pays from his or her own checking account. They keep a large manila envelope into which each puts an equal amount every two weeks, to pay for dinners out, entertainment such as movies or theater, or other things they do together. They are both receiving Social Security benefits, but otherwise neither knows the other's exact income.

○ ○ ○

MAUREEN AND CINDY'S SPENDING PLAN

Maureen and Cindy have learned to adapt to a reduced budget. When both were working, before Joshua was born, their combined income came to about $65,000. Now they live on Cindy's $45,000 salary. They have had to make some sacrifices, cutting back on entertainment, keeping a really sharp eye on the supermarket expenditures, and buying only clothes that will stay in style—when it is on sale. They have a freezer full of fruits and vegetables that they harvest from their huge garden.

○ ○ ○

DICK AND DAVE'S FIRST JOINT CHECKING ACCOUNT

As they lived together for some 30-odd years, Dick and Dave never formalized any division of expenses. They kept separate checking accounts. But when they retired, their incomes were almost the same—closer than they had ever been during working years—and they opened their first joint checking account. From it they pay all household expenses.

On a separate piece of property they own together stands a small cottage. They rent it out, putting the monthly rent into a joint checking account. That gives them enough to take care of household expenses. Dave's feeling—and Dick agrees—has always been, "Let's enjoy what we have now. I'm not going to line my coffin with money." Now that they have retired, they go on many trips and buy the best cars. They believe in mutual trust and live and let live. "When you start making demands," says Dick, "it just doesn't work."

❍ ❍ ❍

EVAN AND BOB'S JOINT ACCOUNT

Their incomes are nowhere near the same, so Evan and Bob have each maintained separate savings and investment accounts. When they started living together, they each had separate checking accounts. To pay the household bills, however, they set up a single joint checking account. Now that is their only checking account—they call it an "us" account. From it, they pay for all household expenses, entertainment, vacations, and the artwork they have been buying together lately. During vacations, and when they are collecting artwork, they charge everything on joint credit cards, paying the card balances in full from the "us" account each month. This builds frequent-flier mileage on two airline credit cards (the card provides one mile for each dollar charged). If the "us" account is running low, Bob, who has the higher income and greater savings, moves some money over from his money-market account.

"We don't divide up who is paying for what," says Bob. He puts his salary into his money-market account, while Evan puts his into the checking account. Bob's transfers from money-market into checking probably add up to more than Evan's contribution. Does it matter? No; Bob earns more. "It's all in the computer," says Bob. They track all income and expenses on a computer. They consider all monies spent on household items as joint.

❍ ❍ ❍

HOW DO THE GOLDENS LIVE ON THEIR SMALL INCOMES?

The chief source of income for all the Golden Guys and Girls is Social Security benefits. From their adjusted gross incomes, they each pay 30 percent to offset the cost of room and board. This money goes directly to the Cooperative Housing Corporation, which pays all the bills on the house—utilities, insurance, cable TV, snow removal, etc.

For food, shopping, and housekeeping services, they each pay $210 each month. The only extras are for such items as snacks (to be kept in their own small refrigerators), their own telephone services, personal care, and clothes. The privacy of having one's own room and telephone is important to them—especially to Frank, whose family gave him a computer whose first e-mail went to the White House. He pays for his monthly online service from his net income.

The household was in luck when the local woman's club furnished it with dishes, pots, pans, utensils, and curtains. Another service club came forward to install curtain rods and shower bars. A garden club built raised-bed areas, making it easier for the residents to grow vegetables and flowers.

The kitchen lacked one key appliance: a state-of-the-art mixer for Frank's bread-making. The Cooperative Housing Corporation understandably declared the mixer not in the budget. So the entire group went to work to earn the funds for the mixer. For a local printing firm they took on labeling, stapling, stuffing envelopes, and tabulating binders—all of which they were able to handle right in the middle of the living room. Result? Funds for a top-of-the-line mixer plus a stronger sense of community. In addition, they have an extra $350 in a savings account. The group is considering whether to use this money for a new four-head VCR that can play the videotapes one of them received as a gift.

❍ ❍ ❍

BOBBIE AND JACK'S SWIMMING POOL

Bobbie was so dependent financially in her marriage that she vowed never again to get into that situation. Now her ex-husband has died. As a surviving divorced spouse, she collects $1,100 a month in Social Security benefits, and she receives interest and dividends. Since she has no mortgage to pay, she is able to pay most of the expenses of maintaining her home, and Jack covers any large maintenance costs. She also buys the groceries and her own clothes.

Jack, who was used to swimming daily laps in the pool at his own home, put in a pool at Bobbie's. He thinks of the pool as a necessity and as a gift to her, but agrees that it has increased the value of her home. He pays for all their entertainment, vacations, club dues, and gifts to family members.

Jack has just started to take his Social Security benefits. In addition, he gets substantial rental income on his real estate investments and from interest and dividends on his portfolio.

❍ ❍ ❍

Each of our couples handles their finances in their own way, finding a comfort level that works for them. Ethel and Bill watch the numbers closely but independently, maintaining entirely separate accounts: each knows next to nothing about the other's finances. Dave and Dick, on the other hand, have established attitudes that are both trusting and lackadaisical about their finances, maintaining few records of who paid for what and never worrying about whether one was paying a greater share than the other. Maureen and Cindy, now that they have two children and are living on one income, work together over the household accounts, keeping careful tabs on every expenditure and stretching every dollar as far as they possibly can. And the Goldens, who share housing, keep all their moneys separate.

Worksheet VIII: Partner 1
SPENDING PLAN

	FIXED EXPENSES	Month 1			Month 2			Month 3			Month 4			Month 5			Month 6		
		Amount Estimated	Amount Spent	Difference	Amount Estimated	Amount Spent	Difference	Amount Estimated	Amount Spent	Difference	Amount Estimated	Amount Spent	Difference	Amount Estimated	Amount Spent	Difference	Amount Estimated	Amount Spent	Difference
1	Rent/Mortgage																		
2	Fuel																		
3	Electricity																		
4	Telephone																		
5	Water																		
6	Homeowner's Insurance																		
7	Automobile Insurance																		
8	Disability Insurance																		
9	Life Insurance																		
10	Personal Property Tax																		
11	Real Estate Tax																		
12	Estimated Income Tax																		
13	Automobile Loan																		
14	Loan Repayment																		
15	Loan Repayment																		
16	Other Debt																		
17	Emergency Fund																		
18	Savings/Investing (IRAs)																		
19	Other																		
20																			
21	TOTAL FIXED EXPENSES																		
22	MONTHLY AVERAGE																		
23	DIFFERENCE																		

Worksheet VIII: Partner 1
SPENDING PLAN

	FLEXIBLE EXPENSES	Month 1			Month 2			Month 3			Month 4			Month 5			Month 6		
		Amount Estimated	Amount Spent	Difference	Amount Estimated	Amount Spent	Difference	Amount Estimated	Amount Spent	Difference	Amount Estimated	Amount Spent	Difference	Amount Estimated	Amount Spent	Difference	Amount Estimated	Amount Spent	Difference
1	**Food**																		
2	Food/Beverages																		
3	Take-Home Food																		
4	Dining Out																		
5	Lunches at Work																		
6																			
7	**Clothing**																		
8	Clothing/Shoes																		
9	Laundry/Dry Cleaning																		
10	Alterations																		
11																			
12	**Gifts**																		
13	**Animals**																		
14	**Personal Care/Toiletries**																		
15	**Periodicals/Books**																		
16																			
17	**Entertainment**																		
18	Recreation																		
19	Travel/Vacations																		
20	Movies/Theater Tickets																		
21	Sporting Events																		
22																			
23	**Household Maintenance**																		
24	Lawn/Snow Removal																		
25	Maid																		
26	Garbage																		
27	Repairs																		
28	Home Furnishings																		
29	Major Appliances																		
30																			

Worksheet VIII: Partner 1
SPENDING PLAN

	FLEXIBLE EXPENSES	Month 1			Month 2			Month 3			Month 4			Month 5			Month 6		
		Amount Estimated	Amount Spent	Difference	Amount Estimated	Amount Spent	Difference	Amount Estimated	Amount Spent	Difference	Amount Estimated	Amount Spent	Difference	Amount Estimated	Amount Spent	Difference	Amount Estimated	Amount Spent	Difference
31	**Transportation**																		
32	Gas/Oil																		
33	Repairs																		
34	Licenses/Registration																		
35	Commutation, Parking																		
36																			
37	**Children's Expenses**																		
38	Allowances																		
39	Lessons																		
40	Camp																		
41	Babysitting/Child Care																		
42	Recreation/Sports																		
43																			
44	**Education**																		
45	Tuition																		
46	Room/Board																		
47	Book/Supplies																		
48	Travel																		
49																			
50	**Medical Expenses**																		
51	Doctor																		
52	Dentist																		
53	Drugs																		
54																			
55	**Contributions**																		
56	Church/Synagogue																		
57	Other Charity																		
58	Home Furnishings																		
59	Major Appliances																		
60																			
61	TOTAL FLEXIBLE EXPENSES																		
62	TOTAL FIXED EXPENSES																		
63	TOTAL EXPENSES																		
64	NET INCOME																		
65	PROFIT (LOSS)																		

Worksheet VIII: Partner 2
SPENDING PLAN

FIXED EXPENSES		Month 1			Month 2			Month 3			Month 4			Month 5			Month 6		
		Amount Estimated	Amount Spent	Difference	Amount Estimated	Amount Spent	Difference	Amount Estimated	Amount Spent	Difference	Amount Estimated	Amount Spent	Difference	Amount Estimated	Amount Spent	Difference	Amount Estimated	Amount Spent	Difference
1	Rent/Mortgage																		
2	Fuel																		
3	Electricity																		
4	Telephone																		
5	Water																		
6	Homeowner's Insurance																		
7	Automobile Insurance																		
8	Disability Insurance																		
9	Life Insurance																		
10	Personal Property Tax																		
11	Real Estate Tax																		
12	Estimated Income Tax																		
13	Automobile Loan																		
14	Loan Repayment																		
15	Loan Repayment																		
16	Other Debt																		
17	Emergency Fund																		
18	Savings/Investing (IRAs)																		
19	Other																		
20																			
21	TOTAL FIXED EXPENSES																		
22	MONTHLY AVERAGE																		
23	DIFFERENCE																		

Worksheet VIII: Partner 2
SPENDING PLAN

	FLEXIBLE EXPENSES	Month 1			Month 2			Month 3			Month 4			Month 5			Month 6		
		Amount Estimated	Amount Spent	Difference	Amount Estimated	Amount Spent	Difference	Amount Estimated	Amount Spent	Difference	Amount Estimated	Amount Spent	Difference	Amount Estimated	Amount Spent	Difference	Amount Estimated	Amount Spent	Difference
1	**Food**																		
2	Food/Beverages																		
3	Take-Home Food																		
4	Dining Out																		
5	Lunches at Work																		
6																			
7	**Clothing**																		
8	Clothing/Shoes																		
9	Laundry/Dry Cleaning																		
10	Alterations																		
11																			
12	**Gifts**																		
13	**Animals**																		
14	**Personal Care/Toiletries**																		
15	**Periodicals/Books**																		
16																			
17	**Entertainment**																		
18	Recreation																		
19	Travel/Vacations																		
20	Movies/Theater Tickets																		
21	Sporting Events																		
22																			
23	**Household Maintenance**																		
24	Lawn/Snow Removal																		
25	Maid																		
26	Garbage																		
27	Repairs																		
28	Home Furnishings																		
29	Major Appliances																		
30																			

Worksheet VIII: Partner 2
SPENDING PLAN

	FLEXIBLE EXPENSES	Month 1			Month 2			Month 3			Month 4			Month 5			Month 6		
		Amount Estimated	Amount Spent	Difference	Amount Estimated	Amount Spent	Difference	Amount Estimated	Amount Spent	Difference	Amount Estimated	Amount Spent	Difference	Amount Estimated	Amount Spent	Difference	Amount Estimated	Amount Spent	Difference
31	**Transportation**																		
32	Gas/Oil																		
33	Repairs																		
34	Licenses/Registration																		
35	Commutation, Parking																		
36																			
37	**Children's Expenses**																		
38	Allowances																		
39	Lessons																		
40	Camp																		
41	Babysitting/Child Care																		
42	Recreation/Sports																		
43																			
44	**Education**																		
45	Tuition																		
46	Room/Board																		
47	Book/Supplies																		
48	Travel																		
49																			
50	**Medical Expenses**																		
51	Doctor																		
52	Dentist																		
53	Drugs																		
54																			
55	**Contributions**																		
56	Church/Synagogue																		
57	Other Charity																		
58	Home Furnishings																		
59	Major Appliances																		
60																			
61	TOTAL FLEXIBLE EXPENSES																		
62	TOTAL FIXED EXPENSES																		
63	TOTAL EXPENSES																		
64	NET INCOME																		
65	PROFIT (LOSS)																		

CREDIT: GOOD OR BAD? SAFE OR SORRY?

"Lease is for 36 mos. based on 1st mos. pymt, $0 down pymt, $495 bank fee, sec. dep., plus tax, tags & reg. fees due at incept."

Dear Ms. : Your ATM card is now a MasterCard card. That's right. You can now use it three ways: to get cash at any automatic teller machine, as a cash card to make purchases at any one of thousands of stores, or to make charges to your MasterCard account . . .

But if we wait until we can afford it, we'll find the price even higher.

Where have you heard—or read—such familiar statements? Almost everywhere in our credit-soaked society. For nearly 50 years, we have been riding high on a wave of credit that is one of the chief reasons why so few of us are financially fit. Through good times and recessions, we Americans have luxuriated in an almost continual spending spree. We have let credit become the rubber that stretches our paychecks to and beyond the breaking point. Buying has become as much a part of life as breathing.

When two people decide to live together, they must each understand this fact of financial life. Credit is here to stay. It offers many benefits. It allows you to do things and purchase products and services that you might never be able to do or get otherwise, or that would take years to save for. Yet credit can be a bane, as well. To determine how much credit you can comfortably afford to carry, your Cash Flow Analysis and your Spending Plan are valuable tools. They provide the only sure way to control abuse of credit and, if abuse occurs, to take charge of the situation and get credit back under control. Control, in fact, is the key word: Either you control credit or credit controls you.

What, then, should they—what should *you*—do about credit cards?

Joint credit cards? Maybe yes. Maybe no.

Probably one of your first questions as live-togethers is, What about credit cards? Think carefully about joint credit accounts. They can create problems. If you set up a joint credit account, so each of you is permitted to sign for a charge, you are each responsible for whatever activity takes place in the account.

That is true even if only one of you carries the card around and uses it. Does one of you tend to be a big spender, likely to owe money all over town? The other partner is equally liable for the debt. Don't laugh. It happens. In fact, when unmarried couples buy real estate together, one partner's negative credit history can affect the couple's ability to qualify for a mortgage. More about this in chapter 11.

What if you break up when you have joint cards or other joint credit obligations? Immediately inform every joint creditor that you want to close the account. Do not simply divide the accounts and agree that one of you may use some of the accounts while the other person uses the others. That will not alter your joint responsibility. You will both continue to be liable for all charges.

If each of you is earning an income, however, you can each have your own credit accounts, deal with your creditors on your own terms, and avoid worrying about the other person's purchases. And if you decide to break up, you each go your own way with your own credit obligations.

Credit is here to stay

Shakespeare knew about credit. He created the creditor Shylock to dramatize the relationship of borrower to lender. Dickens took us inside debtors' prison in 19th-century England. And consumer credit got started nearly 150 years ago when Isaac Singer thought up the time payment: $5 down, $5 a month, to pay for his $125 sewing machine. With the average American in 1856 earning some $525 a year, he generated sales that would have been impossible if people had had to pay the full price up front.

Singer's idea took hold gradually until the concept of buying expensive items on time—automobiles, pianos, boats, airplanes, and, eventually, intangibles such as education—and paying for them while you consume them became commonplace. His inventive mind also launched an industry: bank loan departments, credit unions, General Motors (and other manufacturers') Acceptance Corporation, loan sharks, and countless others that now employ millions to service the world's borrowers.

Next came the all-purpose credit card, started by Diner's Club in 1950, when the American consumer's total outstanding debt was $21.5 billion. Forty-five years later, American Express, MasterCard, Visa, Discover, AT&T, and who knows how many others have raised the total to more than $1 trillion.

Money for rent

The idea of credit is simple. You rent money when you need it, for as long as you need it. It is not very different from renting a car during a vacation trip or renting a sprayer when you paint your house or renting extra dishes and glassware when you throw a big party. The rental firm charges you a rental fee. The credit firm charges you interest. If interest rates rise, you pay the lender more, just as you pay more for the car or sprayer or dishes if the rental company's rates go up.

Getting credit—and using it

Suppose you have never bought anything on credit or borrowed money from any business institution—how do you get credit in the first place?

The catch is that you cannot get credit until you prove that you can be depended upon to pay your debts, and you cannot prove you can pay your debts until someone takes the risk of extending credit to you. When you apply for your first credit card—especially if you are a woman who has always depended on her husband's credit—you may have a rough time. The lender will probably ask you to fill out an application form that is very much like the Net Worth Statement (Worksheet VI) and Cash Flow Statement (Worksheets VIIA and VIIB) in this book. What is the creditor looking for? Three things:

1. Do you have the ability to repay? What is your present total income, including such sources as alimony, child support payments, investments, and full- or part-time employment?
2. What are your assets? Your Net Worth Statement lists them, with their values.
3. Is there evidence that you are *willing* to pay? If you have no history of borrowing, this is the catch. You need a way to convince the lender that you understand the responsibility and will meet it. Most lenders want more than a nice smile and calm assurance.

If you lack a credit history, the lender may insist that you have a cosigner. This means that the cosigner is as liable for the payments on the account as you are, even

NO CREDIT HISTORY, NO CREDIT

During the entire time he was in college and then graduate school, Michael never applied for any credit card—despite the many offers that came in the mail or as "freestanding inserts" in the campus newspapers. He paid cash for everything he bought. But Ellen had taken advantage of a credit-card offer while she was in college. When Michael got his first permanent full-time job with the government and moved to our nation's capital, he applied for a credit card. But he was turned down—because he had not been employed long enough and no credit bureau had any credit history on him. At 31, with his Ph.D. in hand, he couldn't get a credit card. Ellen got him a card by making him a cosigner on her card account.

though the card is in your name and will be reported that way. If, for instance, you co-sign with your live-together, it means you are willing to pay the balance even if your friend cannot pay—or refuses to. As cosigner, you can be sued. If you lose the suit, your wages may be garnisheed.

How to build a credit record

Suppose you are refused credit the first time you apply, and suppose you cannot find a cosigner. What can you do? Try these suggestions:

- Open a checking account in your own name at a local bank. Be sure you don't get overdrawn. Get to know your banker. Let him or her get to know you.
- Apply for a charge account at a local store. Keep it promptly paid up.
- Establish an installment loan at a local store, purchasing something on time, as distinguished from simply charging.
- Apply for a small bank loan, even if you don't need it. Put the money you borrow into a savings account. Withdraw enough each month to make the payments on the loan.
- Apply for a major credit card (MasterCard or Visa) through the bank where you have established your checking account and the banker now knows you and trusts you.

For a moment, put yourself in the shoes of the lending institution. Think like the bank, the store, or American Express or Diner's Club. As a lender, wouldn't you be concerned with your own risk? Wouldn't you look very carefully at the borrower's current income and circumstances before you would take a chance?

TIPS

On your loan application, do not show income that is based on overtime pay or on moonlighting. What if that income should stop? Also, before you take on responsibility for repaying any loan or carrying monthly credit charges, make sure you have enough emergency funds to keep you going and pay your debts if you are laid off. Such funds should include a contingency for a large medical expense. In other words, before you sign up for credit obligations, think about as many "what ifs" as you can.

Obligation. That is the key word. Once you acquire credit, you have an obligation to pay the money back. List that obligation as a monthly fixed expense on your cash flow analysis sheet. Make the payment just as you pay your rent or mortgage or utilities, and don't abuse the obligation.

The credit bureau knows all about you

Now you are building your credit record. The next time you seek credit, the lender may get a credit report on you from a credit bureau (see Exhibit 5, Updated Credit Profile). The report lists all your credit accounts. It shows exactly when you paid—on time or late, current or delinquent. It may also include any civil suits, judgments against you in favor of creditors, or other information that could affect the lender's opinion of you as a credit risk.

Credit bureaus do not make judgments. They do not rate your credit history or your ability to repay. They simply provide the information. Your bank, department store, gasoline company, or credit-card company then uses the information to make its decision on whether you are worthy of credit.

The credit report tells whether, from the seller's point of view, there is a billing problem. If, for example, you are disputing a charge made by a store and are refusing to pay until the matter is cleared up, or if a former spouse fails to pay his or her own debts, the credit report may show such items as unpaid debts. The credit bureau will let you tell your side of the story—up to 150 words of it, anyway—and will add your information to your permanent credit record. How permanent? They keep it for seven years. But they keep bankruptcies on the record for 10 years.

The law says you are entitled to see any credit report that a credit bureau has prepared on you, and that you may challenge any item in the report that you believe is not correct. The bureau must then make an investigation and correct any error. That's especially important if the information is misleading.

If you simply want to find out what the files of a local credit bureau say about you, it may charge you a fee for issuing you a copy of its report. The fee is usually about $10. If any organization reviews your application and credit record and denies you credit, however, you are entitled to receive a copy of your credit history from the credit bureau free of charge.

> *Caution:* Some live-togethers have found that when they have lived together for a long time, or have joint credit cards or bank accounts, their credit histories have become intertwined or even erroneously attributed to each other. If this happens and one of you has a bad credit history, you will find it a disadvantage.

Exhibit 5 page 1
UPDATED CREDIT PROFILE

Subscriber Number — Applicant's Name — Current Address

Previous Addresses — Social Security Number — Year of Birth — Type, Terms and Amount — Employment

Updated Credit Profile

TRW

INQUIRY INFORMATION

► TCA1
RTS 3122250X1J CONSUMER JOHN .S., 10655 B 91502,
P-6613 S 92708,235 E 74202, S-548603388, Y-1944, T-18010005,
E-AJAX HARDWARE/2035 BROADWAY/LOS ANGELES CA 90019

PAGE	DATE	TIME	PORT	H/V	
1	09-30-87	11:23:45	HP26	A60	CONSUMER TCA1 (3)

7-87 JOHN Q CONSUMER
(1) 10655 BIRCH ST
BURBANK CA 91502

3-87 AJAX HARDWARE
(2) 2035 BROADWAY
LOS ANGELES CA 90019

(4) ACCOUNT PROFILE POS	NON	NEG	SUBSCRIBER NAME/COURT NAME STATUS COMMENT	STATUS DATE	DATE OPENED	SUBSCRIBER # COURT CODE TYPE	ASSN CODE TERMS	AMOUNT	BALANCE	ACCOUNT NUMBER/DOCKET BALANCE DATE	AMOUNT PAST DUE	PAYMENT PROFILE NUMBER OF MONTHS PRIOR TO BALANCE DATE 1 2 3 4 5 6 7 8 9 10 11 12
›››››			CHECKPOINT ››› SS# NOT ISSUED AS OF 08/87									
(5)	A		MOUNTAIN BK CURWAS30-2	(6) 1-87	8-84	1139999 SEC SCH MONTH PAY	2 60	(7) ORIGL $43000	 $19330 $956	3562401973 (8) 8-26-87 LASTPAY	 7-30-87	CCCCCCC1C1CC
A			HILLSIDE BK CURR ACCT (9)	7-87	(10) 11-86	3149999 AUT SCH MONTH PAY	5 48	ORIGL $6300	 $3748 $155 (11)	29144508119 7-30-87 (12) LASTPAY	 7-01-87	CCCCCCCC
	A		HEMLOCKS TOO NEW RT	9-87	7-87	3309999 CHG (13) SCH MONTH PAY	2 REV	HIBAL $600	 $437 $44	986543184026 9-05-87		CC
	A		BAY CO CUR WAS 60	3-87	10-Y	3339999 CHG	1 REV	LIMIT $1500	 $0	46812391013 8-21-87 LASTPAY	(14) 3-15-87	CCCCC2CCCCCC
		M	BOWERS CHARGE OFF	3-86	6-80	3369999 CHG	2 REV	C/OAM $200	(15)	212250		
		A	GARDEN FIN DELINQ 120	8-87	8-86	3509999 UNS SCH MONTH PAY	2 24	ORIGL $2200	 $1400 $100	24187010 (16) 8-17-87 LASTPAY	 $325 4-05-87	321CCCCCCCCC
A			WISTERIA FIN PD SATIS	10-86	9-85	8549999 SEC	2 12	 $500		5238610		
	A		HILLSIDE BK INQUIRY	10-18-86		3149999 AUT	(17) 48	 $6300				
		M	CO SPR CT SANTA ANA JUDGMENT	9-19-85		3019999		 $1200	(18)	07505853 ALLIED CO		
›››››			CHECKPOINT ››› SS# IS 524479971/OTHER FILE IDENT:MID INIT IS Q/ STREET INIT IS S, ZIP IS 92708 (19) JOH Q CONSUMER 6613 S 92708									
		A	WYATT FIN REPO	12-84	6-82	3519999 AUT	1 36	 $7500		29416413		
	M		GROVE CREDIT UNION INQUIRY	3-09-87		3789999 H/I	 12	 $5000				
			END — TRW INFORMATION SERVICES									

Confidential

Exhibit 5 page 2

GUIDE TO UPDATED CREDIT PROFILE REPORT

(1) Name and address as recorded on automated subscriber tapes, including date of most recent update.

(2) Employment name and address as reported by a subscriber through an inquiry on the date shown.

(3) A code designating the TRW or Credit Bureau office nearest the consumer's current address, for your use in consumer referrals.

(4) Three columns indicating positive, nonevaluated, and negative status comments.

(5) A (Automated) and M (instant Update or Manual Form) indicate the method by which the credit grantor reports information to TRW.

(6) Name and number of reporting subscriber.

(7) Association code describing the legal relationship to the account.

(8) Account or docket number.

(9) Status comment reflecting the payment condition of the account as of the status date.

(10) Date the account was opened.

(11) Scheduled monthly payment amount.

(12) Date last payment was made.

(13) Type and terms of the account.

(14) The applicant's payment history during the past 12 months. The code reflects the status of the account for each month, displayed for balance reporting subscribers only.

C	—	Current
1	—	30 days past due
2	—	60 days past due
3	—	90 days past due
4	—	120 days past due
5	—	150 days past due
6	—	180 days past due
— (Dash)	—	No history reported for that month.
Blank	—	No history maintained; see status comment.

(15) The original loan amount (ORIGL), credit limit (LIMIT), historical high balance (HIBAL), or original amount charged to loss (C/OAM), represented in dollar amounts.

(16) Balance owing, balance date, and amount past due, if applicable.

(17) Inquiries indicate a request for the applicant's credit information — inquiring subscriber, date of inquiry, and type, terms and amount, if available.

(18) Public Record: Court name, court code, docket number, type of public record, filing date, amount, and judgment creditor. This information may include bankruptcies, liens and/or judgments against the applicant.

(19) Profile report messages alert the subscriber about a credit applicant's social security number, name, address, generation, or year of birth.

Exhibit 5 page 3

NAME OF CREDIT GRANTOR ______________________ TO THE ATTENTION OF ______________________

SIGNATURE ______________________ DATE ______________________

EXPLANATION OF INFORMATION ON FORM

TRW *CREDIT DATA* — *UPDATED CREDIT PROFILE* — *CONFIDENTIAL*

INQUIRY INFORMATION 1

PAGE	DATE	TIME	PORT	H V

2

ACCOUNT PROFILE 3			SUBSCRIBER NAME COURT NAME 4			SUBSCRIBER # COURT CODE 5	ASSN CODE 6	AMOUNT 13	14	ACCOUNT DOCKET NUMBER 7		PAYMENT PROFILE MONTHS PRIOR TO BALANCE DATE 17
POS	NON	NEG	STATUS COMMENTS 8	DATE REPORTED 9	DATE OPENED 10	TYPE 11	TERMS 12	13	BALANCE	BALANCE DATE 15	AMOUNT PAST DUE 16	1 2 3 4 5 6 7 8 9 10 11 12

1 Information used to obtain this Credit Profile abbreviated in computer language
2 Your name and most recent address and reporting subscriber number. your employment on the date shown. and year of birth or age, if on file
3 These columns provide an abbreviated description of the status of the items in your profile POS(Positive) Generally viewed as favorable by credit grantors NEG(Negative) Generally viewed as unfavorable by credit grantors NON(Nonevaluated) May be viewed positively, negatively or indifferently depending on each credit grantor's policy and experience A and M indicate the method by which the credit grantor reports information to TRW (M) Manual. Manually prepared form (A) Automated Automated tapes prepared from the credit grantor's computer
4 Name of credit grantor, lienholder or court name
5 A TRW assigned identification number
6 An association code describes your legal relationship with an account (See below)
7 The number assigned to your account by the credit grantor or court docket number
8 Abbreviated description of the account status. (See Explanation of Status Comments to the right.)
9 The status comment shown in 6 is as of this date
10 Month account opened or month credit transaction took place 5-Y or 10-Y indicates open prior to 5 years or 10 years respectively
11 Credit grantor's abbreviated description of the nature of the credit extended (See chart below)
12 Terms are the periods within which extensions of credit are to be repaid Charge accounts are stated as REV meaning revolving Terms for account types R/E, R F, R V and R C (See #11) are stated in years and for all other account types the terms are stated in months
13 This amount will be either the amount of the original (or revised) credit established, or the highest amount owed
14 Balance owning on date stated under balance date (#15) or the name of judgement creditor
15 Date of the balance (#14)
16 Dollar amount past due on balance date (#15), if any
17 This information is read from left to right This column reflects the status of the account for each of the 12 months preceding the balance date (#15) A blank space indicates we do not maintain a payment history of this account A symbol appearing under one of the numbers (1 through 12) means that the account had such a status (as defined below) in that month under which the symbol appears The following symbols are used in this column

C	= current	5	150 days past due
1	= 30 days past due	6	180 days past due
2	= 60 days past due	-	no history has been reported for that particular month
3	= 90 days past due		
4	= 120 days past due	Blank	no history maintained see status comment

EXPLANATION OF STATUS COMMENTS

BK ADJ PLN	Debt included in or completed through Bankruptcy Chapter 13
BK LIQ REO	Debt included in or discharged through
CHARGE OFF	Unpaid balance reported as a loss by credit grantor
CLOS INAC	Closed inactive account
CLOS NP AA	Credit line closed not paying as agreed
COLL ACCT	Account seriously past due account assigned to attorney, collection agency or credit grantor's internal collection department
CO NOW PAY	Now paying, was a charge-off
CR CD LOST	Credit card lost or stolen
CR LN CLOS	Credit line closed reason unknown or by consumer request there may be a balance due
CR LN RNST	Account now available for use and is in good standing Was a closed account
CURR ACCT	This is either an open or closed account in good standing If the account is a credit card or charge account it should be available for use and there may be a balance due If the account is closed there were no past due amounts reported and it was paid
CUR WASCOL	Current account was a collection account
CUR WAS DL	Current account was past due
CUR WASFOR	Current account Foreclosure was started
CUR WAS 30	Current account was 30 days past due
CURWAS30-2	Current account was 30 days past due twice
CURWAS30-3	Current account was 30 days past due three times
CURWAS30-4	Current account was 30 days past due four times
CURWAS30-5	Current account was 30 days past due five times
CURWAS30 - 6	Current account was 30 days past due six times or more
CUR WAS 60	Current account was 60 days delinquent
CUR WAS 90	Current account was 90 days delinquent
CUR WAS120	Current account was 120 days delinquent
CUR WAS150	Current account was 150 days delinquent
CUR WAS180	Current account was 180 days or more delinquent
DECEASED	Consumer deceased
DELINQ 60	Account delinquent 60 days
DELINQ 90	Account delinquent 90 days
DELINQ 120	Account delinquent 120 days
DELINQ 150	Account delinquent 150 days
DELINQ 180	Account delinquent 180 days
DEL WAS 90	Account was delinquent 90 days now 30 or 60 days delinquent
DEL WAS120	Account was delinquent 120 days now 30 60 or 90 days delinquent
EDU CLAIM	Claim filed with government for insured portion of balance on an educational loan
FORECLOSURE	Credit grantor sold collateral to settle defaulted mortgage
FORE PROC	Foreclosure proceeding started
INQUIRY	A copy of the credit profile has been sent to this credit grantor at their request
INS CLAIM	Claim filed for payment of insured portion of balance
NOT PD AA	Account not being paid as agreed
PAID ACCT	Closed account zero balance not rated by credit grantor
PAID SATIS	Closed account paid satisfactory
PD BY DLER	Credit grantor paid by company who originally sold the merchandise
PD CHG OFF	Paid account was a charge-off
PD COLL AC	Paid account was a collection account insurance claim or education claim
PD FORECLO	Paid account A foreclosure was started
PD NOT AA	Paid account Some payments were made past the agreed due dates
PD REPO	Paid account was a repossession
PD WAS 30	Paid account was past due 30 days
PD WAS30-2	Paid account was past due 30 days 2 or 3 times
PD WAS30-4	Paid account was past due 30 days 4 times
PD WAS30-5	Paid account was past due 30 days 5 times
PD WAS30 - 6	Paid account was past due 30 days 6 times or more
PD WAS 60	Paid account was delinquent 60 days
PD WAS 90	Paid account was delinquent 90 days
PD WAS 120	Paid account was delinquent 120 days
PD WAS 150	Paid account was delinquent 150 days
PD WAS 180	Paid account was delinquent 180 days or more
REDMD REPO	Account was a repossession now redeemed
REFINANCED	Account renewed or refinanced
REPO	Merchandise was taken back by credit grantor there may be a balance due
SCNL	Credit grantor cannot locate consumer
SCNL NWLOC	Credit grantor could not locate consumer consumer now located
SETTLED	Account legally paid in full for less than the full balance
TRANSFERRED	Account transferred to another office
VOLUN REPO	Voluntary repossession
30 DAY DEL	Account past due 30 days
30 2 TIMES	Account past due 30 days 2 times
30 3 TIMES	Account past due 30 days 3 times
30 4 TIMES	Account past due 30 days 4
30 5 TIMES	Account past due 30 days 5 times
30 6 - TIMES	Account past due 30 days 6 times or more
30 WAS 60	Account was delinquent 60 days now 30 days

COURT CODES

CIR	CIRCUIT	IRS	INTERNAL REVENUE SERVICE
CITY	CITY	JUS	JUSTICE
CVL	CIVIL	MUN	MUNICIPAL
CO	COUNTY	REG	REGISTRAR
CT	COURT	ST	STATE
DIS	DISTRICT	SPR	SUPERIOR
		SUP	SUPREME

TYPE OF ACCOUNT

ABBREV	EXPLANATION
AUT	Auto
UNS	Unsecured
SEC	Secured
P S	Partially Secured
H I	Home Improvement
FHA	FHA Home Improvement
ISC	Installment Sales Contract
CHG	Charge Account
R E	Real Estate Specific Type Unknown-term in years
SCO	Secured by Co-Signer
BUS	Business
REC	Recreational Merchandise
EDU	Educational
LEA	Lease
COM	Co-Maker (not borrower)
C C	Check Credit or Line of Credit
F C	FHA Co-Maker (not borrower)
M H	Mobile Home
CRC	Credit Card
R F	FHA Real Estate Mortgage-terms are in years
NTE	Note Loan
NCM	Note Loan with Co-Maker
HHG	Secured By Household Goods
H · C	Secured By Household Goods & Other Collateral
ASL	Auto
R V	VA Real Estate Mortgage-terms are in years
R C	Conventional Real Estate Mortgage-terms are in years
R O	Real Estate Mortgage-with or without other collateral Usually a second mortgage-terms are in months Amount shown in $100 00 increments
SLC	Co-Maker (not borrower)
REN	Rental Agreement
SUM	Summary of Accounts with same status
UNK	Unknown
DCS	Debt Counseling Service
CCP	Combined Credit Plan
QST	Account review by credit grantor
A M	Account monitor by credit grantor
RVW	Account review by credit grantor
EMP	Employment
PSC	Solicitation

ASSOCIATION CODES WITH DEFINITIONS

ASSOCIATION WITH ACCOUNT CURRENTLY ACTIVE — ASSOCIATION TERMINATED AS OF DATE REPORTED

0 — UNDESIGNATED — A
Reported by TRW Credit Data only

1 — INDIVIDUAL
This individual is the only person associated with this account

2 — JOINT ACCOUNT-CONTRACTUAL RESPONSIBILITY — B
This individual is expressly obligated to repay all debts arising on this account by reason of having signed an agreement to that effect There are others associated with this account who may or may not have contractual responsibility

3 — AUTHORIZED USER-JOINT ACCOUNT — C
This individual has use of this joint account for which another individual has contractual responsibility

4 — JOINT ACCOUNT — D
This individual participates in this account The association cannot be distinguished between Joint Account-Contractual Responsibility or Authorized User

5 — CO-MAKER — E
This individual has guaranteed this account and assumes responsibility should maker default This code only to be used in conjunction with Code 7-Maker

6 — ON BEHALF OF — F
This individual has signed an application for the purpose of securing credit for another individual other than spouse

7 — MAKER — G
This individual is responsible for this account which is guaranteed by a co-maker To be used in lieu of Code 2 and 3 when there is a Code 5-Co-Maker

ITEMS OF PUBLIC RECORD

CH 7—FILED	Voluntary or Involuntary Petition in Bankruptcy Chapter 7 · (Liquidation) filed
CH 7—DISCH	Voluntary or Involuntary Petition in Bankruptcy Chapter 7 · (Liquidation) discharged
CH 7—DISM	Voluntary or Involuntary Petition in Bankruptcy Chapter 7 · (Liquidation) dismissed
CH 11—FILE	Voluntary or Involuntary Petition in Bankruptcy Chapter 11 · (Reorganization) filed
CH 11—DISC	Voluntary or Involuntary Petition in Bankruptcy Chapter 11 · (Reorganization) discharged
CH 11—DISM	Voluntary or Involuntary Petition in Bankruptcy Chapter 11 · (Reorganization) dismissed
CH 13—FILE	Petition in Bankruptcy Chapt 13 (Adjustment of Debt) filed
CH 13—DISM	Petition in Bankruptcy Chapt 13 (Adjustment of Debt) dismissed
CH 13—COMP	Petition in Bankruptcy Chapt 13 (Adjustment of Debt) completed
CITY TX LN	City Tax Lien
CITY TX REL	City Tax Lien Released
CONSEL SER	Debt Counseling Service
CO TAX LN	County Tax Lien
CO TAX REL	County Tax Lien Released
FED TAX LN	Federal Tax Lien
FED TX REL	Federal Tax Lien Released
JUDGMENT	Judgment
JUDGMT SAT	Judgment Satisfied
JUDG VACAT	Judgment Vacated or Reversed
MECH LIEN	Mechanic's Lien
MECH RELE	Mechanic's Lien Released
MN MTG FIL	Manual Mortgage Report (Developed credit report prepared for this credit grantor, copy attached.)
NT RESPON	Not Responsible Notice, e.g., husband or wife claims not responsible for debts incurred by spouse
STAT TX LN	State Tax Lien
STAT TX REL	State Tax Lien Released
SUIT	Suit
SUIT DISMD	Suit Dismissed or Discontinued
WAGE ASIGN	Wage Assignment
W A RELEASE	Wage Assignment Released

Note: Federal law bars any creditor from discriminating against you because of race, color, religion, national origin, sex, marital status, or age. While the law does not specifically mention sexual orientation, no cases are known in which gays or lesbians have been denied credit because of sexual orientation. The term "marital status" in the law prevents discrimination against unmarried couples.

The key to credit: your Spending Plan

Don't make the mistake of trying to use credit without setting up and maintaining a well-thought-out Spending Plan. Only your spending plan can tell you how much credit you can safely afford. It will enable you to keep a sharp eye on your monthly repayments to credit accounts, so you do not become overextended. Many people get into trouble by not watching such repayments and running out of money. Then, to buy items that should be included in regular living expenses, they use their credit cards or other charge accounts.

Here's how it happens: No money in the checking account. None in the wallet or purse, either. But must buy something. Use credit. Charge-account balances rise. Credit-card balances rise. Monthly payments cover only the minimum required, if that. Balances due reach approved limits. Apply for more credit on charge cards. Open new accounts at other stores. Minimum payments plus finance charges add up to major expense every month. Available cash for each month gets smaller and smaller. Miss a monthly payment or two. Pay each account less than the minimum due. Juggle—pay this account this month, that account next month. Mail brings past-due notices. Collection agency sends dunning notice. Or phones. Stomach in knots. Head aching. Ulcer kicking in. You add up everything. Your total indebtedness is greater than your annual income.

Credit problems know no economic or social bounds. A junior assistant on a $25,000-a-year salary owes $25,000. An executive earning six figures owes more than $100,000.

Worksheet IX:
LIST OF DEBTS
Date__________

CREDITOR'S NAME	TYPE OF LOAN	DATE OF LAST PAYMENT	MATURITY DATE	MONTHLY PAYMENT From Budget	TOTAL AMOUNT DUE From Net Worth Statement

TOTAL MONTHLY PAYMENTS $

TOTAL AMOUNT OWED $

Chances are, you have already established your own credit history before you decide to live with another person. You each come into the relationship with your own credit cards, automobile loans, maybe educational debts. Before you make a commitment to live together, it is important to look at one another's credit obligations. If one of you is burdened by debt, less money may be available for living expenses. The relationship can erode rapidly if one partner feels that he or she may have to carry the other because of credit obligations. One way to get a clear picture is to look at your debt ratio.

Figuring out your debt ratio

Turn to Worksheet IX, **List of Debts.** Write down all your current consumer debts (your total amount of indebtedness should already be on your Net Worth Statement). This doesn't include your mortgage payment. Your monthly obligations are listed under credit repayment on your Fixed Expenses Worksheet.

Now, on Worksheet X, **Personal Debt Ratio,** figure out a ratio for yourself, based on your total take-home pay and your installment obligations. Your debt ratio is the percentage of your take-home pay (i.e., your net income after all payroll deductions) that you must commit to the repayment of debts.

Most people find that they are in danger if more than 15 to 20 percent of net income is committed to repaying debts. Let the ratio get higher, and you may find yourself robbing Peter to pay Paul, borrowing to meet daily expenses, lengthening the time between payments, charging items that will have a life span less than the time it takes to pay for them.

Check out this test: Can you pay off all your consumer debts within the next 18 to 24 months? If not, your debt ratio is too high.

At any one time, you should know the ratio of all your debts. When you pay off a loan, of course, the ratio changes, and you can then judge whether you can safely borrow again, and whether it makes sense to borrow.

> *Caution:* When you pay off a loan with an obligation of, say, $50 a month, it seems easy to take on another—with maybe a $65 payment. What's another $15 a month? you say to yourself. But if your ordinary non-credit living expenses are rising along with inflation, that $15 a month can lead to disaster. Slowly but surely, if you repeatedly add

Worksheet X:
PERSONAL DEBT RATIO

Your ratio is based on take-home pay. You have figured out the amount of debt that you owe for installment loans. Is this too much for you?

	MONTHLY	YEARLY
1. Your total take-home pay	$	$
2. Use 20% (maximum for most consumers). Divide income by 5. If you feel this is too high, use 15% or divide by 6.7.	$	$
3. Your present installment obligations	$	$
4. Your present safety margin—subtract line 3 from line 2.	$	$
5. Your personal ratio—divide your installments obligation (line 3) by your take home pay (line 1).		

It might be wise to use both the 15% and 20% figures to see the difference in your own situation.

a new debt that is larger than the one you have just paid off, you will rise into a higher and more dangerous debt ratio. Keeping debt within your means, on the other hand, will make more of your monthly take-home pay available for your own security and pleasure. Clamping down on costs that include interest payments will give you more spendable dollars.

Breaking the spending habit

If your debt ratio tells you it is time to cut back on expenses in order to pay off debts, you may have to devote a year or so to being scrupulously careful not to add any new debts while you pay off the current ones. How best to do that?

The best way to go is cold turkey. It is tough—but you can do it. Write out and sign an agreement with yourself. Then gather up all your charge cards—each and every one. Put them into a friend's safe deposit box. And tell your friend not to listen to any plea you make to get them back. Even better—cut each one in half and return them to the creditors, with a note of explanation.

Next, look steely-eyed at your Spending Plan. Cut out every living expense that is not an absolute necessity. Stick to it. Open a separate bank account and deposit a certain amount every payday. Then—*important*—use the money in this account for debt reduction and debt reduction *only*.

If you put yourself on this strict regimen, you will be able to manage on the amount of money you actually have.

You might also think about consolidating all your debts. Some lending institutions specialize in this activity. They lend you enough to pay everyone you owe. You then pay back the single lender over an extended period. Warning: This type of loan can involve a substantial amount of interest, but it does usually give you a lower monthly payment for debt reduction than the total of paying all those separate accounts. Some people use home-equity loans to consolidate their debts. That's a possibility if you have enough equity in your home to get approval of the loan.

Keep these tips in mind for staying out of credit trouble:

- Ask yourself: Would I buy this if I were paying cash? Deferred spending often turns into avoided spending.
- Before you decide on a loan, shop around.
- Refrain from impulse shopping. Never buy anything because it will lift your spirits.
- Never charge everyday expenses on a credit card.
- Track credit-card purchases carefully. Keep good records. Agree with your partner to put all credit-card slips in one place immediately after each purchase. An unexpected charge or unnoticed bill is the worst kind of surprise. It's bad enough if you are the one who forgot; it is worse if you open the monthly credit-card statement to discover that your partner has added a large purchase (especially if you happen to think it was an unnecessary one) that you had not anticipated.

The path to bankruptcy

Suppose you have set up a big loan to consolidate all your debts. Or you have taken on a home-equity loan, which means monthly payments like a second mortgage. And suppose your credit cards are not locked up in your friend's safe-deposit box or cut into pieces. And you start charging again. You are starting the cycle all over again. Within a few months, or a year or two, you will find yourself signing another consolidation loan—if you can get one. The pattern will repeat. It is the path to bankruptcy.

Congress passed the Bankruptcy Act of 1978 to make it easier for one to repay a substantial portion of one's debt, and to ease the actual burdens of going bankrupt. The law acknowledges that people get themselves into economic situations that are often beyond their control, for the ripple effect of our inflationary economy is particularly hard on you if you are extended beyond your safety margin. The act has produced a tremendous increase in personal bankruptcies. In 1995, for example, American creditors lost nearly $5 billion through an estimated one million personal bankruptcies.

Don't forget—if you and your partner are keeping joint credit accounts, bankruptcy for one is bankruptcy for the other. In any case, before you decide to declare personal bankruptcy, talk with a lawyer about various chapters of the Bankruptcy Act and the petitions that you must fill out and file. He or she will tell you that Chapter 13 encourages you to repay your loans. Its so-called "wage-earner plan" lets you consolidate your debts and repay a percentage of them, as approved by the court, over three years. Creditors, in the meantime, must suspend interest and late charges on most debts, and they may not continue any action against you. If you default on Chapter 13 payments, the court will throw you into Chapter 7 proceedings. Chapter 7 covers a straight bankruptcy. That means the court collects, sells, and distributes your (i.e., the debtor's) assets, with certain exemptions.

Bank cards: the incredible selection

More than 19,000 financial institutions offer MasterCard or Visa. Dozens of businesses that are not traditional financial institutions, from AT&T to Sears Roebuck, also compete for your credit-card business. Cards vary in:

- Annual fees—ranging from $0 to $50 (some give you that first year free but charge a fee starting with the second year)
- Interest rates—ranging from 8.5 percent to 21 percent
- Grace periods

Then there are the affinity programs—some 1,500 of them. These set up relationships between charities and nonprofit organizations, including alumni associations and professional organizations. The organizations benefit by receiving a portion of the cardholders' annual fees and/or transaction fees. Your favorite charity or professional group may offer an affinity card relationship and will welcome your application. Affinity groups exist, for example, in the environmental area, with both national and local organizations or chapters of such groups as the World Wildlife Fund, the Zoological Society of Florida, and even the Federation of Fly Fishers.

Many a grandparent flies to visit distant grandchildren two or three times a year on frequent-flyer miles earned by charging frequently on a major credit card that has an affinity relationship to an airline. The usual rate you get is one mile for every dollar you charge. If you have absolute self-discipline, you can break the don't-charge-everyday-expenses rule and build up mileage fast by charging just about everything—even your groceries, since most supermarkets now accept credit cards.

Take a look at the reward programs, too. A number of companies offer a credit card that gives you something back each time you use it. Credits may go toward purchase of an automobile. Or they may bring you gift certificates.

It's almost free money

Take advantage of the billing cycles of your credit cards. If you pay the full amount due each month, you can gain a real advantage. Here's how.

Before they assess finance charges, most credit cards allow a grace period of 25 to 30 days after the date on which they bill you. If you make a purchase immediately after your billing date (you'll find the date imprinted on your bill), and if you pay in full when you pay, you can gain free credit for almost two months. Example: Your billing date is July 1. You buy something on July 2. The charge does not appear on your bill until August. You then have until September 1 (or the due date stated on the bill) to pay for it. If you pay the full amount of your new balance by September, no interest will be charged. You will gain the advantage of free use of your July 2 purchase until the first of September—just about two months.

> Evan and Bob charge everything—even their art acquisitions—on an airline MasterCard, so they get one frequent-flier mile for every dollar they spend. This pays for their vacation flights.

Finance charges: do you need an interpreter?

If you do not pay the amount due in full, your credit-card company will add finance charges. Any of several methods of calculation may be used by your company. The most common is the average daily balance method, including newly billed purchases. In this method, the grace period for newly purchased items (see the preceding paragraph) is not allowed. Note also that, under this method, the finance charge is based on the *average* amount you have charged during the preceding month. As soon as your latest purchase goes into the computer, your average changes and your finance charge goes up. The finance charge continues to be calculated on your latest average daily balance until it changes again. If your creditor uses this method, it is better to pay as soon as you receive the bill rather than waiting (as you might have done when paying in full) until the end of the month. Why? Because, if you decide to leave part of a bill unpaid for only one month, you will be charged interest.

The two-cycle method is now being used by a few credit-card issuers. It calculates the interest on last month's balance and on this month's, then adds them together. If you sometimes pay in full and sometimes carry a balance, this method can be very expensive, for you can be charged interest even for months when you have made full payment.

If you make only partial payments month after month, you invite high finance charges—and trouble. The reason is that, no matter how much you pay, the creditor takes its full finance charge out before it deducts anything from the balance you owe. So, if you pay only the minimum required, you reduce your debt only by that amount *less the finance charge*. And as you continue paying only the minimum, the finance charges are compounding. Suppose, for instance, you show a balance of $2,500. You make a minimum payment of 2 percent ($50 the first month). If the interest rate is 18 percent, it will take you just under 28 years to pay off the balance, and you will pay a total of $5,896 in interest over that time. As you pay off the loan, the minimum payment will drop slightly each month.

If you owe a rather large balance, your required minimum payment may be mostly interest (or finance charge) month after month while the principal amount you owe reduces very, very slowly—much too slowly to be considered sound money management.

Exhibit 6
FINANCE CHARGE CALCULATION

FINANCE CHARGES AS CALCULATED USING AVERAGE DAILY BALANCE WITH NEWLY PURCHASED ITEMS INCLUDED. The finance charge *depends on the date the payment is received* as illustrated. In the first example the payment is made on the 15th of June and in the latter on the 24th. Note there is $1.13 difference by paying it 9 days later.

6/1	Previous Balance	$300.00 × 5	1500.00
6/5	Purchase of $10.00	$310.00 × 5	1550.00
6/10	Purchase of $65.00	$375.00 × 5	1875.00
6/15	Payment of $200.00	$175.00 × 6	1050.00
6/21	Purchase of $18.00	$193.00 × 3	579.00
6/24	Purchase of $7.00	$200.00 × 7	1400.00
		31 days	7954.00

7954.00 divided by 31 (number of days in billing cycle) equals 256.58 (average daily balance) times 1½ equals $3.85 (finance charge).

6/1	Previous Balance	$300.00 × 5	1500.00
6/5	Purchase of $10.00	$310.00 × 5	1550.00
6/10	Purchase of $65.00	$375.00 × 5	1875.00
6/15	Purchase of $18.00	$393.00 × 5	1965.00
6/21	Purchase of $7.00	$400.00 × 6	2400.00
6/24	Payment of $200.00	$200.00 × 5	1000.00
		31 days	10,290.00

10,290.00 divided by 31 equals 331.93   331.93 times 1½% equals $4.98 finance charge

Watch for sneaky tricks

Among issuers of credit cards, competition is fierce. Often they come up with offers that sound too good to be true. Heed the old adage: If it seems too good to be true, it probably is. Read the fine print with great care, for that is where the ploys are buried. Some examples:

- The no-fee card with ultralow interest. The headline, or the lead paragraph in the letter, says "no fee" and promises a delightfully low rate of interest. The small print discloses that after a certain amount of time (usually six months to a year) the interest jumps higher and an annual fee may be imposed.
- The reduced rate. If the bank that issued your card suddenly announces it is reducing the interest rate, don't assume you will get the lower rate. You may first have to pay off your entire remaining balance at the old rate. You may save money by simply switching to another credit-card issuer—one that is competing by also offering the lower rate.
- The spending requirement. The card offering a very low rate of interest may demand that you charge a certain amount annually. Otherwise, it keeps your rate higher than for someone who is spending at the required level.
- The bait-and-switch tactic. You get an invitation to apply for a "pre-approved" gold card with no annual fee. But then, despite the "pre-approved" promise, you are turned down. The issuer may then send you the standard non-gold card instead, with a higher interest rate, lower spending limit, and an annual fee. You do not have to accept it, however. You can cut it up and send it back. But

remember: You filled out and signed an application, so the account may show up on your credit history even if you never use it, leading some other creditor who is looking you over to think you are already overextended.

- The tier-rate system. Many credit-card issuers offer lower rates to preferred customers. If you are unhappy with your current card, or have been offered a better deal elsewhere, the issuer may waive your annual fee or offer you another card with a more attractive rate. It never hurts to ask for a better deal, for credit-card issuers do not want to lose your business. It costs more to land a new customer than to hang on to an old one.

How to apply for a low-interest card

Those who issue low-interest cards are working on a tight profit margin. They can't afford to take on customers who may default or declare bankruptcy. So they ask you to fill out an application that is longer than usual, and they look you over very carefully and approve fewer people. If you want to be sure you get approval for a low-interest card, here's how to increase your chances:

1. If you are behind on any of your bills, get caught up before you apply.
2. Avoid looking like a high risk. If you have more than four credit cards with large outstanding balances, pay off one or more of them by transferring the balances to one of your other cards—preferably one that offers lower interest rates.
3. Pay off your outstanding balances down to not more than 70 percent of your approved credit limit.
4. Reduce the total amount of credit that is available to you. Got any cards you are not now using? Cut them up, if they have no outstanding balances, and write the issuer saying you want to close the account. *Important:* Be sure to request that this information be reported promptly to the credit bureau, and then check your credit history to verify the cancellation.
5. Don't apply for too many low-interest credit cards all at the same time. When your application for a new credit card comes in, the issuing company will request your credit history. All requests show up on the credit bureau's computer, and too many inquiries over a period of a few months or a year can make you look like a poor risk.

Splitting big-ticket costs

Suppose you two want to split the cost of buying something that's quite expensive. Say it's a $2,000 computer. You can charge $1,000 on each of your credit cards. Or one of you can buy the CPU (central processing unit) while the other buys the monitor and printer—each paying for his or her purchases by card, cash, or check. If you're the type who keeps absolutely everything separate, you can even split restuarant checks, each using your own credit card.

How about buying a car? Probably, like most folks, you cannot afford to buy a car, at today's prices, with cash. Should you take out a loan jointly, or lease jointly? The best way is for each of you to lease or buy your own car, taking out your own loan. But what if one of you needs a new car and the other is advancing part or all of the down payment? The borrower should sign a written contract to repay the loan to his or her partner. If you want to have joint ownership of the vehicle, you should sign an agreement that outlines the details—especially if one of you is signing a bank loan but both of you are contributing funds to repay it.

Your state's motor vehicle department must prepare title documents on your car, to show its type of ownership. If you are setting up joint ownership, be sure to check with them for specific details.

❍ ❍ ❍

MAUREEN AND CINDY PAY OFF DEBT

When Maureen left her full-time job to stay home with Joshua, she had $15,000 in her 401(k). She decided to take it and pay the penalty and the taxes in order to pay off several debts. Less debt meant lower monthly expenses.

❍ ❍ ❍

WHY BILL PAYS CASH

Bill's habit of paying cash stems from the time when he made the mistake of investing in a friend's business. It went belly up, and Bill was out nearly $100,000 and had to declare bankruptcy. That's why he and Ethel save cash in an envelope for entertainment and dining out. Using this method, they won't run up charges on Ethel's credit cards and he can pick up the check at the restaurant table.

❍ ❍ ❍

CHAPTER SEVEN

SAVING AND INVESTING: WHERE TO KEEP VERSUS WHERE TO PUT YOUR MONEY

❍ ❍ ❍ ❍

"Should we own our investments jointly?"

"Should we keep our savings in a passbook account?"

"What makes saving 'passive' and investing 'active'?"

"Why not buy Treasuries through the mail?"

"CDs, stocks, bonds, mutual funds—how can I decide among all these types of investments?"

"Is there any single most important key to investing?"

"Can you please explain 'phantom income'?"

❍ ❍ ❍

Saving is one thing. Investing is another. There is a big difference.

When you save, you accumulate money for a specific purpose or to use in an emergency. You use saving as a way of preserving your capital and guaranteeing that you will have funds to pay your expenses if other income dries up. You also maintain liquidity; money you have put into savings is always immediately available.

Investing is something else. It involves some risk—how much depends on the type of investment. You accept the risk on the premise that you will get returns that are higher than you get from the dependable but conservative practice of ordinary saving. When you invest in a stock, for example, you are assuming that you will sell later on at a price higher than you paid when you bought the stock.

Investing involves more than risk. It demands your time and effort. You must be willing to take the time to study, listen, compare, and sometimes make difficult choices. So investing is active—much more active than saving, which is passive.

If you want your money to grow, you have to start an investment program. Your most important consideration, at the outset, is to understand that investing takes time and patience. You will be foolish to try to rush it or to outguess the market. Over the long haul, you will see slumps and you will see rallies.

The second most important thing about investing is this: Don't get into it until you have established saving as the foundation of your financial pyramid. Several fundamental elements are needed for a solid and successful investment program, including:

- Savings for an emergency
- Savings for one or more specific goals
- Enough life insurance
- IRAs and 401(k)s
- A home of your own

You need one more fundamental: enough income to meet living and saving expenses and to maintain a positive cash flow—i.e., liquidity. If you have that solid foundation in place, you can consider yourself ready to take the risks that come with investing in stocks and bonds or any of the possibilities of the market.

The passive side: saving

One of the facts about money is that when it is in a checking account it gets spent. That means you must have at least one savings account. If you are opening checking accounts—joint or individual—open savings accounts at the same time. Get into the habit of paying yourself immediately after every payday. Put money away for your emergency fund and for fixed expenses—preferably the same predetermined amount each time.

You can use any of several types of savings accounts:

1. *Passbook or regular savings account.* This is the good old standard. You can get your money out of it any time, without paying a penalty for the privilege. Most automated teller machines (ATMs) are glad to serve up your savings just as easily as they let you get money out of your checking account. The main disadvantage of a passbook or regular savings account is that it pays low interest—less than most other accounts. But in many banks you can avoid monthly charges on your checking account by keeping a minimum balance in a savings account.

Another disadvantage: Some banks quietly take a service charge (typically, $5) monthly out of any savings account that has a balance under $300. That's $60 a year gone forever.

When you talk with a banker about opening a savings account, ask how interest is credited. Is it compounded daily, quarterly, semiannually, or annually? The more frequently the interest is compounded, the higher the effective yield, and the faster your money grows. The effective yield is the total interest the account pays. You can figure out compounding, and its effective yield. Start with your current balance, or principal amount. Calculate the interest paid for a given period—year, half-year, month, or day—and add that to your current balance. That gives you a new balance or principal amount. Using that new total, calculate the interest again, and add it to get yet another new principal.

What is the ideal rate of compounding interest? Daily, from day of deposit to day of withdrawal.

Just *when* is the interest credited? is another important question. Some banks may compound interest every day but withhold crediting that earned money to your account until three months go by. Not so good, if you should need to withdraw money before the end of the three months. You could lose all the interest. Again, day-of-deposit to day-of-withdrawal is how you want your interest compounded.

2. *Bank money-market account.* Usually you can get higher interest in this type of account than in a regular passbook savings account. You will probably have to make a minimum deposit of $1,000. The money-market account has advantages and disadvantages:

- The bank may prescribe its own rate of interest, determined by what it sees in market conditions, so shop carefully.
- The bank is not allowed to guarantee its interest rate for longer than a month. Most banks guarantee the rate only for a week, so they can be competitive with Wall Street's money-market funds, which are in popular demand.
- You can maintain your money-market account in the bank where you have your checking account, transferring funds when you need them. This lets you earn interest right up to the moment when you need the cash.
- Bank money-market accounts carry Federal Deposit Insurance Corporation (FDIC) coverage up to $100,000.

3. *Mutual fund money-market account.* You can expect this one to earn higher interest than a bank money-market account, but the rules are more strict. You will probably get check-writing privileges, for example, but you will not be allowed to take less than $500 in any one withdrawal and your number of withdrawals per month may be limited. The mutual fund will probably invest your money in CDs and government securities, and it will not be insured by the FDIC.

4. *CDs or TDs.* If you buy certificates of deposit or time deposits, you will be committed to keeping that money on deposit for a minimum period. Such certificates are called "deregulated." That simply means that the government does not set the rates. Any bank may decide on the minimum investment size it is willing to handle, and may set its own interest rate. Duration is not limited, either. You may buy a certificate that runs

for just about any term you want, from three months to 10 years. You are welcome to pick your own maturity date. Looking ahead to a child's or grandchild's birthday? Anticipating a big celebration for a major anniversary—a business date, a when-we-met date? Tell the bank when you buy the certificate. They'll set up the interest rate and maturity date you want.

You have to look closely at deregulated investments. Ask tough questions. Read folders and brochures—and especially small print—with care. You will find that many choices are facing you.

> *Note:* One nice advantage is that deregulation reduced the penalties that were formerly exacted if you cashed in a CD or TD before its maturity date.

Investing

Investing means looking ahead—far ahead. Three years, five years, maybe longer. You cannot think short-term.

That means you must sit down and seriously consider your objectives, figuring out just what you want your investments to accomplish. You must do your homework, gaining an understanding of what "investments" are and how they work.

Your understanding must include the fact that investing can produce anxiety. Investment "vehicles" and investment "products" (the jargon of Wall Street for how you describe whatever you are investing your money in) can be highly complex, so you need to acquire enough knowledge to make informed decisions. That takes time and effort and a willingness to read, listen, and learn. It also means not listening to non-experts and not chasing after will-o'-the-wisp tips.

The wide-ranging market

The number of choices you face is almost staggering. It ranges from stocks and bonds to precious metals, from mutual funds to real estate, from tangible goods to collectibles. Dozens of experts are waiting with tons of advice: from stock brokers to certified public accountants, from lawyers to securities analysts.

The many risks

When you hear about someone who has made it big in the market, remember that for every winner there is a loser—someone who willingly took a risk and suffered a loss. But if that person had a solid financial foundation established beforehand, and understood how investing works, he or she was prepared for the loss.

Investing is risky, yes. It demands that you understand just how much you yourself—or you and your partner, if you are investing together—can live with. You have to build up enough knowledge to know whether you are more comfortable investing in blue-chip stocks or in tax-sheltered limited partnerships, in municipal bonds or in high-grade corporate bonds. "Comfortable" is a key word. You must not let anyone talk you into any investment in which you feel uncomfortable.

The risk spreads itself out over the long term. Look at what happened in and after October 1987. Within a few days, the stock market lost 24 percent of its value. Countless investors, not willing to think long-term (or perhaps just incapable of thinking long-term) cashed out, taking major losses. But in 1988, the market—as measured by Standard & Poor's 500 Stock Index—gained 16.5 percent, and the next year it went up 31.7 percent. Those who had not cashed out, but held on to their stocks, made solid gains and were better off than ever.

Exhibit 7
COMPOUND INTEREST CHART

Investing small amounts of money over time can prove to be very profitable. The chart below shows the effect of $1,200 per year ($100 per month) invested at varying rates compounded *annually*.

END OF YEAR VALUES	6%	8%	10%
5th year	$7,170	$7,603	$8,059
10th year	16,766	18,774	21,037
20th year	46,791	59,307	75,602
30th year	100,562	146,815	217,131
40th year	196,857	335,737	584,222

You should be aware of a number of risks, but—let's face it—you will have very little control over them. They include:

- *Macroeconomic risk.* These are the big ones, such as: a change in the federal government's monetary policy . . . or a change in policy by the Organization of Petroleum Exporting Countries (OPEC) . . . or a world crisis such as the threat of war.
- *Market risk.* Changes in interest rates (e.g., a major change in the prime rate) . . . or changes in psychology and perception that are not connected to economic events.
- *Industry risk.* Changes within a specific industry, such as the computer world, where rapid obsolescence can be a key factor.
- *Business risk.* Changes in share of market held by a given company because a competitor has attracted new customers by earning greater share of voice through advertising or by introducing a new or improved product.
- *Management risk.* Mergers and acquisitions, top-level reorganizations, poor judgment—such management events can affect the value of your shares in a company. Even an unforeseen news event—an accident, a fire—can spell trouble.
- *Information risk.* Perhaps this one should be labeled "misinformation" risk, for it usually involves rumor or other false and misleading information.
- *Natural disaster risk.* A hurricane, flood, tornado, or drought can severely affect an investment, especially in agricultural or livestock companies or those in the paths of natural disasters.
- *Liquidity risk.* This is the one that brings disillusion to any investor who does not maintain a long-term viewpoint. It is the risk that you won't get your money out, with at least some profit, when you want to sell. Many who bought tax-sheltered investments in the early to mid-1980s, for example, found in the 1990s that their expectations could not be met. Commercial real estate, oil and gas exploration, and a number of other investments simply stayed flat or lost all or most of their value.

The liquidity risk is the one most likely to affect you. If you cannot risk liquidity—if you *must* maintain liquidity—put your savings where they will not only preserve the asset (i.e., the basic amount you have saved) but will give you a nice steady rate of return or income. Never forget that whether you can handle the liquidity risk is your primary criterion in deciding whether or not to get into investing.

Determine your investment objectives

The best way to decide on your investment goals is to ask yourselves some key questions:

- How important is income? Do we want, or need, high yield—steady, dependable income at a relatively high percentage of the investment?
- How important is growth? Can we set aside our interest in income for now and put our money into investments that will grow steadily and, in the future, be worth a lot more?
- Or do we want *aggressive* growth—some quick bucks, so we can sell at a good profit and repeat the process?
- What about tax advantages? Do we want to defer taxes, or even pay no taxes at all by buying tax-free municipal bonds?

Your answers to questions like these can give you direction on your investment objectives. Your goals will fall into one or more of four basic types:

1. *Income return.* Income-producing investments will bring you regular, current income. Use them if you want to supplement your other income or add to your retirement income. But don't forget that, over the long haul, inflation may rob you of purchasing power while you are enjoying the privilege of safe investing. What kinds of investments produce income? Bonds, whether government, municipal, or high-grade corporate. And certain stocks—talk with a reliable broker about which ones—that pay regular dividends.

2. *Safety of principal.* If you want to protect yourself against any possible loss of principal, you will probably have to accept a low rate of return. You cannot expect high yields, and you should expect inflation, again, to steal purchasing power. Ultimately, when you sell, each dollar will be worth less than when you first put it away. Money-market accounts, regular savings accounts, U.S. Treasury bills, and certificates of deposit (CDs) all suffer in this regard.

3. *Long-term capital growth.* Ideally, this is exactly what you want. As you acquire capital and it accumulates in the future, you are looking ahead to the day when it will have increased substantially and you will be able to realize a profit or capital gain. In short, your money is working not only to keep ahead of inflation but to give you financial security and fitness in years far ahead. Examples? Real estate, stock mutual funds, and certain stocks (again, talk with a knowledgeable broker).

4. *Minimizing taxes.* This one is just what it says: Your goal is to protect your earnings from taxation, either entirely or as long as possible, under laws passed for just that purpose. Municipal bonds give you permanent tax-free protection. Such savings plans as 401(k)s

and Individual Retirement Accounts (IRAs) defer taxation until the time when you are in a lower tax bracket.

Work out your investment goals and strategies together before you start making specific investments. Don't think about, or be influenced by, where the market is today. Rather, think about your needs for tomorrow. And be realistic: Consider your ages and temperaments, your current financial needs, and what you think your future needs will be.

Write things down. Put your objectives on paper. Keep a copy with your investment papers. Don't deviate from them unless you have an excellent reason to do so, and stick to them until you know it is time for a change. A couple of basic guidelines: Invest for growth and for tax advantages if you know your income level is rising and if you do not have children or other dependents to feed, clothe, and educate. Invest for income and high yield if you are on the threshold of (or in) your retirement years, or if you have dependents (expensive teenagers? college undergrads or grad students?) whose financial needs you must meet or help meet.

What should you invest in?

Have you looked at your Spending Plan carefully? Reviewed your net worth? If so, and if you are confident that you have enough income to maintain a positive cash flow and cover your expenses, think about two types of investments: fixed-income and equity.

In a fixed-income investment, you lend your money to a corporation or a government agency (at the federal, state, county, municipal or other local level). This makes you a creditor of the corporation or government, which pays you interest at a rate that is set, or fixed, when you buy the bond. *Note:* In the past, bonds were never quite as glamorous as stocks, because their prices did not fluctuate as dramatically. Recently, however, bond prices have swayed as widely as stock prices.

In an equity investment, you buy stock, or equity, in a company. In effect, you own a part of the company, however small or large your investment may be, and you expect to take advantage of its growth and profits.

Fixed-income investments

These include a wide range of bonds:

1. *Government securities.* With the U.S. government borrowing some $200 billion every year, new issues are often available. These investments are safe simply because the government can print new dollars to repay old debts. Government securities come in three types:

- Treasury bills. Sold every week, these reach maturity within three, six, or 12 months. You must invest at least $10,000. If you buy a three-month Treasury bill worth $10,000, you get it at a discount. You might pay $9,850, or more, or less, depending on the interest rate. After the three months, you present it for full payment of $10,000. You realize the difference in interest.
- Treasury notes. These are sold every four weeks or so. Maturity is anywhere from one to 10 years. The usual minimum purchase is $1,000, and you pay the full price of the note you buy. Then the government pays you cash interest twice a year during the length of the note.
- Treasury bonds. You won't find a regular schedule for the sale of these. You must watch for them. If you are interested, check in regularly with your banker to see when they will be offered. These bonds take anywhere from 10 to 30 years to mature—definitely in the long-range category. The usual price is $1,000 each. Like Treasury notes, you buy them at full price and then get cash interest twice a year. Treasury bonds are considered a barometer of the bond market.

Where do you buy Treasuries? You can buy them directly (i.e., without a broker or middleman) at any Federal Reserve Bank. Or you can get them through the mail, but you must send a certified check one week in advance of the offering. To find the nearest Federal Reserve Bank, ask your local banker or librarian. Or you can buy them through a bank or a broker, who will add a sales charge.

Note: If you buy Treasuries through the mail, you will have no way of knowing what interest rate they are paying until after you have made the purchase.

Hold on to Treasuries until they mature. You can always borrow against them, or sell them in the secondary market, where you will get more or less what you paid for them—depending on whether the interest rates have risen, fallen, or stayed the same since you bought them.

Tax note: The interest you earn from Treasuries is not taxed at the state or local level. So if you live in a state that taxes interest income, Treasuries can give you a certain tax advantage.

2. *Government savings bonds.* These savings bonds are not marketable. That is, they may be bought only from the U.S. government and may not be traded among investors. Effective May 1, 1995, the government made some changes in the rules on Series EE bonds. Rather than guaranteeing a minimum interest rate, as in the past, it now pays market-based rates and credits interest to all bonds twice a year. This interest is exempt from local and state taxes, and you pay no federal tax until the bonds mature or you cash them in. *Note:* You may buy Series HH bonds only in exchange for Series EE bonds; interest is also deferred until maturity.

Savings bonds have excellent liquidity. You may cash them in at any bank after holding them for only six months. They are extremely safe. But their yields are lower than other investments that are just as safe. Why buy them? One reason: If you cannot afford any larger kind of government security. Another: To force yourselves to save, by buying them through a payroll deduction plan.

3. *Corporate bonds.* When you buy any bond—government or corporate—you lend your money to that particular government or corporation for a certain length of time. At the end of that time, on the date of maturity, the government or the corporation that issued the bond pays you back the full amount of the bond—i.e., its face value. In the meantime, while you hold the bond, you receive a fixed rate of interest that, in most cases, is paid twice a year. You can find the rate of interest printed on the bond. If the rate is 9 percent on a $1,000 bond, for example, you will get $90 a year. Once the bond is issued—that means, once you have bought it—the rate does not change, no matter how much bond prices fluctuate.

How risky are bonds? Think about two factors. First, bonds are as risky as the creditworthiness of the corporation that issues them. If the perception of the value of the corporation deteriorates, the bonds are likely to lose value. Second, if interest rates rise, the value of the bonds drops. Bonds issued just a few years ago are likely to have gained in value because interest rates have fallen since they were issued. Sometimes you can buy a bond at less than its face value. The seller is offering it to you at a discount, in effect, to induce you to own a bond that is worth less than the going rate. Such a bond is known as a discount bond.

How do bonds work? Bond prices move up and down with changes in interest rates because yields on existing bonds must compete with those on new bonds that are being issued. Suppose you buy a $1,000 bond that pays a 9 percent rate. If interest rates then rise to 10 percent, no one will want to pay $1,000 for your 9-percent bond. The price of your bond will drop to roughly $900, so that its current yield to maturity will be 10 percent. The yield to maturity takes into account the coupon rate of 9 percent and any gain or loss in the price of the bond between the time when you bought it and the maturity date. If you are buying a bond after it has been issued, be sure to ask the broker what the *yield to maturity* is.

Bond prices also depend on the length of time between purchase and maturity. The longer the time to maturity, the more volatile the price. If interest rates rise one percentage point, the price of a 10-percent coupon bond with a 30-year maturity is likely to fall about 8.7 percent. But, assuming a similar rise in rates, a 10-percent bond that is due in only three years will drop only about 2.5 percent. So a change in interest rates has a greater effect on the price of a bond with a long time to maturity than on the price of one with shorter maturity. This is a danger that you may see identified as "interest-rate risk."

But what if interest rates go down? Then you see the opposite effect. Your bond increases in value. You can sell it at a premium, because—when interest rates are down—buyers are willing to pay a premium to get a bond with a higher interest rate. Yield, don't forget, is not the same as interest rate. Your yield may be higher or lower than the interest rate—depending on whether you bought the bond at a discount (i.e., below face value) or at a premium (above face value). In short, bonds adjust to interest movements by changing price.

If you are buying bonds, how can you measure risk? What's the chance that the issuer will fail to repay you? Most bond buyers get the answers to such questions by looking at rating services. The two best known are Standard & Poor's and Moody's. These companies don't report the market attractiveness of the bond. They study the financial stability of the issuer. Their job is to inform the investor about how much risk is involved in buying any particular bond. Bonds of the highest quality are rated as AAA by S & P's and as Aaa by Moody's.

Here's how current yield can fluctuate:

	Interest Payment	Current Yield
If you buy at par—$1,000	$80.00	8%
If you buy at discount—$800	$80.00	10%
If you buy at premium—$1,200	$80.00	$6\frac{2}{3}$%

4. *Tax-exempt bonds.* Issued by states, communities, or their agencies, these bonds are generally called municipal. Their yields are not taxed by the federal government. Because of their tax advantages, they are usually recommended for people in high-income brackets. If you want to decide whether to buy tax-free or taxable bonds, you have to figure the tax-equivalent yield—i.e., the yield a taxable bond would need to produce *after* taxes in order to equal the yield of a tax-exempt issue. The answer, of course, depends on your particular federal and state income-tax rates. If you are in the 28-percent tax bracket, for example, and live in Connecticut, a tax-exempt yield of 6 percent would be equivalent to a 8.33 percent taxable bond. Bonds that have longer maturities will give you extra yield.

Exhibit 8
COMPARING TAX-EXEMPT AND TAXABLE BONDS

With a federal tax bracket of	A tax-free yield of 5%	6%	7%	8%
	is equivalent to a taxable yield of			
15%	5.9%	7.1%	8.2%	9.4%
28	6.9	8.3	9.7	11.1
31	7.2	8.7	10.1	11.5
33	7.4	9.3	10.9	12.5
39.6	8.2	9.9	11.5	13.2

Tip: When you buy a bond issued by the state in which you live, you avoid not only the federal tax but any state or local taxes.

5. *Mortgage-backed securities.* These are pools of mortgage loans. Among the most popular are those backed by the Government National Mortgage Association or "Ginnie Mae." If a borrower on a mortgage in the pool fails to make a monthly payment of principal and interest, the agency will make good in the event the issuer of the security does not. Ginnie Maes pay interest and a small amount of principal each month. The actual yield of a mortgage-backed security depends on how rapidly its underlying loans—i.e., the mortgages held by the lending institutions participating in the pool—are paid off ahead of time. If interest rates drop, for instance, borrowers may either sell their homes or refinance them. As a result, you may receive a return of a large share of your principal, which you will have to invest at lower interest rates.

The yields on GNMAs are usually higher than on long-term Treasuries. GNMA certificates come in $25,000 lots. Many investors, however, find managed funds of mortgage-backed securities in which they can invest in lots of $1,000 or more.

6. *Zero-coupon bonds.* These are sold at a deep discount from face value, and your interest is figured on the difference between what you paid and the face amount you collect at maturity. The longer the maturity, the higher the yield, so they are good for such long-term investment goals as retirement or a child's education. You will find zero-coupon Treasuries, corporate, or municipal bonds available, but be aware that the zeros do not pay interest on any current basis. Instead, you receive all the interest, plus your original investment, when the bond matures.

Why buy zero-coupon bonds? Because you can get more for your money. Why are they sold? Because the issuer can keep and use its money for longer than if it were required to make periodic interest payments.

But watch the tax aspect. Unless you buy tax-free or municipal zeros, you must pay income tax on the deferred or phantom income you would have received if payments had been made periodically.

The value of a zero will fluctuate as interest rates change. But you will find no effect on the value of the bond if you hold it to maturity. And if you are buying zeros, you can take advantage of the fact that you can buy varying maturity dates that coincide with such goals as retirement or education.

Equity investments: the stock market

A stock market investment makes you a part owner of a corporation. You buy a share in it. Why make such an investment? For two obvious reasons: First, you believe that the company will succeed and that, as a result, the price of its stock will rise so that eventually you can sell your share in it for more than you paid for it. And second, you believe that while you own a share in it, the company will be so well run that it will make a profit and that it will divide that profit among its shareholders—including you.

Don't look for guarantees in the stock market. A company may or may not do well. Stock prices change every day. If you are the type who lies awake wondering whether the market price of your stock will go down tomorrow, you probably should stay out of the market. Also, you have to be willing to do your homework. Never buy a stock that you have not studied carefully, so you know the goals of the company, who runs it, what kind of record it has. You may find it valuable to consult with a securities analyst, a professional who specializes in this kind of analysis.

Where do you buy stocks? They are bought and sold—or traded, to use the jargon of the business—on exchanges. The largest and probably best known in the United States is the New York Stock Exchange. It is where the major shares of blue-chip corporations are traded. You will find the stock of smaller, less well-known companies traded on the American Stock Exchange (AMEX). And regional exchanges are located in other major cities. In addition, the stocks of many companies are unlisted or are sold over the counter.

The business section of a good daily newspaper contains stock listings, organized by the exchanges on which they are traded. The most comprehensive, of course, are in *The Wall Street Journal* and *The New York Times*.

But you cannot go to an exchange to buy stocks. You must go to a broker or bank that is a member of an exchange. The broker or bank charges you a commission on each transaction—whether buying or selling—it handles for you. The rate of the broker's commission varies, depending on whether it is a full-service or discount brokerage.

A good stockbroker can be a real asset. Shop for one as you shopped for a lawyer or accountant: Find someone who is willing to take the time and make the effort to understand you and your particular goals. Let's put it this way: If a stockbroker whom you are considering neglects to ask for a thorough overview of your entire financial situation—including your respective incomes and insurance coverage and net worth—he or she is not the stockbroker for you. Why set yourself up to pay commissions to such a person?

If you are willing and able to do the research yourselves, if you can choose your own stocks and bonds without outside help, and if you feel comfortable doing so, consider using a discount broker. This type of broker's commissions for executing trades are usually 40 to 70 percent less than those of a regular broker.

Take the long view

In planning your future financial security, remember that when you buy stocks you own something. When you buy fixed-income investments—the Treasuries, CDs, guaranteed income contracts (GICs), and money-market accounts—you are lending money. Owning is better than lending. Here's why.

Over the long term, the stock market has performed much better than other means of investing. Take the decade of the 1980s, for example. Standard & Poor's 500 Index of common stocks revealed an average return of 17.5 percent. In the same period, Treasury bonds produced 12.6 percent, while Treasury bills came in at 8.9 percent. And all that time, inflation was steadily doing its dirty work.

Look at it this way: If you had invested one dollar in a Treasury bill on the last day of 1925, you would have had $12.87 by the last day of 1995.

If you had put one dollar in a long-term government bond at the same time, it would have increased to $34.04.

But if you had put your dollar in large company stocks at the same time, you would have had $1,113.92 by the end of 1995.

Which would you prefer?

Yet many people feel safe with fixed-income investments, and they forget that inflation is always eating away at the value of their holdings. Furthermore, the longer they hold them, the more inflation consumes.

Yes, you may say, but the stock market can decline suddenly, and it can stay down for a long time. Agreed. That is why you must think long-term when you buy stocks. The longer you hold them, the lower the risk.

With that background on stocks versus other investments, what are the various options you may consider when you are going into the market?

1. *Common stock securities.* As described earlier, buying common stocks makes you a part owner, or shareholder, of a corporation. From its earnings, the company pays you dividends. But if earnings are slim, or if there are none, the company can reduce its dividends—or pay none at all. And if things get really bad and the company is liquidated, the holders of common stock are the last to be paid.

2. *Preferred stocks.* These also make you an owner of the company. But you get paid before any earnings are distributed as dividends to those who own common stock. Your dividends are fixed and stated in advance. However, they are not guaranteed. If the company is liquidated, you get paid (as a preferred stockholder) before any common stockholder—but after those who own the company's corporate bonds.

3. *Stock options.* These put you into a higher level of risk. You should not get into them unless your base of savings and other investments is really solid. What the stock option gives you is the right to buy or sell shares in a certain stock at a stated price until a certain date. The time frame *may be* any period from tomorrow morning to nine months hence. After that, the option expires. If you think the stock is going to rise in value, you buy a call option. The call gives you the right to buy a particular stock at a specified price during a certain period. If the price of the stock goes up, you can sell the option at a profit or exercise your option to buy the stock at the specified price. If the price doesn't go up, you will have to sell the option at a loss. If you do not, it will expire and you will have lost your entire investment in the option. If, on the other hand, you buy

a put option, the process is reversed—you hold the right to sell the stock at a specified price during the time period. In either case, when you hold a stock option you are not legally obliged to exercise it.

4. *Commodities.* A commodity is any tangible property that is traded on a commodities exchange. Such commodities range from silver to corn, from pork bellies to orange juice. If you trade in commodities, you are buying or selling contracts for future delivery of the properties. You are also a gambler, for commodities are highly speculative. Their prices can fluctuate wildly as they are affected by everything from weather conditions to world crises. They are not for the inhibited.

5. *Precious metals and gemstones.* You may have a fondness for gold or silver or diamonds. They are among the precious metals and stones in which you can invest. But get good advice; prices in these properties can rise and fall without warning or explanation. Connect with a reliable and trustworthy dealer before you make any buys in this area. In addition, there is a considerable difference between the price at which a dealer will sell you a gemstone and the price he will pay to buy it from you at any given time.

6. *Real estate.* Over the long term, real estate has always been a good area of investment. It has usually appreciated in value, despite some ups and downs. If you are thinking of buying real estate, always bear in mind the corny old adage that the three most important words in real estate are location, location, and location.

What kind of real estate should you look at? Most investors' first venture is a simple one: a second home, usually a vacation retreat. But you may find good opportunities in apartment houses or business buildings (commercial rental properties, in the jargon) or land that is either available for development or likely to become available and thus more valuable.

Real estate investment gives you a tax advantage, as the interest you pay on a first or second mortgage is deductible—if your mortgage loan is not greater than the amount you pay for the property plus any improvements you make. Taxes on your real estate are also deductible. Another important note: Any profit you make in selling your principal residence is exempt from taxes if within two years you turn around and buy another residence that is equal or greater in value. Furthermore, if you do make a profit but are 55 or older, you do not have to pay taxes on the first $125,000 of profit.

Suppose you become a landlord by renting out some property that you own. Or suppose the two of you are business partners as landlords. You can write off a number of costs—all maintenance, depreciation, and other expenses, including the interest you repay on your mortgage—up to $25,000 more than the income you get from the rent *if* your own income is under $100,000 a year and you are handling the regular daily management of the property yourself. If your income is between $100,000 and $150,000, you may deduct a part of such costs.

The landlord's role is not always easy. You have to deal with contractors who don't show up for repairs. You have to placate demanding tenants, not all of whom are clean or show respect for your walls and floors and windows and fixtures. And you have to pay your mortgage whether or not your tenant has paid the rent or you have space vacant and available.

One way to invest in real estate but head off such headaches is to buy shares in a Real Estate Investment Trust (REIT). Various brokerage firms and financial institutions sell REITs. Ask your stock broker or your banker about them.

When your money is in real estate, it is tied up. The risk is that the market may be down at a time when you want to liquidate, and liquidation—no matter where the market is standing—can always be slower than you expected. It usually takes time to negotiate a deal and for your buyer to get approval from lenders.

7. *Collectibles.* In addition to the precious metals and gemstones discussed earlier, you may want to think about other collectibles, from antique automobiles to baseball cards, from stamps and coins to cut glass. Collectibles bring you no income. But they can provide hours and even years of enjoyment, and if you have collected something that other people want, and that becomes more and more rare over time, it can bring you a big payoff some future day. Ask anyone who happened to pick up a Mickey Mantle baseball card in The Mick's rookie year.

8. *Annuities.* An annuity is an investment contract that you buy from an insurance company. The idea is that the insurance company will provide you with payments at regular intervals over a fixed period, starting on some date in the future. When you buy an annuity, it accumulates interest that compounds, tax-deferred, until funds are withdrawn.

You can buy either of two types: *fixed annuity* or *variable annuity*. In a fixed annuity, the insurance company guarantees the principal and a minimum rate of return. How can it do that? By investing your funds in fixed-income investments, such as bonds and mortgages. In a variable annuity, neither the principal nor the minimum payout is guaranteed. Your money is invested in stocks, bonds, and mutual funds. Some insurance companies allow you to split your investment between fixed and variable accounts.

When it is time to start taking payouts from an annuity, you must make some choices. See chapter 9 on retirement.

Do you have to buy an annuity outright? No. You can buy it in installments if the single-premium price is beyond reach. The insurance company will tell you its minimum dollar investment for either way of paying. It will also impose a penalty if you want to start early on withdrawals—usually 6 or 7 percent in the first year, then decreasing by 1 percent each year until there is no penalty. In addition, because an annuity gives you tax deferral, the government discourages early withdrawal. It takes 10 percent of any amount you withdraw before you reach 59½. And you must pay income tax on the dollars you withdraw.

To avoid risk, diversify

You can make money in the stock market. You can lose money in the stock market. You always face risk. How much risk depends on the economy, on your particular investment goals, and on how you balance your investment program to meet those goals. The key word is *diversification*. When you are building a portfolio of stocks for the long term, you must diversify. Buy stocks of various companies in several different industries. Make various types of investments. Need income? Buy stocks that pay regular dividends. Willing to forego income now for greater growth over a long period? Buy stock in companies that are growing now and expected to keep growing. They may be paying relatively low dividends now, but are plowing profits back into research and expansion to assure their future growth.

When you are thinking diversification, think about all your assets. Try to diversify not only among various types of assets but also within classes of assets. For example, you might buy several different utility stocks in various parts of the country. Or you might buy both government and corporate bonds.

Some other things that can help keep risk under control:

- *Build your foundation first.* Make sure you have money put away for specific goals and rainy days. Life insurance, too—be sure you have as much as you are both likely to need. Review cash flow—for each of you, and for your household. How about the house itself? Are you satisfied it is what you want, so you won't be tempted to pull money out of investing to cover major changes or improvements?
- *Develop an investment plan.* Set your objectives, both middle-range and long-range. Are you in a hurry to build up a down payment for a house? Is security, over the long term, your first order of business? Or are you out to make a killing? Is your

Exhibit 9:
CHECK YOUR ASSET MIX

Time Horizon	Amount Needed	Investment Characteristics To Look For	Trade-Offs	Appropriate Measures	Current Investments
Short-Term (0-5 years)	$________	• Conservative investments–price that doesn't change at all or only changes slightly • Maturity of no more than five years • Regular income payments • Easy access to money; no withdrawal penalties	• Lower overall returns • Vulnerable to inflation	• Money-market funds • CDs or bank deposits • Short-term notes or bonds	$________ $________ $________ $________ $________ Total________
Intermediate-Term (6-10 years)	$________	• Moderately aggressive investments–higher income or appreciation potential • Regular income payments • Price that moves within a fairly narrow range • Bonds: maturity of less than 10 years, or flexibility to shorten maturities	• Greater price fluctuation than short-term investments • Lower returns than more aggressive investments • Bonds vulnerable to inflation	• Bonds with intermediate maturities • GNMAs • Preferred stocks and high yielding common stocks	$________ $________ $________ $________ $________ Total________
Long-Term (11+ years)	$________	• Aggressive investments–history of high yields or high returns over time • Capital growth potential • Returns that consistently outpace inflation • Maturities of more than 10 years	• Potential high price volatility • May be less liquid	• Long-term bonds • U.S. common stocks, especially growth stocks • Foreign stocks and bonds	$________ $________ $________ $________ $________ Total________

Source: T. Rowe Price Associates, Inc.

Exhibit 10:
COMPARE YOUR INVESTMENTS WITH YOUR GOALS

Time Horizon	Current Investments		Growth Factor*		Assets Would Grow To This	Amount I Need For My Goals	Shortfall (Or Excess)		Monthly Investment Factor*		Amount I Need To Invest Monthly
Short-Term (5 years)	$______	x	1.5	=	$______	$______	$______	÷	74.0	=	$______
Intermediate-Term (10 years)	$______	x	2.2	=	$______	$______	$______	÷	184.2	=	$______
Long-Term (20 years)	$______	x	4.7	=	$______	$______	$______	÷	592.9	=	$______

* Factors reflect an 8% pre-tax return, compounded monthly. This table is hypothetical and does not represent the results of any particular investment.
Source: T. Rowe Price Associates, Inc.

basic point of view long-term or short-term? If it is long-term, can you provide the patience to keep it that way?

- *Get a good fix on your current financial situation.* You must not only do a Net Worth Statement and a cash-flow analysis, you must redo each one at least once a year. Regular review is indispensable.
- *Check your risk pulse and take your risk temperature.* Financial fitness for a live-together calls for informed self-knowledge. You are the only one who knows exactly how much stress you can stand. You've got to be able to recognize it when an investment is likely to put too much strain on you, so you will be able to back off.
- *Stay well informed.* Keep reading up on money matters. Read the financial publications. Ask your broker or financial adviser educated questions.
- *Don't be afraid to make changes.* If a stock turns out to be a loser, get rid of it. If your goals change, review your portfolio and evaluate it in light of new goals. Never fall in love with a stock.
- *Don't look for magic or miracles.* You won't find any. You will find some gains, and some losses. To get high returns, if that is your goal, you will have to take high risks.
- *Put your eggs in more than one basket.* No single type of investment performs best at all times or under all conditions.
- *Keep liquidity in mind.* What if you need cash? What will you sell? You should always know which stocks will be the first you will let go if you have to.
- *Try the water first.* If you have never bought stocks, and if you are a little wary about getting started, you can get a feel for it—find out what your initial risk temperature is—by buying shares in a mutual fund.

To help organize your thinking about what to look for that will meet your short-term, mid-term, and long-term goals, see Exhibits 9 and 10.

CHAPTER EIGHT

SPREADING THE RISK: MUTUAL FUNDS HELP THE SMALL INVESTOR

If you and your company are putting money into a 401(k) (more about that later, in chapter 10) or profit-sharing plan, chances are the company asks you to select a mutual fund to invest in. Probably it offers several choices, ranging from fixed-income to stock funds. Most people, lacking sophistication on the subject, choose guaranteed-income contracts (GICs), which are nice and safe but will not give you long-term growth.

Some 5,000 mutual funds are alive and well today in America, up from about 500 back in 1979. The secret of their success is the simple fact that a mutual fund puts together the money of many participants and buys a large portfolio that is widely diversified. The risk is thus spread among many—ideal for a small investor.

Any mutual fund buys securities and receives dividends and interest from them. If it sells a security at a profit, it usually gives you a capital gain distribution in proportion to the number of shares you have bought in the fund. If shares in the fund increase in value while you own them, you profit when you sell them. If you must sell when the value of the fund's shares is down, of course, you suffer a loss.

If you buy one or more mutual funds with your 401(k) money, you are in a tax-deferred plan and the mutual fund will automatically reinvest any capital gains or income it declares. If you are simply buying the mutual fund directly, you take your choice: Tell the company to put your profits into buying more shares, or tell them you want the cash. Such distributions may be made annually or more often—some as frequently as every month. Check the policy of the fund you are buying to be sure its distribution schedule fits with your particular needs.

When you buy mutual funds, you avoid the headache of doing your own research on stocks and bonds. Instead, you let the fund management do the analyses. But, of course, you have to make the decision on just which fund or funds to buy. You will find plenty to choose from. They vary according to their investment objectives. You can even find a "family of funds"—a group, all run by the same basic company and each with its own management, that aims at a variety of objectives.

Types of mutual funds

Among the types of funds are these:

- A *money-market fund* usually invests for high yield, concentrating on Treasury bills, certificates of deposit, and commercial paper. These are called "cash" or "liquid" funds.
- A *corporate bond fund* or *income fund* seeks to return a high level of income. It invests heavily in corporate bonds, but also in preferred stock and U.S. Treasury bonds.
- A *high-yield bond fund* purchases lower-rated bonds of corporations. While producing a rate of return that is usually better than that of higher-rate bonds, it runs greater risks.
- A *growth fund* looks toward long-range capital growth by buying the common stocks of established companies. Its goal is increased value rather than current dividends.
- An *aggressive growth fund* is less concerned with established companies. It invests in smaller firms and in developing industries, where capital appreciation is likely. In this one, you think capital gains, not current income, and you face greater risks.
- A *balanced fund* and several others—equity/income fund, total return fund, growth-and-income fund—are all similar. They balance their portfolios between bonds and stocks, in varying proportions with the goal of conserving your capital, promoting long-term growth, and at the same time providing you with current income.
- A *specialized fund* concentrates on one field: banking, health, utilities, high technology, or whatever, but buys stock in many firms within the field in order to gain diversification. The risk? Often, a specialized fund is more volatile than the overall market.
- A *tax-free fund* or *municipal bond fund* is for those who, in high-income tax brackets, want tax-free income. It invests in municipal bonds. Some concentrate on the bonds issued by a single state, giving residents of that state the advantage of earning income that neither the state nor the federal government may tax.
- An *international fund* invests in companies in foreign lands, mostly Europe and Asia, expecting to gain from economic growth around the world.
- A *U.S. government income fund* buys such government securities as U.S. Treasuries, guaranteed mortgage-backed securities (GNMAs) backed by the federal government, and other notes.

When you think about a mutual fund, you must have one or more of three basic goals in mind: Stability (your principal is protected), growth (your principal increases through capital gains), and income (the fund produces consistent income for you). You must decide among these goals, and pick funds oriented to the objectives you want. No single fund can give you all three.

What determines a mutual-fund share?

When you buy shares in a mutual fund, how many shares you get depends on the *net asset value* of that fund on the day you buy. To get net asset value, the fund divides the total value of all stocks and bonds it holds by the number of outstanding shares in the fund. Net asset value is figured daily. It goes up or down depending on the market price of the securities it holds. If, for example, you invest $1,000 and the net asset value is $12.23 on the day you buy into a given mutual fund, you will get 81.776 shares.

What about taxes?

When you are to be taxed is determined by the kind of savings you put into a mutual fund. If it is retirement savings, the money you put in and its earnings—interest, dividends, or capital gains—will not be taxed until you take it out. It will then be treated as ordinary income. If you are not yet 59½ you will also face a penalty for early withdrawal. Retirement savings plans that fit this category are your 401(k) plan, IRA, Keogh, SEP, or company profit-sharing.

You must pay taxes, on the other hand, on any money that you put into a mutual fund and that is *not* in one of those plans. The tax is on any interest, dividends, or capital gains, whether you take those profits as cash or direct the mutual fund to reinvest them in additional shares.

Watch out for double taxation. Make an accurate record of what you pay when you first buy any mutual fund. Any time the fund reinvests your interest, dividends, or capital gains, you are, in effect, buying more shares. Add the cost of those shares to your original purchase price. When eventually you sell your shares (or any portion of them), that total cost is what you use to determine whether you have had a capital gain or loss.

In January, your mutual fund will send you forms 1099-DIV and 1099-B for the year before to use in preparing your tax return. Copies will go to the IRS. Some other key points:

- Whenever you sell shares, you must pay taxes —even if you are simply moving your money from one member of a family of funds to another.
- Remember the FIFO rule: First in, first out. When you sell shares, it is assumed that those you bought first are the ones you are selling first. Figure your gain or loss accordingly.

Exhibit 11

MUTUAL FUND COST BASIS

CONFIRM DATE	TRADE DATE	TRANSACTION		DOLLAR AMOUNT	SHARE PRICE	SHARES THIS TRANSACTION	SHARE BALANCE
10/3	10/3	Purchase		1,000.00	19.97	50,058	50.058
01/06	12/23	INCOME REINVEST	.550	27.53	22.15	1.243	51.301
01/06	12/23	SHORT TERM C G	.430	21.52	22.15	0.972	52.273
01/06	12/23	CAP GAIN REINV	1.670	83.60	22.15	3.774	56.047
03/28	03/14	INCOME REINVEST	.300	16.81	24.16	0.696	56.743
04/15	04/15	PURCHASE		695.00	24.37	28.519	85.262
06/28	06/14	INCOME REINVEST	.300	25.58	25.17	1.016	86.278
09/27	09/13	INCOME REINVEST	.300	25.88	24.98	1.036	87.314
Cost basis 9/27				1,895.92			

- If you don't like the FIFO rule, you are permitted to order specific shares sold. This means you can calculate gain or loss on the price you paid for those particular shares.

Invest steadily

If you are putting money into a 401(k) plan through payroll deductions, you are automatically getting dollar cost averaging. This is good. It means that because your payroll deduction is always the same amount, you buy more shares when the market for them is down, and fewer shares when it is up. It averages out in your favor, giving you a better average cost-per-share than the price you would be likely to get for a single purchase.

If you are not in an automatic payroll deduction plan, you must discipline yourself to do your own dollar cost averaging. Decide how much you can put into mutual funds on the same day each and every month, and stick to it—without looking up market prices all the time. Even better, ask the fund to arrange for your bank to make an automatic transfer every month into your mutual fund account. The fund may set a minimum—probably between $100 and $250.

Study before you buy

Before you make a commitment to buy any mutual fund, look it over carefully. Get the fund's prospectus. Study it. What are the fund's objectives? How has it performed over the years? What fees does it charge for sales or for maintaining your account? What procedures must you follow in buying or selling shares? In particular, look for:

- A *statement of investment objectives* that reveals exactly what kind of fund this is. If it is an aggressive growth fund, look for the words "maximum capital appreciation" as a goal. If it is a balanced fund, look for such words as "income," "capital growth," and "stability."
- A *per share table* that tells you how much each share of the fund has earned annually since its inception, or over 10 years or so. Earnings will include dividends as well as capital gain distributions. The table portrays the fund's performance—erratic or steady—in both an up market and a down market. Some tables include comparisons with the Standard & Poor's 500 or the Dow Jones. Don't count on the table as a guarantee of future performance, however, because changes in the market or changes in its own management can nullify the best promises.
- A *fee table* that lets you know whether you must pay a sales commission—known as a "load"—on purchases, or whether it is a "no-load" fund that does not charge up-front when you buy in. Watch out for funds that charge you for "re-loading" when they reinvest a distribution for you. Some fees to look for:
    a. *12b-1 fee*. Some funds make this assessment as high as 1.25 percent per year. These charges are used to defray the cost of marketing and distributing funds.

b. *Redemption fee.* This may be a small fixed charge, or it may be a percentage of your redemption price. Funds use it to cut down on recurrent buying and selling.

c. *Contingent deferred sales charge (CDSC).* This one is imposed to discourage you from holding shares for very short periods. It may be as high as 5 percent if you sell during your first year, then 4 percent the next year, down to no fee after 5 years. It is a sort of "back-end load."

d. *Operating and management fee.* This covers the handling of your account. Expect it to average from 0.5 percent to 1.0 percent annually. You will probably find it defined as a percentage of the fund's average assets. Be sure to compare, against other funds you are considering, to see how earnings have been affected by fees not only in the past year but over earlier periods—say, from 3 to 10 years.

- A statement of *investment policies and risks.* Look this over carefully. Imagine yourself dealing with the risks it describes. Check out what kinds of securities, in terms of quality and grade, the fund buys. See what risks its managers take—or avoid—in working to meet their objectives.
- A description of *distributions* that informs you on just when dividends or capital gains are distributed, and what choices you have about how you receive them. The fund should permit you to take both dividends and capital gains any way you want—either one in cash, either one reinvested.
- A policy on *how to buy and redeem shares* that establishes the minimum purchase you must make to open an account as well as the minimum for additional purchases. Check on whether telephone transfers may be made. Note whether you get the advantage of dollar cost averaging.

Why mutual funds are a good investment

You get a number of advantages when you put retirement savings into mutual funds, including:

- *Low minimum investment.* The required initial investment in many funds is as low as $250. Top minimum is seldom more than $1,000. In a word, getting started is within easy reach.
- *Professional management.* This is one of the major attractions of mutual funds. You yourself don't have to become a Wall Street expert. Professional managers study the market for you, analyze trends, keep reading up on financial information, and work hard to make smart decisions about the fund's portfolio.
- *Easy record-keeping.* Mutual funds are well disciplined on record-keeping. They send year-to-date statements on your account frequently. Well ahead of tax time, they provide forms 1099-DIV and 1099-B so you can conveniently report on your income and capital gains to the IRS.
- *Automatic reinvestment.* Setting up your fund so that dividends and capital gains are reinvested is easy and will maintain continual growth of your account.
- *Automatic withdrawal.* If you so desire, you may order your fund to pay you regularly—even to make direct deposits to your checking account. Retirees find this feature particularly practical.
- *Liquidity.* Your mutual fund must buy back your shares any time you want to sell them. The best time, of course, is when they are worth more than when you bought them.
- *Convenience and flexibility.* Switching from fund to fund, as the market changes or your needs or objectives change, is easy within a family of funds. Usually you can switch funds or sell shares with only a phone call. This advantage is called "investment timing" in the jargon of the business.
- *Diversification.* When you buy shares in a mutual fund, your investments are automatically diversified in stocks, bonds, and other types of investments. How widely diversified, of course, depends on how specialized the fund is.

CHAPTER NINE

RETIREMENT: IT'S NOT THAT FAR IN THE FUTURE

No matter how far off in the future it seems to be, you must think today about your retirement. And the first fact you must accept is that you have to take responsibility for it yourself. That means putting yourself first—ahead of any company, large or small, that is employing you. That was not the thing to do, only a few years ago, when company loyalty was encouraged by employers who were willing and able to play the paternal role, setting up pension plans for employees who stuck around until it all paid off, and running the plans carefully as retirees lived out their lifetimes.

What happened? The 1980s happened. The business climate changed drastically. Mergers, acquisitions, corporate restructuring, downsizing, tighter and tighter profit margins—one management factor after another put the squeeze on whatever could be squeezed. American businesses in large numbers turned away from the attractive pension plans that had provided retirement income for millions ever since the Great Depression. Instead, they began asking workers not only to pay for their own retirement plans but to *manage* them. After decades in which the retiring worker was promised a steady benefit check until he or she died, corporate pension plans have been rapidly replaced by individual 401(k) plans. The 401(k) demands that you put in your own money and that you decide how it is to be invested.

Another factor contributes to the picture. In today's business climate, workers don't stay put. They move from company to company. They switch careers and career skills. Few indeed stay with the same employer for 25 or 30 years. So the company's loyalty to the employee has withered alongside the employee's loyalty to the company.

All of which means you are unlikely to build up the kind of pension benefits that were built by long-time employees in earlier years. Rather, you must make planning for retirement a part of your total financial fitness program. That means saving. Nothing can be more important or, in the long run, more valuable to you.

Another important factor: You must be aware that many of the benefits that are available to married couples, both from Social Security and from pension plans, are denied to live-togethers.

Face it—life will be different

In retirement, you will have plenty to think about. Psychologically, you may sense an emptiness, a loss of identity, especially if you have not established interests or hobbies that you can carry over into retirement. Medically, you may face physical changes that come with what doctors like to call "the mature years." Socially, you may find yourself moving from familiar circles into new lifestyles in new places. All such changes will reflect differences from the long period when your work structured your day, defined who you were and how you felt about yourself, and gave you a sense of worth and accomplishment.

But economic changes have the potential for giving you the biggest headaches. Think about what the late Florida Representative Claude Pepper, chairman of the Select Committee on Aging of the U.S. House of Representatives, said in a hearing on September 17, 1980. He could have said it yesterday.

> The current retirement income system has not kept its promise to the workers who faithfully paid into the Social Security [system], placed their faith in private pension plans, and tried to frugally invest in savings accounts during their working lives. Inflation has ravaged their retirement savings or made it impossible to save, while their pension expectations have vanished into an incomprehensible mass of requirements or often disappeared because of the requirements that a worker participate in a plan for ten years before he becomes entitled to pension benefits . . . We must come to grips with the failure of pension plans and savings plans to play their intended role in contributing to retirement income security.

Although inflation is not nearly as staggering as it was when Representative Pepper made this statement, his comments—made some years before corporate America began its drastic changes—ring true today. The "broken promise of retirement" has shattered dreams and created despair and want. Social Security and a pension no longer do the job. In fact, the Social Security Administration itself estimates that a single retiree with annual earnings of $57,600 is deriving only about 43 percent of his or her income from Social Security benefits and a pension.

What, then, makes the difference? Saving and investing. Chapter 7 gave you a detailed discussion of saving, but look first at what you will need after retirement and what Social Security can be expected to provide.

What will be your income—and your needs—after you retire?

You and your partner must sit down and figure out what your sources of income in retirement will be. Write it all down: Social Security for each of you, payments from a pension (or two), payouts from Individual Retirement Accounts (IRAs) and 401(k) plans. *Important:* Put down amounts you expect to receive in terms of today's dollar, no matter how far into the future you are planning.

That brings up the question of inflation. Did you ever stop to think that inflation is selective? It doesn't hit everyone in the same corner of the pocketbook, nor with the same severity. Its effects vary, depending on where you live and on what you buy and in what proportions. For example, if you live in a rent-stabilized apartment in a large city with a good public transportation system, you are not likely to feel the impact of inflation in oil prices. But if you live in the suburbs or down on the farm and are dependent on the internal combustion engine to take you places and an oil burner to keep your house warm, inflation can be a factor in your economic life.

Probably the eldest are the hardest hit. Usually, their incomes stay essentially the same no matter what inflation does. It can leave you, in retirement years, with less and less to spend on nonessentials. Many retired people have found that inflation has reduced their standard of living to the point where their incomes barely cover food, shelter, transportation, and medical care. Large numbers have been driven to moving into smaller homes or to shared households in order to cut expenses.

What will your needs be, after retirement? Let's hope that all payments for the education of offspring will have been completed. The same for the mortgage on the house. Business lunches, commutation fares, work clothes (whether blue-collar or white-collar) will all be in the past. But you should think about three key areas:

1. *Emergency fund.* Maybe you haven't needed more than a few months of living expenses in a set-aside fund all these years. But special emergencies are more likely to come up as you get older. Unreimbursed medical and dental expenses. Home repairs that used to be paid from your salary. New appliances. Set up a fund.
2. *Lifestyle.* Rethink your priorities. Will the two of you still need two cars? Will travel become a larger item in your Spending Plan than before? How about entertaining—will you be doing more, or less? Be prepared for some expense items to stretch, others to shrink, as your retirement lifestyle evolves. *Important:* Don't set anything in concrete. Expect change. Try to build in the opportunity for fun and variety.
3. *Spending Plan.* If you have kept a regular Spending Plan in force, you have a good fix on where the money now goes. Usually, a retired couple can live on 75 to 85 percent of the gross income they had before retirement. How come? Deductions from your gross income go down. You no

longer pay into Social Security (unless you keep on working on a part-time basis) and you no longer face payroll deductions for savings plans, medical insurance, and such. Your income taxes will probably be reduced.

Some expenses will go down or disappear altogether, yes. But some others, such as medical costs, are almost certain to increase. And inflation will play its hand. The bottom line of your Spending Plan will show a difference between the sources of income that you estimate and the expenses that you estimate, and that difference will be your *retirement gap*—the additional income you will need during retirement.

Social Security

Just what is Social Security? Few people seem to know the answer, or understand what benefits it provides if you become disabled or when you retire.

Social Security is a form of social insurance that is run by the United States government and reaches nearly every U.S. citizen. In the vernacular of the bureaucrats, it is "contributory." That simply means that you contribute to it and whoever employs you at any given time also contributes to it. It provides continuing income to you if your income stops because you have retired or are incapacitated by a disability, and it provides income to others, under certain conditions, on your behalf if you die.

During your working career, you build up protection under Social Security until you are fully insured and entitled to all its benefits. You achieve this by earning what Social Security calls *quarters of coverage*. A quarter of coverage is three months, even if you worked only part of the quarter. Once you have contributed to Social Security for 40 quarters—10 years—you are fully covered from then on. Until then, the number of quarters of coverage you must have recorded in order to draw benefits depends on your age.

The baby-boomer worry

The fast-approaching day when the baby-boom generation—those born between 1946 and 1964—start collecting Social Security benefits is cause for big worry. The baby-boom population is 77 million. By 2030, most of them will have retired. At that point, only two workers will be paying into Social Security for every one who is retired, whereas in 1995 the ratio was 3.2 to 1. Statisticians figure that, unless Washington either beefs up the financing of Social Security or cuts down its benefits, the system will start going into the red in the year 2015.

It's always changing

The important thing to keep in mind about Social Security is that the amount of benefits available is constantly changing. So is legislation involving Social Security. Therefore, you must consider the following

Exhibit 12
AGE AT WHICH YOU CAN RECEIVE FULL SOCIAL SECURITY BENEFITS

YEAR OF BIRTH	FULL RETIREMENT AGE
1937 or earlier	65
1938	65 and 2 months
1939	65 and 4 months
1940	65 and 6 months
1941	65 and 8 months
1942	65 and 10 months
1943–1954	66
1955	66 and 2 months
1956	66 and 4 months
1957	66 and 6 months
1958	66 and 8 months
1959	66 and 10 months
1960 and later	67

figures as only examples and not as the final word. (With Social Security, there is never a final word.)

The rules change again in 2000

Starting in the year 2000, and because life expectancies have become longer than when the original rules were made, the age of eligibility for full retirement benefits will gradually rise from 65 to 67. If you were born in 1938 or later, this change affects you. See Exhibit 12.

What do 40 quarters of coverage entitle you to?

If you become disabled, or retire, or die after completing 40 quarters of coverage and becoming a fully insured worker, you or your dependents are entitled to receive:

1. *Retirement benefits.* This brings you a monthly payment, starting at any time after you reach age 62. At 65, a spouse receives a payment amounting to 50 percent of a retired worker's amount, even if the spouse has never been employed. The spouse may receive a reduced benefit as early as age 62.

   But note: A live-together is not a spouse. A person who is currently in a live-together situation, however, is entitled to receive Social Security benefits based on *one of the following:*
   - His or her own record
   - A deceased spouse's record *or*
   - The account of a former spouse from whom she is divorced but to whom she was married for at least 10 years. The divorced spouse may receive benefits at age 62 but must be unmarried when applying. She will receive the same as a married spouse—50 percent of her ex's benefit if she is 65 or 37.5 percent if she is 62. Such a benefit will cease if she remarries. A divorced spouse whose former spouse dies may receive full widow's benefits, if she is unmarried and over age 60.
2. *Unmarried children's benefits.* If you die, your children who are under 18 and unmarried are entitled to a benefit equal to 75 percent of your benefit. If you retire or become disabled, the entitlement of each of your minor offspring is equal to 50 percent of your benefit. In either case, the amount is subject to a maximum for the whole family.
3. *Disabled worker's benefit.* If you become disabled at any age, you are entitled to a monthly benefit that continues as long as you are considered fully disabled.

○ ○ ○

BOBBIE COLLECTS ON HER DECEASED EX-HUSBAND'S RECORD

Bobbie was married for many years to her corporate executive husband. Then they were divorced. He died a few years ago, in his late sixties. As a surviving divorced spouse, she receives $1,000 a month from Social Security—the same amount her late ex-husband was receiving at the time of his death. Now she and Jack are live-togethers. If they were married, her Social Security benefits would not change, because she was over 60 and unmarried when she applied for benefits. She would not have to give up the benefit based on her ex-husband's Social Security status.

If you are a surviving spouse, you are entitled to a monthly payment starting when you are 60, even if your spouse died before you reached that age. If you are caring for a child or children under age 16, you get additional payment, up to a family maximum.

○ ○ ○

TWO WIDOWS: CHRIS AND MARTHA

When Chris' husband, who was only a few years older than she, died of a massive heart attack when she was in her thirties, she was left with children five and seven years old. She began receiving Social Security benefits, as did the kids. When she met Randy, who was 15 years her senior, they wanted to get married, but knew she would lose her Social Security benefits if she remarried—and they needed her share of those benefits to make ends meet because his small-appliance business was not producing enough profit. Worried that he might go out of business, they decided to live together until his situation improved or they could both find jobs. They may even wait until the youngest child reaches 16, at which time her benefits will stop. (The children's will continue until they reach age 18.)

If you are a widow who is not yet 60 and you remarry, you are not entitled to benefits from your late husband's Social Security. Rather, you will receive benefits based on the record of your new spouse. Take Martha's experience, for example. Married to a physician who would receive maximum Social Security benefits when he retired, she was widowed while in her mid-fifties. She had held part-time jobs, but her own Social Security benefits were not expected to come anywhere near the monthly amount she would get from her late husband's account. If she waited until she reached 65 to start receiving a monthly check, she would get (in 1996 dollars) about $1,200 per month. Now she has met Andy, an artist, whose Social Security benefits will be substantially less than those of Martha's late husband—about $800 a month. If she marries Andy before she turns 60, she will lose her widow's benefit. And, as Andy's spouse, she will get just 50

Exhibit 13
INCREASES FOR DELAYED RETIREMENT

YEAR OF BIRTH	YEARLY PERCENTAGE INCREASE
1916 or earlier	1%
1917–1924	3%
1925–1926	3.5%
1927–1928	4%
1929–1930	4.5%
1931–1932	5%
1933–1934	5.5%
1935–1936	6%
1937–1938	6.5%
1939–1940	7%
1941–1942	7.5%
1943 or later	8%

Important: Even if you are delaying your retirement, be sure to sign up for Medicare to start when you are 65.

percent of his benefit, or $400 per month. If she waits until she is 60 to remarry, she will be entitled to have either one's benefits—but not both.

○ ○ ○

If you work beyond age 65, what are you entitled to?

Suppose you are feeling great, you like your work, your employers need you and want you—can you increase your Social Security benefits by continuing to work full-time after you reach 65? Yes. You can gain two ways. First, remember that the higher your lifetime earnings, the higher your benefits. Adding even one year of earnings can help your total picture. Second, don't forget that the longer you delay retirement—up to age 70—the larger your Social Security checks will be. The percentage of increase depends on when you were born (see Exhibit 13).

How can you tell how much your benefits will come to?

Social Security benefits are based on your total earnings over all the years you have worked. This figure is on file at national Social Security headquarters. It is updated regularly. It's a good idea to check up on your records at least every three years. How do you do that? Get a Request for Earnings and Benefit Statement from your nearest Social Security office, or by writing to Social Security Administration, P.O. Box 57, Baltimore, Maryland 21230 (see Exhibit 14). Fill in your name, address, date of birth, Social Security number, and current earnings, and send it in. Allow at least six to eight weeks for a response.

If you are over 60, contact the Social Security Administration and it will send you your statement of earnings and estimate of benefits if you are not already receiving benefits (see Exhibit 14). The Social Security Administration plans to start sending current status statements to all workers annually, starting by the year 2000.

Checking Social Security records is important. If an error occurs, and if you wait more than three years, three months, and 15 days to report it, you may find it is too late to get a correction in.

With the estimate of benefits, you should be able to determine how much you will be entitled to receive during retirement, how much you would receive if you were disabled, and how much your survivors would receive if you died. *Note:* The estimate may be lower than what you will actually receive at 65.

In figuring the amount of your retirement benefit, the Social Security Administration will consider all your

Exhibit 14

SOCIAL SECURITY ADMINISTRATION

Form Approved
OMB No. 0960-0466 ☐ SP

Request for Earnings and Benefit Estimate Statement

To receive a free statement of your earnings covered by Social Security and your estimated future benefits, all you need to do is fill out this form. Please print or type your answers. When you have completed the form, fold it and mail it to us.

1. Name shown on your Social Security card:
   John Q Public
   First / Middle Initial / Last
2. Your Social Security number as shown on your card:
   987-65-4320
3. Your date of birth: ____ Month ____ Day ____ Year
4. Other Social Security numbers you have used:
   ☐☐☐-☐☐-☐☐☐☐
   ☐☐☐-☐☐-☐☐☐☐
5. Your Sex: ☐ Male ☐ Female
6. Other names you have used (including a maiden name):

7. Show your actual earnings for last year and your estimated earnings for this year. Include only wages and/or net self-employment income covered by Social Security.
   A. Last year's actual earnings:
   $ 61,200.00
   Dollars only
   B. This year's estimated earnings:
   $ 65,000.00
   Dollars only
8. Show the age at which you plan to retire: 65
   (Show only one age)
9. Below, show the average yearly amount that you think you will earn between now and when you plan to retire. Your estimate of future earnings will be added to those earnings already on our records to give you the best possible estimate.

   Enter a yearly average, not your total future lifetime earnings. Only show earnings covered by Social Security. Do not add cost-of-living, performance or scheduled pay increases or bonuses. The reason for this is that we estimate retirement benefits in today's dollars, but adjust them to account for average wage growth in the national economy.

   However, if you expect to earn significantly more or less in the future due to promotions, job changes, part-time work, or an absence from the work force, enter the amount in today's dollars that most closely reflects your future average yearly earnings.

   Most people should enter the same amount that they are earning now (the amount shown in 7B).

   Your future average yearly earnings:
   $ ☐☐☐,☐☐☐.00
   Dollars only
10. Address where you want us to send the statement:

   Name

   Street Address (Include Apt. No., P.O. Box, or Rural Route)

   City State Zip Code

I am asking for information about my own Social Security record or the record of a person I am authorized to represent. I understand that if I deliberately request information under false pretenses I may be guilty of a federal crime and could be fined and/or imprisoned. I authorize you to send the statement of earnings and benefit estimates to the person named in item 10 through a contractor.

Please sign your name (Do not print)

Date (Area Code) Daytime Telephone No.

ABOUT THE PRIVACY ACT
Social Security is allowed to collect the facts on this form under Section 205 of the Social Security Act. We need them to quickly identify your record and prepare the earnings statement you asked us for. Giving us these facts is voluntary. However, without them we may not be able to give you an earnings and benefit estimate statement. Neither the Social Security Administration nor its contractor will use the information for any other purpose.

Form **SSA-7004-SM**-OP1 (9-91) Destroy prior editions

Exhibit 15

FACTS, CREDITS, AND EARNINGS

February 15, 1996

THE FACTS YOU GAVE US

Your Name .... John Q. Public
Your Social Security Number 987-65-4320
Your Date of Birth .... Dec. 3, 1939
1994 Earnings $60,600
1995 Earnings $63,600
Your Estimated Future Average Yearly Earnings $65,000
The Age You Plan To Retire 65
Other Social Security Numbers You've Used .... None

We used the facts you gave us and the information in our records under your Social Security number to prepare this statement for you.

When we estimated your benefits, we included any 1994 and 1995 earnings and any future estimated earnings you told us about. If you did not estimate your future earnings, we did not project any future earnings for you.

YOUR SOCIAL SECURITY CREDITS

To qualify for Social Security benefits and Medicare, you need credit for a certain amount of work covered by Social Security. The number of credits you need will vary with the type of benefit. Under current law, you do not need more than 40 credits to qualify for any benefit or for Medicare.

Our review of your earnings, including any 1993 and 1994 earnings you told us about, shows that you now have at least 40 Social Security credits.

YOUR SOCIAL SECURITY EARNINGS

The chart on the next page shows the earnings on your Social Security record. It also estimates the amount of Social Security taxes you paid in each year to finance benefits under Social Security and Medicare. If you have government earnings that help you qualify for Medicare, those earnings also are included on the chart under the heading "Medicare—Your Taxed Earnings."

We show earnings only up to the maximum yearly amount covered by Social Security. These maximum amounts are shown on the chart. The chart may not include some or all of your earnings from last year because they may not have been added to your record yet.

YOUR EARNINGS RECORD

	SOCIAL SECURITY			MEDICARE	
YEARS	Maximum Yearly Earnings	Your Taxed Earnings	Estimated Taxes You Paid	Your Taxed Earnings*	Estimated Taxes You Paid
1937-50	$3,000	$ 0	$ 0		
1951	3,600	0	0		
1952	3,600	0	0		
1953	3,600	0	0		
1954	3,600	0	0		
1955	4,200	0	0		
1956	4,200	0	0		
1957	4,200	4,200	94		
1958	4,200	4,200	94		
1959	4,800	4,800	120		
1960	4,800	4,800	144		
1961	4,800	4,800	144		
1962	4,800	4,800	150		
1963	4,800	4,800	174		
1964	4,800	4,800	174		
1965	4,800	4,800	174		
1966	6,600	6,600	277	$ 6,600	$ 30
1967	6,600	6,600	290	6,600	30
1968	7,800	7,800	343	7,800	40
1969	7,800	7,800	374	7,800	40
1970	7,800	7,800	374	7,800	40
1971	7,800	7,800	405	7,800	40
1972	9,000	9,000	468	9,000	45
1973	10,800	10,800	864	10,800	108
1974	13,200	13,200	1,042	13,200	135
1975	14,100	14,100	1,113	14,100	140
1976	15,300	15,300	1,208	15,300	150
1977	16,500	16,500	1,303	16,500	160
1978	17,700	17,700	1,070	17,700	180
1979	22,900	22,900	1,403	22,900	220
1980	25,900	25,900	1,587	25,900	240
1981	29,700	29,700	1,975	29,700	272
1982	32,400	32,400	2,170	32,400	334
1983	35,700	35,700	2,391	35,700	374
1984	37,800	37,800	2,532	37,800	397
1985	39,600	39,600	2,591	39,600	514
1986	42,000	42,000	2,701	42,000	609
1987	43,800	43,800	2,765	43,800	635
1988	45,000	45,000	2,853	45,000	652
1989	48,000	48,000	2,976	48,000	696
1990	51,300	51,300	3,180	51,300	702
1991	53,400	53,400	3,335	53,400	730
1992	55,500	55,500	3,458	55,500	749
1993	57,700	57,700	3,636	57,700	778
1994	60,600	60,600	3,757	60,600	879
1995	61,200	Not Yet Recorded			
1996	62,700	Not Yet Recorded			

*Earnings were taxed for Medicare beginning in 1966. From 1983 on, these earnings include Medicare-Qualified Government Earnings (see page 7). In 1991, the maximum yearly earnings taxed for Medicare are $125,000. For 1992, the amount is $130,200.

earnings that are covered by Social Security, up to the time when you apply for benefits, based on estimated future earnings that you give them. If between now and the day you retire you have more earnings that are covered by Social Security, your monthly payments will probably turn out to be higher than Social Security has estimated. With such figures in hand, you can calculate how much income you will need, in addition to Social Security benefits, to provide the kind of comfortable retirement you have earned.

How much can you earn during retirement without giving up Social Security benefits?

If you are 65 or older, but not yet 70, you will lose some of your Social Security benefits if you earn income that totals more than $12,500 a year. If you are not yet 65 but are getting Social Security benefits, that maximum is $8,280. Once you reach 70, however, Social Security doesn't care how much you earn. You're home free.

How do the limits work? If you are under 65, you will have to give up $1 for each $2 you earn above the

Exhibit 15 *continued*

ESTIMATED BENEFITS

Retirement

You must have 40 Social Security credits to qualify for retirement benefits. This is the same number of credits you need to qualify for Medicare at age 65. Assuming that you meet all the requirements, here are estimates of your retirement benefits based on your past and any projected earnings. The estimates are in today's dollars, but adjusted to account for average wage growth in the national economy.

If you retire at 62, your monthly benefit in today's dollars will be about .... $ 998

The earliest age at which you can receive an unreduced retirement benefit is 65 years of age. We call this your full retirement age. If you wait until that age to receive benefits, your monthly benefit in today's dollars will be about .... $ 1,248

If you wait until you are 70 to receive benefits, your monthly benefit in today's dollars will be about .... $ 1,680

Survivors

If you have a family, you must have 22 Social Security credits for certain family members to receive benefits if you were to die this year. They may also qualify if you earn 6 credits in the 3 years before your death. The number of credits a person needs to qualify for survivors benefits increases each year until age 62, up to a maximum of 40 credits.

Here is an estimate of the benefits your family could receive if you had enough credits to be insured, they qualified for benefits, and you died this year:

Your child could receive a monthly benefit of about .... $ 936

If your child and your surviving spouse who is caring for your child both qualify, they could each receive a monthly benefit of about .... $ 936

When your surviving spouse reaches full retirement age, he or she could receive a monthly benefit of about .... $ 1,248

If more family members qualify for benefits (other children, for example), the total amount that we could pay your family each month is about .... $ 2,184

We may also be able to pay your surviving spouse or children a one-time death benefit of .... $ 255

Disability

Right now, you must have 22 Social Security credits to qualify for disability benefits. And, 20 of these credits had to be earned in the 10 year period immediately before you became disabled. If you are blind or received disability benefits in the past, you may need fewer credits. The number of credits a person needs to qualify for disability benefits increases each year until age 62, up to a maximum of 40 credits.

If you were disabled, had enough credits, and met the other requirements for disability benefits, here is an estimate of the benefits you could receive right now:

Your monthly benefit would be about .... $ 1,248

You and your eligible family members could receive up to a monthly total of about .... $ 1,872

These estimates may be reduced if you receive workers' compensation or public disability benefits.

IF YOUR RECORDS DO NOT AGREE WITH OURS

If your earnings records do not agree with ours, please report this to us right away by calling the 800 number shown below. We can usually help you by phone. When you call, have this statement available along with any W-2 forms, payslips, tax returns or any other proof of your earnings.

IF YOU HAVE ANY QUESTIONS

If you have any other questions about this statement, please read the information on the reverse side. If you still have questions, please call 1-800-537-7005.

Social Security considers all calls confidential. We also want to ensure that you receive accurate and courteous service. That is why we may have a second Social Security representative listen to some calls.

limit. If you are between 65 and 69, Social Security takes away $1 for each $3 you earn. For example, suppose you are 66:

Social Security Benefits	$ 9,600 a year
Earned Income	$20,000 a year
Earnings Limit	-12,500
Difference $20,000 - $12,500 =	$ 7,500 divided by 3
	= $ 2,500

Your Social Security benefits will be $9,600 less $2,500, or $7,100. With your $20,000 in earnings, your gross income will come to $27,100.

But suppose you limit your earnings to $10,700. You will get your full Social Security benefits of $9,600, plus your $10,700 in earnings, for a gross of $20,300.

In any case, of course, you will face some further reductions. You must pay income taxes and Social Security tax on your earned income, and if your total earnings are above certain limits, you may have to pay federal tax on a percentage of your Social Security benefits.

> *Important:* The limits on earnings will increase $1,000 a year from now until the year 2000, when the limit will hit $17,000. Then it will jump to $25,000 in 2001 and $30,000 in 2002.
>
> *Note:* During your first year of retirement, special rules apply. Check them out when you notify Social Security of your official retirement date.

Important points to remember about Social Security

- If your adjusted gross income, plus tax-exempt interest, plus one-half of your Social Security benefits total more than certain base amounts, a certain percentage of your Social Security benefits can be taxed as income. The base amount for a single taxpayer is $25,000, with a tax on up to 50 percent of Social Security benefits.
- If you are a single taxpayer whose total of those three items—adjusted gross income, tax-exempt interest, and one-half of Social Security benefits—comes to more than $34,000, you must pay tax on up to 85 percent of your Social Security benefits. *Note*: 85 percent is how much of your benefit is subject to federal income tax, not how much tax you pay.
- The latter (i.e., the tax on up to 85 percent of benefits) hits at upper-income taxpayers more than at people whose income is $55,000 or less. Take Bobbie and Jack, for example. By not marrying, they have sidestepped the substantial "marriage penalty" that is built into this tax rule. The penalty they avoid arises from the fact that there is only a $10,000 difference between the $34,000 base for single taxpayers and the $44,000 base for couples filing jointly. Bobbie's income of $40,000 includes $12,000 of Social security benefits, of which $4,500 are taxable (i.e., $40,000 - $12,000 = $28,000; $28,000 + [$12,000 × 50% = $6,000] = $34,000; $34,000 - $25,000 = $9,000; $9,000 × 50% = $4,500). Jack will pay at a higher rate because his income exceeds all thresholds. If they were married, they would immediately be well above the $44,000 base, so 85 percent of their total Social Security benefits (i.e., $20,400) would be taxable. As a result, they save substantial taxes by not marrying.
- Since live-togethers file separate tax returns, either or both of you can work without affecting the other's Social Security benefits.
- When a married couple receives Social Security benefits, the earned income of one can affect the Social Security benefits of the other. Live-togethers avoid that disadvantage, for each can work without affecting the other's Social Security benefits since they file separate tax returns..
- Some states tax Social Security benefits. Others do not. Most states that impose income taxes follow federal guidelines. But be sure to check out the laws in your state, and check on any state you may be considering a move to.
- Until you actually make a claim, Social Security can only estimate your benefits. The exact amount will be computed when you file your claim.
- Nothing happens unless you make it happen. You will receive no benefits unless you file for them. You must notify Social Security of your retirement, your disability, or any death that may result in Social Security paying you benefits. Such notification must be made within six months after the

Exhibit 16:
MARRIAGE PENALTY ON SOCIAL SECURITY

	Household Income		
	Single	Live-togethers	Married
Adjusted Gross Income (without Social Security)	$26,000	$52,000	$52,000
Taxable Social Security	3,500*	7,000	20,400**
Adjusted Gross Income	29,500	59,000	72,400

*Tax on 50% of excess over $25,000 (i.e., $32,000 - $25,000 = $7,000 × 50% = $3,500).

**Tax on 85% of Social Security

Assumption: Each receiving $12,000 in Social Security Benefits

Exhibit 17
SOCIAL SECURITY BENEFITS AS PERCENTAGE OF PRIMARY INSURANCE AMOUNT (PIA)

OLD-AGE BENEFIT	
Starting age 65 or over	PIA
Starting age 62–64	PIA reduced
DISABILITY BENEFITS	PIA
WIFE'S BENEFIT (wife of retired or disabled worker)	
Caring for child (under 16 or disabled)	50% of PIA
Starting age 65	50% of PIA
Starting age 62–64	50% of PIA reduced
HUSBAND'S BENEFIT (husband of retired or disabled woman worker)	
Starting age 65	50% of PIA
Starting age 62–64	50% of PIA reduced
CHILD'S BENEFIT	
Child of retired or disabled worker	50% of PIA
Child of deceased worker	75% of PIA
MOTHER'S OR FATHER'S BENEFIT (widow or widower caring for child under 16 or disabled)	75% of PIA
WIDOW'S BENEFIT (widow not caring for child)	
Starting age 65	100% of PIA
Starting age 60–64	100% of PIA reduced
WIDOWER'S BENEFIT	
Starting age 65	100% of PIA
Starting age 60–64	100% of PIA reduced
DISABLED WIDOW'S OR WIDOWER'S BENEFIT	
Starting age 50–60	50% to 71½% of PIA
PARENT'S BENEFIT (dependent parent of deceased worker)	
One dependent parent	82½% of PIA
Two dependent parents	75% of PIA (each)

retirement, disability, or death. In almost all cases, the law does not permit any retroactive payment of benefits for a period longer than six months.

- If you are 65 and you are delaying making a claim for Social Security benefits, be sure to notify the Social Security office. Why? Because at 65 you are entitled to Medicare coverage (parts A and B) even if you are still working. But you must sign up for it.
- Allow plenty of time. Notify Social Security at least three months ahead, if you want benefits to start promptly on your retirement date.

- In the case of a death, notify Social Security immediately. Don't forget that a divorced person who was married for at least 10 years can receive benefits as a widow or widower when an ex-spouse dies, subject to meeting other conditions.
- If you are the survivor (widow or child) of a fully insured or currently insured worker and are entitled to Social Security benefits based on that worker's record, you are entitled to an immediate lump-sum benefit of $255.
- Social Security benefits are adjusted annually, based on the Cost of Living Index. The increase is automatic.
- Never forget that Social Security rules and regulations are changed frequently. Stay up-to-date on how they affect you. Carefully read all bulletins, letters, and notices the Social Security Administration sends to you.

○ ○ ○

BARBARA, 63, AND SAM, 66. BOTH RETIRED. BOTH NOW WORKING

Barbara earns $8,000 annually as a part-time secretary in a lawyer's office. Sam is earning close to $11,000. Their total earned income: about $19,000. Since they file as single taxpayers, they do not have to give up any of their Social Security benefits. If they were married, their earnings would be subject to the rules for people who are working and are less than 70 years old.

○ ○ ○

C H A P T E R T E N

YOUR PENSION PLANS: NOBODY'S GOING TO DO IT FOR YOU

If both of you are working, you probably each have pension plans in place. If you have both retired, you may be collecting on two different plans. Basically, participation in any plan is the same whether or not matrimony is a part of your present lives. But what you must look at closely are the designation of beneficiaries and the options for receiving the benefits of the plans.

In recent years, a major shift has occurred in the responsibility for pensions. Plans sponsored and managed entirely by employers have been disappearing fast. In their place have come plans that require voluntary contributions from employees as well as knowledgeability on their part. You've got to know how it all works and watch out for your own best interests. So it is imperative that you gain not only a basic understanding of what pensions are but an appreciation of the importance of your own long-term financial fitness.

A form of deferred wages

Think of your pension plan as a form of deferred wages. Under some plans, the employer puts in all the money; these are called non-contributory plans. In others, the employee puts in some percentage of his or her earnings; these are called contributory plans.

Only slightly more than half of all American workers in the private sector (i.e., not in government jobs) are covered by pension plans—either contributory or non-contributory—provided by their employers. Altogether, the field includes such a bewildering array of basic plans, with many diverse provisions, that we cannot describe a single sample plan. Rather, you must look hard at any plan your employer offers, become thoroughly familiar with it, and get to know its every detail so you understand it now and can understand changes that come along, as they surely will, in the future.

There are two basic types of pension plans:

1. *Defined benefit plan.* This is considered the traditional pension plan. It specifies in advance the benefits that you will receive. Your employer funds it and takes responsibility for investing the money that goes into it, usually hiring a professional money manager or management firm to handle the investment. Under this

plan, you may find either of two ways of paying benefits to you when you retire:

To make sure the money will be ready and available when you retire, the law requires your company to fund this type of plan in advance. Your benefits are based on your earnings over a specified period of service with the company. How much you get is usually figured as a percentage of your earnings. For example, suppose you work for the ABC Company. And suppose you have worked for 30 years with average base earnings of $25,000, or $2,083 per month. The company agrees that when you retire it will pay 1.1 percent of your average monthly earnings (figured by counting the highest 60 months out of your last 120). Your benefit in retirement is $687.00 per month—$2,083 × 1.1% × 30.

Sometimes it is figured on a flat rate plan. In this one, you get a fixed dollar amount for each year of service. If, for example, you receive $20.25 per month for each year of service, and if you have 30 years of service, you will get $607.50 a month. The rate under this plan varies according to job classification, so you get a higher pension if you had a better-paying job.

Over the four years from 1990 through 1994, the number of such traditional pension plans fell by 40 percent. Company after company has been discontinuing them in order to reduce costs. Usually, they replace them with defined contribution plans.

2. *Defined contribution plan.* This one is also called an individual account plan. The typical plan relies on you to put in your own money toward retirement and make your own decisions on how to invest it. The amount of your contributions is flexible and the benefits you ultimately get are based on how much is accumulated in your account by the time you retire.

a. *The 401(k) plan.* The best known and most common type is the 401(k) plan. Between 1990 and 1994, these plans grew by 12 percent nationwide. First introduced in 1978 and named after a section of the Internal Revenue Service code that created it, the 401(k) plan is a voluntary retirement savings plan to which you make contributions from your gross income before taxes (one of its great advantages). Your employer is permitted under law to make matching contributions (another great advantage) that typically range from 25 to 100 percent of your contribution—up to a certain limit.

A typical plan may say, "The company will match $0.50 for each $1.00 of the first 6 percent of your pay." Your contribution is limited to either a percent of pay or a dollar amount. Suppose, for example, you are making $50,000 a year and contribute 6 percent. Your account will be credited with $4,500—$3,000 from your payroll deductions, and $1,500 put in by your company. Now suppose you increase your contribution to 10 percent—$5,000. The company's contribution will still be $1,500, so your total for the year is $6,500.

The tax deferment is valuable. You pay no taxes until you start withdrawing money from the plan, usually when you retire. You get other advantages, too. Your plan may allow you to make contributions from your after-tax dollars, in addition to the before-tax payroll deduction. Some limitations apply: The maximum amount you may contribute in 1996 is $9,500; the total amount that may be contributed in any one year by you and your employer together is $30,000 or 25 percent of your gross salary minus your 401(k) contributions—whichever is less.

Exhibit 18
401(k) PLAN ACCOUNT GROWTH

Projected account at the end of:	Current salary	
	$35,000	**$50,000**
10 years	56,748	$81,070
20 years	214,953	307,076
25 years	370,677	529,538

Source: Hewitt Associates

Assumptions: 5% salary increases, employeee contributions of 6%, employer contribution of 3%, interest rate of 8% (credited quarterly on employee contributions and at end of year on employer's contributions).

❍ ❍ ❍

BOB'S 401(k) PLAN

Ever since his first job, Bob has contributed the maximum allowed to a 401(k) plan. His employers have always matched what he put in. As a result, he has built up a sizable nest egg that is approaching a quarter of a million dollars—and he's not even 40.

❍ ❍ ❍

CINDY'S PLAN IS DIFFERENT

Because Cindy works for a nonprofit organization, her plan is different. Called a 403(b), the plan welcomes contributions from employees but does not require them. The university is allowed to contribute up to a prescribed maximum even if she does not contribute. Cindy has not made any contributions to the plan but, over the eight years she has worked there, it has reached $25,000. One reason why she has not contributed is that she is so confused by all the investment choices that are offered. Even though the university provides informative seminars on the subject each semester, she has yet to attend one. She knows she should, but she just hasn't gotten around to it.

○ ○ ○

Where is the best place to put the money?

Your employer will offer various investment alternatives, from money-market accounts to fixed-income investments to stock funds. Often, company stock is offered. As you consider possibilities, note that the number of mutual funds out there keeps growing, adding to the choices you face.

One of the biggest problems in the whole pension world is that those who put money aside in defined contribution plans do not invest it as well as the professionals who manage defined benefit plans. About half of all the 401(k) assets in America are sitting quietly in low-interest guaranteed investment contracts. The fact is, most people play it too safe with their retirement earnings. The growth of your retirement funds can be seriously impeded, especially in the early years of long-term investing, if you are too conservative.

How about getting your money out? You are allowed to start taking money from your 401(k) plan under the terms of your particular plan document. Usual conditions are: 1) you terminate employment; 2) any time after you reach age 59½; 3) if you become disabled; or 4) if you are undergoing a financial hardship. If you withdraw money before age 59½, however, you must pay a penalty of 10 percent of the amount you withdraw unless you are 55 and met your plan's early retirement conditions. You will also be subject to income taxes on the amount withdrawn. But suppose you are changing jobs and not yet 59½. In that case, take the lump-sum amount and roll it over either into an Individual Retirement Account (IRA), where it will continue to grow on a tax-deferred basis or into your new employer's 401(k) plan.

Another advantage of the 401(k) plan: You may borrow from it if the plan permits. However, you may not borrow more than $50,000 or one-half of the amount in your account, whichever is lower. Unless you are using it to buy a principal residence, the amount you borrow must be repaid within five years and you must make payments at least quarterly.

b. *Money purchase plan.* Your employer must contribute a fixed percentage of your salary each year.

c. *Profit-sharing plan.* In this one, your employer's contributions may vary from year to year as profits of the firm vary. There may be a formula spelled out in the plan or the contributions may be decided by your employer each year.

Think about vesting

In today's job world, pensions and profit-sharing are well worth thinking about even when you are first contemplating being hired by a particular company. Ask about its pension plan. And if you are already employed, pay attention when your company offers any change in its existing plans.

Just what does "vesting" mean? When you become vested, it means that the money credited to your name in the company's pension accounting is legally yours, without question or qualification, from then on. Vesting varies from company to company. In most plans, you become vested in the employer's contributions only after you have worked a certain number of years or reached a certain age. You are always vested in the money you yourself contributed plus the interest it has earned. Two typical vesting situations:

1. *Partial vesting.* Under (for example) a seven-year schedule, you are entitled to 20 percent of the employer's money in your account after you complete three years. You get another 20 percent at the end of each of the next four years, until you reach 100 percent.
2. *Full vesting.* You have no vested right to the employer's money until you complete five years of employment, at which point you become 100-percent, or fully, vested.

If you are contributing to your plan, you may walk away at any time with the amount you have put in, before you have any vesting whatever. If you depart after you have become vested, you can not be forced to forfeit your pension benefits—the money in which you are vested is yours, with very few exceptions.

But there is a catch in many pension plans: In order to receive your pension upon retirement, you must have fulfilled the requirement for duration of service. At most companies, the longer you work, the larger your pension. For instance, look again at our previous example under the flat-rate plan. If you have 30 years of service, your pension is $607.50 per month. But a worker the same age who has been with the company for only 20 years will get $405 a month.

Suppose you move to a job at another company after you are fully vested. Then what? You will have to consider several questions:

1. May I take a lump-sum distribution and roll it over into another form of retirement account, such as an IRA?
2. Will I have to pay a tax if I take the lump sum?
3. May I move the money into another company's pension plan? Will my new employer accept it?

4. May I leave the money with the company I'm departing from, and, if so, how much will I receive monthly when I do retire?

Getting your pension benefits

Whether you are retiring or moving to another company and claiming your vested interest in your former employer's pension plan, you must make the critical decision on how to take the money. Your options include:

1. *Lump-sum distribution.* Whether you can take the lump sum depends on what kind of plan you are in. If it is a defined contribution plan, such as a 401(k), you may take the lump sum. If it is a defined benefit plan, you have to find out how your company has it set up. The lump sum may not be available to you and you will have to take your pension in monthly installments as an annuity.

Suppose you do take the lump sum. Now you must decide whether to roll it over into an Individual Retirement Account (IRA) or into your new employer's pension plan and thus delay paying taxes on it or not roll it over and pay the tax on the full amount. To make that decision, you should be aware of certain rules that govern lump-sum distributions:

a. *Taking the cash.* If you want to take the money now rather than roll it over into an IRA, it will be taxed as ordinary income. If you are over 59½ and have been a participant for five years, you will be allowed to use a five-year forward averaging provision. Pending legislation, however, may eliminate this. You may use this only one time. (If you were born before 1936, you are allowed a 10-year forward averaging.)

In figuring the tax, the Internal Revenue Service considers you a single person with no exemptions. No other income is taken into consideration in calculating the tax. In addition, if you are under 59½, you must pay a 10-percent penalty unless you are over 55 and meet the plan's conditions for early retirement.

b. *Salting it away.* If you do not need the funds immediately, the rollover is your best bet. From the day you receive the money, you are allowed 60 days to put it into a rollover account. The distribution, as it is called, must come from a qualified retirement or profit-sharing plan (i.e., the plan must be one that is approved by the IRS).

Why is the rollover attractive? Because your money continues to grow, tax deferred, and there are no taxes to be paid at the time of a rollover.

The government wants to discourage you from spending money that is being put away for your retirement. If you are younger and changing jobs, it especially urges you to roll over funds. To back up its point of view, it requires that your plan administrator withhold 20 percent of any lump-sum distribution you take. The plan administrator must send that 20 percent to the Internal Revenue Service. If, within 60 days, you deposit your remaining 80 percent in an IRA or other tax-deferred account and add to it, from some other source, an amount equal to the 20 percent withheld, you may then get the IRS to refund the 20 percent it took. How? By adjusting your estimated tax payments, or by waiting until you get a refund on your tax return the following year. Either way, the government gets to use 20 percent of your money, without paying you interest, in the interim.

You can avoid this procedure. Don't take the lump-sum payment. Instead, have your plan administrator transfer the money directly to an IRA or another trustee account, either at your new place of employment, if permissible, or with a bank or mutual fund or wherever you wish to put it—as long as that place is approved by the IRS. Discuss this with your accountant. Make your decisions before you leave the company.

Lump-sum distribution has real advantages: You keep control over your money, and you decide what kind of investments you want to make. You can put your rollover money in a variety of IRAs: savings and money-market accounts, certificates of deposit, stocks and bonds, mutual funds or an annuity contract (see Exhibit 19).

2. *Annuity.* Rather than taking the outright lump-sum distribution, you may prefer to receive an annuity distribution. But be aware that, as live-togethers, you do not get the automatic survivor benefits that married couples get from an annuity. To protect one spouse from losing the other spouse's pension when he or she dies, a law passed in 1984 requires the payment of a joint-and-survivor annuity of at least 50 percent to the surviving spouse. It provides, for instance, that if a husband who is receiving a pension dies before his wife dies, she will automatically receive at least 50 percent of the amount he was being paid. This means that the monthly payment in the meantime, while both are living, will be lower than would be paid by an annuity set up on a single life. If a husband and wife decide that they don't want this feature, and would rather get the higher payments while both are living, the spouse must sign a waiver and have it notarized before filing it with the plan administrator.

The key to heading off a problem in this regard is *anticipation.* You must be well informed and anticipate what can happen. If your company requires you (under a defined benefit plan) to take an annuity, or if you prefer to take one, your employer—knowing you are not married—will pay it to you as a straight life annuity. That means you will receive a monthly payment as long as you live but, when you die, it will end. *Nothing* will

Exhibit 19
LUMP-SUM DISTRIBUTION: 5-YEAR AVERAGING VERSUS ROLLOVER

$100,000 lump-sum distribution versus IRA rollover		
	Lump-sum distribution	**IRA rollover**
5-Year Averaging Tax:	$15,000	N/A
Amount Available to Invest	85,000	$100,000
Accumulated Value—5 years	108,484[a]	146,933[b]
Accumulated Value—10 years	138,456[a]	215,892[b]
$200,000 lump-sum distribution versus IRA rollover		
	Lump-sum distribution	**IRA rollover**
5-Year Averaging Tax:	$42,733	N/A
Amount Available to Invest	157,227	$200,000
Accumulated Value—5 years	200,666[a]	293,866[b]
Accumulated Value—10 years	256,106[a]	431,785[b]
$250,000 lump-sum distribution versus IRA rollover		
	Lump-sum distribution	**IRA rollover**
5-Year Averaging Tax:	$56,878	N/A
Amount Available to Invest	193,122	$250,000
Accumulated Value—5 years	246,478[a]	367,332[b]
Accumulated Value—10 years	314,575[a]	539,731[b]

[a] Funds are invested tax-free at a 5% rate of return. Though the funds could be invested for a higher rate of return in a taxable investment, income taxes would be due each year on the interest and dividends that the money earned. The accumulated value, therefore, at the end of the period might be the same. (See chapter 10 on saving and investing for taxable versus tax-free equivalents.)

[b] Funds are invested at an 8% rate of return. At the end of the five- or ten-year period, the money may be withdrawn in a single lump sum, paying income taxes on the full amount, or annually, paying income taxes only on the amount withdrawn.

Source: Dworken, Hillman, LaMorte & Sterczala, PC

be provided for your partner. How, then, can you provide for your partner? The most important thing to do is to find out if your employer's plan allows a joint-and-survivor benefit with a non-spouse. If it does, tell your plan administrator *before you retire* that you want to arrange a joint-and-survivor annuity. Once the annuity payments start, it is too late. You cannot then change the way you receive it.

How much do you get each month? That depends on the plan (either a defined contribution or defined benefit), and on how much you or the company, or both, have put into the plan. It probably also depends on the age at which payments are to begin. If you start receiving payments when you are 65, for instance, they will be smaller amounts than if you wait until you are 70. If your partner is much younger, and thus can be expected to live much longer, the monthly payments will be lower.

Another important angle: If you take a straight life annuity and give up any survivor benefits, your monthly check will be higher. This means that when you die the remaining money that has not been used in payments will belong to the plan or the insurance company.

When does it make good sense to choose a straight annuity paid on your life only, so you get a larger monthly check than if you built survivor benefits into the plan? When the survivor's own pension is substantial enough that he or she will not need survivor's benefits. Or when you and your partner figure out that, with income from Social Security, investments, and proceeds from life insurance policies, he or she will probably not need a survivor annuity after you die—the income from these other sources will enable your partner to live comfortably. And meantime, while you are alive, you can both have the advantage of receiving the larger check. So do some good hard thinking. And planning.

What is the advantage of an annuity over a lump-sum distribution? For a start, you never have to worry about managing the money. The annuity guarantees you a fixed monthly income, and you know you will never outlive your capital.

But the annuity has a disadvantage. Your monthly check remains exactly the same, no matter what inflation does. You have no protection. As many a retired person has learned from bitter experience in recent years, the value of an annuity can be eroded by inflation. And there is no changing your mind: Once you have signed the contract and paid for the annuity, that is it. It has no cash value.

○ ○ ○

THE SURPRISE DICK GOT WHEN HE RETIRED

When Dick retired from the back office of his insurance company, he took his pension as a lump sum—all $400,000 of it. He had worked for the same company for 40 years. Even he was amazed at how much had been salted away for him.

Dick transferred his lump sum into an IRA account at a brokerage house, where it is invested in stocks and bonds and maintains its tax-deferred status.

○ ○ ○

Plan years ahead

Considering these alternatives, and the seriousness or consequences of each, makes it vitally important that you think your pension plans through with great care well in advance of your retirement. Six months before retirement is too late.

As you think about your plans, many questions will occur to you. Here are a few of them—and some answers:

1. *What if I take early retirement?* If your pension plan stipulates 65 as retirement age but you want to retire at 60, you are likely to lose one-third of it. Retiring at age 55 may cost you up to 50 percent or even more. And that does not include what you would lose by having fewer years of service.

2. *What if I decide to stay on at work after I turn 65?* The chances are your pension will continue to increase as long as you work. This will be specified in your particular plan.

3. *What happens to my plan if I take a leave of absence or if I'm laid off temporarily?* Check this carefully with your company. For pension purposes, the employer will usually honor all service before and after the break. Some, however, insist on a waiting period—usually one year—before they will let you back into the plan.

4. *Are my pension benefits affected by my Social Security benefits?* Do not be surprised if your employer reduces your defined benefit pension by a percentage of the amount you are to get from Social Security. This can range from 25 percent to as high as 50 percent—depending on your company's plan. This can be a real shocker.

5. *What if I die before I retire?* You can name your partner to receive any death benefits. Or you can name your estate to receive the benefits and, under your will, give your partner the rights to this money. Usually, it is easier to name your partner as beneficiary of the retirement plan because, if you break up, the designation is revocable. Of course, a will can also be changed, but involves paying a lawyer—and a will can be contested. If you die before pension payments begin, your named beneficiary can receive payments based on her or his life expectancy.

When the money is distributed through your will to your estate, tax deferral is lost and both income and estate taxes will have to be paid. If you die at a time when you are eligible for early retirement, your partner (if named as your beneficiary) will receive benefits just as he or she would have if you had already retired before you died and were covered by a joint and survivor annuity. Under a defined contribution plan, the death benefit is usually determined by the amount of money that the pension plan holds in your name.

6. *What if I become disabled?* Under many plans, if you are permanently disabled, you become fully vested regardless of the usual vesting rules. If your disability is temporary, so that you are unable to work for a while, most plans will simply hold the benefits that have accrued to you to date. Or, if you have reached early-retirement age, you may be entitled to an immediate annuity based on the amount that has accrued in your account up to that date. Some plans provide for a disabled employee to receive early retirement benefits at a younger age, and with fewer years of service required, than an able-bodied employee would be entitled to.

7. *How can I find out the status of my plan?* The law requires your company to give you a summary report on the money in your plan at least once a year. Make sure you thoroughly understand this statement. If you have any questions, talk to someone in authority where you work. Get it explained. Do not simply accept the interpretations—or the guesswork—of fellow workers.

It is your money, and your retirement. You want to be as comfortable as possible. Nothing is more important than checking regularly on your pension situation and knowing well in advance just what your benefits will be.

❍ ❍ ❍

BOB'S BENEFICIARY

Bob has not named Evan as beneficiary of his retirement accounts. Rather, he has named his sister. Why? Because Evan's future is more secure. He will be coming into a substantial inheritance, whereas Bob's sister is struggling to make ends meet.

❍ ❍ ❍

IRA—Individual Retirement Account

Before 1982, you were not permitted to establish an Individual Retirement Account (IRA) unless your employer provided no pension or profit-sharing plan. From 1982 through 1986, anyone who was earning income could contribute to an IRA and deduct the contribution—up to a $2,000 maximum—from his or her federal income taxes. In effect, you could reduce your taxable income. Starting in 1987, however, the rules on IRAs changed. The maximum yearly contribution of $2,000 per worker continued, but the rules on tax deductibility were changed. If you are not covered by a qualified pension plan, you may deduct the full $2,000 you put into your IRA, regardless of how much your income is, as long as it is at least $2,000 a year. Furthermore, if you are a single person, if your adjusted gross income is not higher than $25,000, you may still deduct the full $2,000—even if you are covered by a qualified plan. If your adjusted gross income is between $25,000 and $35,000, and if you are covered by a qualified plan, the $2,000 maximum will drop, going down by $200 for each $1,000 of additional income. For example, if your adjusted gross income on a single return is $27,500, you may take a deduction of $1,500. The deduction drops to $1,000 if your adjusted gross income is $30,000 and to $500 if your adjusted gross reaches $35,000. If you are an individual taxpayer with an adjusted gross over $35,000, the deduction phases out completely.

A BIG ADVANTAGE

Live-togethers get one advantage that married couples do not get. For a married couple in a qualified retirement plan provided by an employer, if one spouse is covered and if their combined incomes are higher than $40,000, the deductible IRA contribution by either spouse is reduced or eliminated. Live-togethers do not face that disadvantage. If one of you is covered by a qualified plan, the other can make a deductible contribution to his or her own IRA, if eligible (i.e., if his or her income does not exceed the limits—see Exhibit 20).

Even if you cannot take the deduction, you may nevertheless continue to make contributions up to the $2,000 maximum and thus put off taxation of the interest that money earns until you withdraw the funds. And if you are unable to deduct your contributions, you will not have to pay income tax on those amounts when you withdraw them upon your retirement. (In other words, the government will not tax you twice.) You will, however, have to pay income tax on the interest they have earned.

Are you required to put the maximum into your IRA each year? No. You may put as much as you want to or feel you can afford. You may make a single deposit of your entire amount for the year, or you may put in dribs and drabs. Amounts may vary from deposit to deposit and from year to year, and if necessary you may skip one or more years. An IRA may be opened and the first

Exhibit 20
IRA DEDUCTIBILITY

(If you are in an employer-sponsored plan)			
If you are:	**If your adjusted gross income is:**		
Single	$25,000 or less	Between $25,000 & $35,000	$35,000 or more
Married filing jointly	$40,000 or less	Between $40,000 & $50,000	$50,000 or more
Married filing singly	Not applicable	Under $10,000	$10,000 or more
Your IRA contribution	Fully deductible	Partially deductible	Not deductible

Exhibit 21
HOW MUCH CAN AN IRA ADD UP TO?

	Amount of annual contribution (assumes 8% annual interest)					
	$500		$1,000		$2,000	
Starting at age	**At age 59½**	**At age 65**	**At age 59½**	**At age 65**	**At age 59½**	**At age 65**
25	$89,085	$132,897	$178,169	$279,781	$356,339	$559,562
35	37,495	61,173	74,990	122,346	149,980	244,692
40	23,276	39,477	46,552	78,954	93,125	157,909

deposit made as late as the due date of your income tax return, April 15 of the year following. You may continue to make deposits until you are 70½, if you are working. But not after that.

Self-employed? Use the Keogh plan

If you are self-employed, think seriously about starting a Keogh plan. It provides a nest egg for retirement. In all respects, Keogh imposes the same rules and regulations as an IRA, but with one important exception: You may contribute as much as $30,000, or 20 percent of your income (whichever is less) each year.

○ ○ ○

DAVE'S KEOGH PLAN PAYS OFF

As a doctor in independent practice, Dave was delighted when the Keogh plan came along. He took advantage of it immediately, and over the years put away a large amount. Even today, after withdrawing the minimum amounts for the last seven years, he still has about $200,000 in the account.

○ ○ ○

TAKE HOW MUCH? WHEN?

The IRA rules for withdrawing are ambiguous. Few banks, brokers, or employers understand them. Their clearest rule is that you must start withdrawing your money by the time you are 70½ or face some stiff penalties.

Now look far down the road. How much you take out of your IRA or any other savings plan between the ages of 59½ and 70½ is your own decision. (IRA is synonymous with any qualified tax-deferred plans.) You are allowed to take as much as you want, or leave it all to grow on a tax-deferred basis until you are 70½. But be aware there might be a 15-percent excess tax if you withdraw more than $155,000.

Minimum distributions

Once you reach 70½, the rule is hard and fast: You have to start cashing in. The deadline for starting? April 1 of the calendar year after the calendar year in which you turn 70½ But there is a catch: If you wait that long—until the year after the year in which you become 70½—you will have to take your first distribution by April 1 and then take a second distribution by December 31. This, of course, could substantially increase your taxable income, because each distribution counts as income in the same single year.

To avoid that catch, take your first distribution in year one (i.e., the calendar year during which you turn 70½). Don't wait until April 1 of year two, even though the law allows you to wait that long. Each year after that, you will be required to take a distribution by December 31.

How much should you take? As little as possible, so your money can last as long as possible. The required minimum distribution is based on the amount you have in the account, and on whether you take the distributions based on your own single life expectancy or on a joint life expectancy with another person. The IRS provides life expectancy tables based on single life expectancy and on a joint life and last survivor expectancy. (See Appendix, Tables I and II.)

There are two withdrawal methods:

1. *Recalculation method.* Say, you are a male who reaches 70½ this year and is using a single life expectancy, which at age 70½ is 16 years. You decide to take your first withdrawal from an IRA by the end of the year. If your account balance on December 31 is $75,000, and your life expectancy is 16 years, divide $75,000 by 16. You must withdraw $4,687.50. $75,000

minus \$4,687.50 will leave you \$70,312.50. Next year, the balance will increase by the interest earned by the fund, but it will be reduced by the distribution you took last year. If you assume an 8-percent return on your funds, your account balance at the end of the second year will be \$75,937.50. And now that you are a year older, your life expectancy will be 15.3 years, so you divide \$75,937.50 by 15.3 for a minimum withdrawal of \$4,963.23. You must use the life expectancy tables every year.

2. *Term-certain method.* Here's another method for withdrawing IRA funds. It lets you *lock in* your payout period, based on your life expectancy. Using the same figures as in the previous example, your first withdrawal would be \$75,000 divided by 16, for a minimum withdrawal of \$4,687.50. At the beginning of the second year, the balance will be \$70,312.50—i.e., \$75,000 minus \$4,687.50—but at the end of that year the balance (assuming an 8-percent return) will be \$75,937.50. You divide that by 15, for a minimum distribution of \$5,062.50. The following year, divide the year-end balance by 14, and so on.

What is the difference? In the recalculation method, the money is drawn down at a slower rate while you are alive. In the early years, true, you withdraw smaller amounts. But the biggest difference comes when you die. If you have named a beneficiary, under the recalculation method, the minimum distribution is recalculated using the life expectancy of your beneficiary. This increases the amount of the withdrawals, incurs more taxes, and drains the estate more quickly. At the death of a beneficiary, all of the remaining money goes to his or her estate the year after death and becomes subject to income and estate taxes.

With the term-certain method, however, the payouts to a beneficiary continue at the same pace as before. Upon the death of the beneficiary, the remaining money is paid to the estate over the remaining period, thus prolonging the tax-deferred growth. (See chapter 14: Estate Planning.) If you want to protect a beneficiary's right to do this, you must arrange it in advance. Write to *each* bank or other custodian where you have an IRA account, specifying the original joint life expectancy, acknowledging that you will use the MDIB rule while you are living, and saying that the original life expectancy will apply if you die before your beneficiary. This "timely selection" must be made before your required minimum distribution date of April 1, following the year you turned 70½. You might write something like this: "I hereby elect the term certain method of distribution subject to the MDIB rules while I am alive for myself and my beneficiary."

Speaking of custodians, you can make everything easier if, before you retire or die, you consolidate your IRAs in a single custodian—either one mutual fund company (through which you may invest in any number of distinct funds) or with one stockbroker. However, this can be a problem if you have many beneficiaries. If, for example, you have three children from a previous marriage as beneficiaries, it might be easier to set up three equal accounts.

Excess distributions have some rules of their own. Any annual withdrawals that are larger than \$155,000, and any qualified employee-sponsored lump-sum distributions greater than \$775,000, are subject to a 15-percent excise tax. If you find yourself in this category, you might want to take distributions before 70½, rather than risk falling into this excise-tax trap—as do so many people who wait until they are 70½ because they want to keep the money tax-deferred as long as possible. Note, however, that in the year you are rolling over a distribution from a qualified plan, it is exempt from the excise tax.

Withdrawals based on two lives: joint life expectancy

Suppose you want to withdraw your money from your IRA as slowly as possible. Minimum distributions are allowed on the joint life expectancies of two or more people—you and your partner, or you and your children from a previous marriage. If you have named a beneficiary who is not a legal spouse, she or he will be treated as no more than 10 years younger than you are, while you are alive. Say you are 71 and your partner is 55. For the purpose of figuring the minimum distribution that it insists on, the government considers your partner to be 61 years old. According to the IRS actuarial tables, your joint life expectancy is 29.7 years. But going by the

KEY POINTS

- Unless you elect the term-certain method before April 1 of the year after which you turn 70½, you will be stuck with the recalculation method.
- Be sure to write to all custodians, specifying which method of distribution you want.
- Once you make the choice, it is irrevocable.
- Before you start minimum distributions, you may well find it valuable to consult an attorney who specializes in pension law.
- In any year in which you do not take your required minimum distribution, an excise tax of 50 percent of the excess in your IRA will be imposed.

IRS Minimum Distribution Incidental Benefit (MDIB) table and the 10-year rule, your life expectancy is 25.3 years. (See Appendix, Table III.)

In a word: *Plan*. This is not something you leave until the last moment.

Taxes on IRAs

While the money you put away in IRAs, and the interest it earns, have not been taxed all this time, the minute you start to make withdrawals you have to pay tax on any amount you take out. It is treated as ordinary income. That means, of course, that if you take it all out in one lump sum, you will be taxed for the entire amount in the year in which you take it out. But there is a wrinkle. If you have made contributions to an IRA that were nondeductible (i.e., you made them with after-tax money, after you had already put in the maximum before-tax contribution allowed) the portion of any distribution you take that comes from that money is now tax-free—because you have already paid tax on it. How does the IRS decide what that portion is? Here's an example:

Let's say you withdraw $2,000 from your IRA, after making deductible contributions of $6,000 and nondeductible contributions of $10,000 over some eight years. At the end of this year, the balance in your IRA account is $22,000, including earnings over the eight years. Add the IRA balance at the end of the year and the withdrawal you made, and divide that figure (i.e., $24,000) into the total amount of nondeductible contributions (i.e., $10,000). This will give you 41.7 percent of your withdrawal tax free, with the remaining 58.3 percent (i.e., $1,166) taxable.

Don't forget to keep good records. File away copies of Form 8606, which lists your nondeductible contributions every tax year. Put them with your tax returns for such years. And also keep all forms sent to you by banks or other institutions that hold your IRA savings and that show your contributions to IRAs and your distributions from them.

Suppose you withdraw the money before you reach 59½? It will be taxed as ordinary income and, in addition, you will be charged a penalty of 10 percent of the amount you withdraw. That means you pay a $200 penalty on top of the tax itself if, for example, you take out $2,000 before you are 59½.

IRA money is allowed to move around

Must you always keep the money in the same IRA account? No. You may move it to another account, in another bank, either by direct transfer or by rollover. In a direct transfer, you do not get your hands on the money, even momentarily. It is moved directly from one trustee to another. You may ask your bank, for example, to transfer the fund directly to a mutual fund. But if you ask for a rollover, you do get your hands on the money—either cash or a bank check. You then have 60 days in which to deposit it in another IRA account. If you fail to do so, on the 61st day you will owe tax on the total—as ordinary income—and you will also owe the 10-percent penalty.

Important: The law prohibits you from making more than one rollover in any 12-month period. (Clearly, the government doesn't want you borrowing from yourself for 59-day periods over and over.) You may make direct transfers as often as you want to.

How about *when* you put money into an IRA—does it make any difference? Yes. If you make an IRA deposit early in the year—say, in January—that money and the interest it immediately starts to earn are tax-deferred (i.e., protected from any tax) for that year. And your money gets that much more time to grow. If, on the other hand, you put the money into a regular savings account or money-market fund, waiting until the April 15 deadline the following year before you move it into an IRA, the interest it earns will be taxable.

Does an IRA really make a difference?

It does. If you contribute the maximum of $2,000 a year for 10 years and it earns 10 percent you will have about $35,062 in the account at the end of 10 years. If you put the same amount, at the same interest, in an account where you pay taxes on it, you will have about $23,000 in 10 years—assuming you are in the 25-percent tax bracket.

What about *where* you put the money—does that make a difference? Yes. Banks, insurance companies, brokerage firms, mutual funds—they will all be delighted to get your money. You can put IRA funds into almost any type of account. So you must do some homework. Think about every aspect of your situation before you make any decision. How long do you plan to make contributions? What types of risks are you willing to take? If, for instance, you are now in your fifties, you may want to choose an investment with a guaranteed yield. But if you are much younger, you may be willing to take some risks, knowing that if you sustain losses you will have time to make up the difference.

Think also about how much you are willing to contribute each year. Some IRAs permit you to make small or frequent contributions, while others do not. Before you decide on any one type of IRA, get specific information from the institution you are considering. Here are some of the ways you can go:

1. *Banks.* At most banks, you will find a variety of options, all patterned on the conventional certificate of deposit (CD). The various options include the kind of

interest, amount of interest, and length of time of the certificate. Some offer variable or floating interest, while others do not—so compare the interest rates offered by various institutions. The minimum deposit? In most, it takes only $100 to get started.

2. *Credit unions.* These organizations, in most cases, design their IRAs to fit the size and nature of the union. The interest rate is set by the board of directors. Probably you may make a very low initial deposit, and deposits may be deducted directly from your paycheck—if your employer is willing to provide that benefit. It gives you some real convenience.

3. *Insurance companies.* If you set up an IRA with an insurance company, you are buying an annuity. The company will set a minimum rate of interest through the years, possibly higher in the early years and lower later on. You may have to pay an annual fee and some sales costs, and you will probably face a sizable penalty if you withdraw the money prematurely—even higher, it is likely, if you withdraw in the early years of the policy.

4. *Mutual funds.* Here, you buy shares in a pool of money that is invested in securities selected by professional money managers. In some, your IRA is in a money-market fund, where the investment is in short-term securities and the rate of return will vary each day. In others, the investment is in stocks and bonds—some in blue-chip companies, others in riskier emerging companies. Most mutual funds require a minimum deposit. It may be as low as $100. And most mutual funds charge a yearly maintenance fee of about $10.

As your investment objectives change, you may want to move your IRA from one mutual fund to another. To do this, some people choose a large company that operates several funds.

5. *Investment brokers.* Here you will find the widest range of IRAs. You can build your own portfolio, setting up a self-directed plan in which you make the decisions on investing in stocks, bonds, mutual funds, and government securities. You will pay administrative fees, and each time you buy or sell you must pay a commission. Most brokers expect you to invest your entire annual $2,000 deposit at one time, and the fact is that it is best to accumulate from $10,000 to $15,000 before you get into self-directing. Never forget that investing in securities involves the risk of loss as well as the hope of gain. It is, however, the most flexible route you can choose for your IRA money.

It's never too soon

To summarize: It is never too soon to start an IRA. Your commitment is a long-term one, but it is well worth it—especially when you think about all the concern in recent years over the future of Social Security, pension plans, and inflation.

Think of IRAs, Keoghs, and 401(k)s as bonuses offered by your government. They may well be the most important keys to the perplexing question: How can I maintain my lifestyle during retirement? But they can effectively head off disappointments in retirement only if you do your homework, making the effort to learn how they work, analyzing your own needs, asking questions, understanding the many options, and keeping a weather eye out for changes in Social Security and the laws and regulations about pensions.

It takes discipline. Retirement planning is not simple. You have to look far ahead, projecting income and expenses. Then, as your age of retirement draws near, you must closely track interest rates, inflation, retirement benefits, and surges and trickles in the economy. The sooner you get going, the sooner you will begin to feel comfortable about looking toward those promised golden years.

If you are as human as most people, probably two questions have been nagging at you as you made your way through these pages on Social Security and pension plans: Will I have enough to live on when I retire? Or will I need additional income?

You can develop practical answers by looking at your assets and figuring whether they can produce more income for you. You may suprise yourself by discovering that you have more alternatives than you think you have.

CHAPTER ELEVEN

HOUSING: WHAT KIND OF ROOF IS OVER YOUR HEADS?

When you live together, just *where* do you live together? For unmarried couples, what kind of housing is probable—let alone possible—from the standpoint of financial fitness?

More and more, joint ownership of residential real estate by unmarried individuals is becoming common. But when you get into such arrangements, you must expect some daunting implications, especially if you and your partner break up later on. How will the title to the house be held? This question will have significant consequences if the property is to be sold while both of you are living, or if one of you moves out or dies. What is the potential liability of a partner's debt? What are the difficulties of removing a partner's name from a mortgage and deed?

When married people get divorced, the house is often the largest asset, and the courts decide who gets what. But if you and your partner break up, there is neither court nor judge to allocate or distribute property. You are likely to find that you have to settle the distribution of an asset like a house through a costly and complicated civil action. Lawyers may call upon each of you to prove your respective contributions to the property over the years, which can mean digging up checkbooks or canceled checks from years past. If you paid for things out of a joint account, the problem becomes even larger.

Three ways to buy in

Let's suppose you are moving into a house that is already owned by someone else. You can handle this in several ways:

1. The simplest way is for you to forget buying a share and to pay rent. Your monthly payment should be less than half of the monthly mortgage, tax, and insurance costs, because your partner owns the house and is getting the tax deductions and building up equity. Check out rents for similar properties in the neighborhood and work out a fair price.
2. The owner of the house can sell you one-half of the equity in the house at fair market value. You may pay outright for your half share, or you may give a promissory note to secure the payment, paying the owner a certain amount with interest over a length of time. The owner deeds one-half of the house over to you and the two of you become owners in joint tenancy. If the house is sold or refinanced, the note must be paid in full.

3. You gradually become a co-owner. This is not a simple way of doing it. Usually it takes many years before you reach 50-50 ownership. You pay one-half (or any other portion) of the monthly expenses. In exchange, you get a percentage of the equity in the house over a period of time.

Important: No matter which method you use, it is essential that you draw up a contract. Consult a tax accountant and a lawyer before you leap into any arrangement.

Even if you get into joint ownership, you will probably find that your bank issues only one Form 1098: Mortgage Interest Statement. The IRS is likely to check the mortgage interest deductions you claim on your tax return against this form, and it will holler if the two do not agree. That means that if the form is issued in the name and Social Security number of your live-together partner, you must enter your share of the deduction on your tax return's line 11 of Schedule A, which reads, "Home mortgage interest not reported to you on Form 1098." Attach a statement to your return listing the name, address, and Social Security number of the person named on Form 1098. And before next year's tax time, tell your bank to issue separate 1098s.

Tax consequences

Keep taxes in mind. If the title to the house changes but the owner or owners receive no money, there is no immediate taxable gain and, therefore, no tax to pay. However, the chances are that you owe gift taxes. If you decide just to make a gift of half of the property to your partner, and if you later split up, you will find that you have no recourse to get the property deeded back to you. If you want to leave your partner the house, it is better to do it in a will or trust, which can always be changed.

If an owner gets money from a sale, he or she must determine what percentage was a return on capital investment or capital improvement, which is not taxed, and what percentage was profit on the sale or interest on a note. Capital gains taxes must be paid on the latter.

If you and your live-together decide that you want the disposal of either partner's share in a house to be settled by a will, be sure to supplement the will with a written agreement that contains the entire understanding of both parties. Remember, a will can be changed or destroyed at any time by the person who made it and without the knowledge of anyone who is named in it. For live-togethers, a written agreement is imperative if you are going to own property together.

The advantages of home ownership

To own your own home is to realize the American dream. It symbolizes financial security. For the typical American, it is probably the best single investment available. A house bought for $20,000 some 30 years ago is now worth (if it has been maintained well) $100,000 or more, depending on location. In the United States, among people between the ages of 25 and 29, home ownership has declined during the late 1980s and the 1990s. Why? Because the median price of a typical first home has risen to $115,000.

Owning your own home gives you four basic advantages:

1. It is your best way to accumulate tangible capital. And it is an investment that you can not only walk around but add to and improve.
2. It is one of the few almost foolproof ways to shield an investment from inflation. (Real estate values are a barometer of economic changes.)
3. It gives you tax advantages. By allowing you to lower your income taxes through itemized deductions of the interest you pay on your mortgage and the taxes you pay on the property, your Uncle Sam provides an indirect subsidy for your house.
4. It gives lesbian and gay couples some privacy from the sometimes hostile world.

How much house can you afford?

Today you must ask yourselves a number of questions and do plenty of figuring before you can determine how much house you can afford. Start with the following checklist, and make notes as you go, for you are sure to come up with more questions than these. Many of them will pertain to your own particular situation.

1. Where will we feel comfortable? This is probably the most important question for all live-togethers. You don't want to live in a neighborhood that is hostile to your lifestyle or is only for people who are related by blood or marriage. In some areas, you will find sellers who prefer not to sell to a couple who is not married. Such moral judgments are, of course, their privilege. Your best step, almost always, is to find a real estate agent who understands your lifestyle and is willing to work with you.
2. How large a down payment can you make? Obviously, the more you can put down, the lower your monthly payments will be.
3. How long a mortgage term should you sign for? Mortgages can be set up to span 15, 20, 25, or 30 years. The shorter the time, the less you spend on interest—but the higher your payments will be.
4. How large a monthly payment can you comfortably make? Your Spending Plan determines this.

After you have figured out how much you need for non-housing expenses (including savings and an emergency fund), what is left is what you have to work with for housing. But remember: Insurance, utilities, property taxes, and maintenance are part of your monthly housing costs, too. This question also calls for plenty of thoughtful long-term planning. Look not only at what you are both making now but how much more you can reasonably expect if you get raises regularly . . . at what will happen to your joint income if you adopt a child and one of you leaves the work force either temporarily or permanently . . . at what the cost of child care, if necessary, will do to your Spending Plan.

5. What does the location of the home you are buying do to your expenses? Will you be adding commuting costs? A major increase in the weekly mileage on one or two cars? Where are the stores? Services? Recreation facilities? How far will you have to drive to get a loaf of bread?
6. Just how much will utilities add to your monthly housing expenses? What about heat? Heat was part of the deal if you were renting an apartment. Now you must pay for it. Better check with the fuel company that has been supplying the house and see how much fuel was used last winter, or the last two or three winters, so you can average it out.
7. How much more will insurance cost? It is bound to be greater than you have been paying to cover your apartment.
8. How much will the property taxes be? This one can be ticklish. Find out when the last reassessment in town occurred. If it has been a while, another could come around soon and hit you with an unexpected hike in taxes after you move in. Check with a resident who is knowledgeable about what the local policy is. Ask at the town hall or city hall.
9. What local services do you get? Are they free? Do your local taxes pay for garbage collection, or will you get a monthly bill from the garbage collector?
10. What about child-care facilities? Any nearby?
11. How about schools? This could be the most important question on your list. If you are planning to raise a family in this house, take the time and trouble to investigate the schools thoroughly. Stop in at the school superintendent's office, or at any school principal's office, and ask questions. What is the average ratio of pupils to teacher in the classroom? How much does the community spend each year per pupil and where

Exhibit 22
MONTHLY PAYMENTS ON A $100,000 FIXED-RATE MORTGAGE

Interest rate (%)	15-year period monthly payment ($)	Total payments ($)	30-year period monthly payment ($)	Total payments ($)
6.5	871.11	156,799	632.07	227,544
7.0	898.83	161,789	665.30	239,509
7.5	927.01	166,862	699.21	251,717
8.0	955.65	172,017	733.76	264,155
8.5	984.74	177,253	768.91	276,809
9.0	1,014.27	182,569	804.62	298,664
9.5	1,044.22	187,960	840.85	302,708
10.0	1,074.61	193,430	877.57	315,926
10.5	1,105.40	198,972	914.74	329,306
11.0	1,136.60	201,588	952.32	342,836
11.5	1,168.19	210,274	990.29	356,505
12.0	1,200.17	216,031	1,028.61	370,301
12.5	1,232.52	221,854	1,067.26	384,214
13.0	1,265.24	227,743	1,106.20	398,232
14.0	1,331.74	239,713	1,184.87	426,554

does it rank among cities and towns in your state? What percentage of the high-school graduates move on to higher education, and what colleges do they go to? Some basic demographic statistics about the school system can tell you a lot about whether or not you really should be buying this home. And finally, what hostility is your child likely to face because of your living situation or lifestyle?

12. What about closing costs? At the time of the closing, you may have to pay some points. This is a one-time expense. Each point equals 1 percent of your mortgage (e.g., $1,000 on a $100,000 mortgage). Most lenders charge two to three points. A lender who wants a higher interest rate may demand fewer points than one charging lower interest rates. And don't forget about title and mortgage insurance, attorneys' fees, title search, prepayment of taxes and insurance, credit report, and appraisal. Altogether, you should figure closing costs of 2.5 to 3.5 percent of the amount of your mortgage.
13. Do you have enough reserves to pay the cost of moving and to buy incidentals that you may not realize you need until you actually start to live in the house: fuel, insulation, lawn mower, garden hose, gardening tools, rake, snow shovel, etc.? How about landscaping? If you are buying a brand-new home, it is likely to come with a minimum of trees and shrubs. Probably it will lack screens, storm windows, and storm doors.
14. What are you willing to compromise on? In today's market, almost everyone must trim desires to fit pocketbooks. You don't want to buy a house that you may later come to regret buying. That is, you don't want to find yourself "house poor," paying so much for the house that you can't afford to live in it. So establish your priorities firmly before you start to look. And don't set foot in any house that does not meet your most important priorities. If you do not set priorities, you may find yourselves compromising on less important features.

❍ ❍ ❍

MAUREEN AND CINDY'S HOME

Cindy drives a one-and-one-half-hour commute to work every day. Why? Because she and Maureen bought a house in a community near their families, and it was cheaper than housing in the university town where Cindy works. While both were working, they had a total income of $65,000. They were able to manage a 15-year mortgage. Then, when they decided to have a child, and before Cindy became pregnant, they refinanced their home to get a lower rate of interest and spread payments over a 30-year loan, to lessen monthly costs.

❍ ❍ ❍

A lot to think about? You bet. But the amazing thing is that millions of Americans have survived the entire process.

How much for a down payment?

If you have asked yourselves all the foregoing questions, and have come up with a firm yes on the ultimate one—can we afford a house?—you must now produce the down payment.

Let's say you have worked hard to put away $200 every month for five years. Assuming 8-percent interest on your money, compounded quarterly, you should have close to $15,000 salted away. This should give you enough for a down payment of $10,000, with the balance to be used for closing costs, moving, and all the incidentals already mentioned. You have watched the pot grow. Now you can put it to work. The next question is: What type of housing? House and lot? Condominium? Cooperative apartment? Mobile home? Let's look at each.

House and lot

Any house you look at is going to be either new—or old. If you are looking at a new house, you are pretty much assured that everything will function properly. The builder should stand behind the work. Furnace and appliances will come with guarantees. You may have plenty to do in the area of landscaping and perhaps painting the interior, if it has been left undecorated.

If it is an older house, you will want to be sure it is in acceptable condition. It takes expertise to evaluate an older home. Don't hesitate to get it. If you are not an expert yourself, pay a professional to make an inspection. Don't just ask a friend. This will give you a reliable check on plumbing, heating, paint condition, roof, electrical wiring, insulation—a million and one details that could make the difference between frustration and satisfaction for you as buyers. Nothing is worse than having to buy a new roof or a new septic field for a house just after you bought the house itself. If the inspection reveals that something is wrong, you can start to renegotiate the price with the seller, taking into account the cost you face in fixing the problem.

Condominium

The condo is rather new on the American home-owning scene. It is usually a structure on the order of an apartment house, in which you are deeded the title to, or ownership of, your unit. It becomes your property.

You also own a proportionate interest in the common facilities, such as hallways, grounds, elevators, and recreational areas (tennis courts, swimming pool, even a golf course in some condos). Each month, you pay common charges that cover taxes on the property (the tax portion of your common charge is deductible on your income-tax return), maintenance, heat, and utilities. *Warning*: Common charges have a way of increasing, so make sure your Spending Plan is elastic enough to accept increases in them. As owners, you will join a condominium association in which each member has one vote when decisions about the condominium must be made (all members will have agreed to abide by the provisions of a condo agreement).

As a condo owner, you have the same advantages as the owner of a house and lot. Your equity builds up as time goes by (generally, condos have appreciated to match inflation, just like houses). The tax benefits that you can itemize on your income-tax return are the same. Your responsibility for repairs and maintenance within your individual unit is also the same as in a house. And, generally speaking, you are entitled to sell your unit to anyone you choose.

> *Tips:* Watch the recreational facilities. Don't be fooled into buying into a condo where the swimming pools and tennis courts are "going to be built soon." And turn your back on any place that has a tiny swimming pool or a single tennis court for a hundred or more condo units.

Cooperatives

In a co-op apartment, a nonprofit corporation owns your unit. What you own is stock in the corporation. The amount of stock you own depends on the size and value of the apartment you take. There is one common mortgage on the building (unless the corporation has bought the building outright or already paid off the mortgage) and all the owners make monthly payments, varying in size according to the value of the individual units, to the corporation. These payments cover, in effect, taxes, interest payment, and maintenance. As a shareholder, you are entitled to list as deductions on your income-tax return your share of the property taxes and the interest on the mortgage. When you want to sell the apartment, you are really selling your shares in the corporation.

Note: Some co-ops stipulate that any prospective owner must be approved by the other shareholders. The corporation may exercise the option of buying back the shares if the prospective owner isn't approved.

Some questions to ask before you buy into a co-op or purchase a condo:

- What are the rules and regulations? Do you want to agree to abide by them?
- Are those now living there pleased with the living conditions? Is the place noisy? Too hot? Too cold?
- Is it clean and well-maintained, indoors and out? Trees and shrubs healthy? Lawn green and manicured?
- Are the recreational facilities adequate? Well-maintained?
- How's the parking? Plenty of space?
- What about lighting? Parking areas well-lighted? Paths and entryways clear and bright?
- Who pays the utilities? How are the costs apportioned?
- Are you permitted to rent your unit?
- What are the costs of settlement?
- Are there any lawsuits pending against the developer or officers of the association?
- Are most owners living on the premises or have they rented out their units?

Mobile homes

This is probably the cheapest form of home ownership. It can be your first way—maybe for now your only way—to own low-cost housing.

Here's how it works. Either (1) you rent a small piece of property in an open park, then have your manufactured house installed on that property at your own expense, or (2) you buy a home from the management of a closed park. This is what many retired people do. In fact, many closed mobile-home parks are designed mainly for retired people.

In some parks, the mobile-home owners may buy their land instead of renting it. This has a certain advantage: If your mobile home is set up on your own land, some banks will offer you a regular real estate mortgage. Otherwise, they want you to finance the purchase of your mobile home like an auto loan, with a low down payment, short repayment period of three to five years at best, and high monthly payments. Recently, the U.S. government has begun insuring mobile-home loans through the Federal Housing Administration (FHA) and the Veterans Administration (VA).

A mobile home may well be a viable start for you. Before buying one, check with a number of lenders about the type of financing they offer. It is worth the effort to find the best possible deal.

Financing

You've analyzed the possibilities. You have the down payment in hand. Are you each contributing equal amounts for the down payment? If not, how will this affect ownership? You've reviewed your Spending Plan and tried to answer the nagging questions about the future. You've decided to do it. Now, how do you finance the purchase of the home you want?

In the distant past, many lenders refused to lend to gay or lesbian couples. By and large, this situation has changed, but there are still instances where it occurs. So present yourselves as knowledgeable buyers, learning all you can about various types of mortgages before you go to a lender.

Not many people can come up with the full purchase price of a home. So they buy with the help of some kind of mortgage financing. Banks now look at debt-to-income ratios. Most banks believe that mortgage debt, which includes property taxes and homeowner's insurance, should not exceed 28 percent of total household income. The bank will also look at total debt—i.e., mortgage debt plus such other monthly debt obligations as car payments and student loans. They don't like this ratio to get any higher than 36 percent. These ratios usually apply to buyers who have 10 percent of the purchase price available for the down payment. Some lenders, however, will let you have financing with a down payment of as little as 5 percent. This means that, if you have very little debt and a spotless credit history, you can buy a house sooner. Usually, because they figure you have a higher risk of defaulting on your mortgage, such lenders will say that your mortgage debt must not go above 25 percent, and your total debt not above 33 percent, rather than the 28- and 36-percent limitations already mentioned.

Just what is a mortgage? By definition, it is simply a pledge of property to a creditor as security for a loan. As the borrower, you are the mortgagor. You give the mortgage to the lender, or mortgagee, who takes the mortgage and holds it until you have paid the debt.

A mortgage has three elements: the amount the lender provides, the repayment period, and the rate of interest. Until very recently, once a mortgage loan was closed, none of these elements could be changed. You got a mortgage for a certain number of years at a certain rate of interest and that was it—period. But lately, lenders, finding themselves stuck for years with mortgages that bring them low payments of interest at a time when they have to pay out high interest on savings deposited with them, have been eager to adapt to changing conditions. The result is that today you may choose between the old-fashioned conventional fixed-rate mortgage and a new type, the adjustable-rate mortgage (ARM). Let's look at each.

- *The conventional fixed-rate mortgage.* With this type, you pay a fixed monthly payment, at a fixed rate of interest, for the life of the loan—as long as 30 years. Many banks still offer the fixed-rate mortgage, but today the cost is likely to be higher initially—maybe 2.5 percent higher—than the cost of an adjustable-rate mortgage. If interest rates do go up over the long haul, you get the advantage and the bank, or lender, finds that it has loaned you money at a lower rate of return, or profit, than it might have gained by some other investment.
- *The variable, or adjustable-rate, mortgage.* With this type, the initial cost is lower, because you start off at the lowest interest rate the bank, in order to meet competition from other lenders, dares offer today. But you agree to abide by regular review and escalation or de-escalation as interest rates are adjusted up or down by the lender to meet the conditions of the money market. Interest adjustments are usually scheduled every six months or once a year, with the rate permitted to increase usually no more than a maximum of 2 percent a year. The rate changes are tied to a number of interest-based indexes published by the federal government, and usually there is a cap, or ceiling, beyond which the rate may not be raised, as well as a downward floor.

While the interest rate is usually lower at first than that on a fixed-rate mortgage, the risk you take is that it will eventually equal it or even exceed it. If, on the other hand, the adjustable rate holds steady or goes down, you may come out ahead.

Under an ARM, the amount you have to pay to the bank could change at every adjustment date. With most ARMs, you sign up for a fixed monthly payment that will stay the same through a given period before an adjustment is made. For instance, the lender may tie the rate to the one-year Treasury bill rate plus 2 percent, with the rate adjusted annually. Suppose at the time you negotiate the loan, the Treasury bill rate is 5.5 percent. Your rate would be 7.5 percent. But to meet competition the lender might offer a come-on rate of 6 percent. Find out how these bargain rates are adjusted and what you would be paying if you weren't getting the come-on rate because that is what you will be paying at the next adjustment date, even if interest rates don't go up.

If you are hit with an upward adjustment that is more than your Spending Plan can stand, see if the bank will keep the payments the same and extend the life of the loan. What the bank does is determine, based on the current interest rate, the amount of interest due with the remainder of your payment going to pay down your principal. If the interest rate goes down, the bank puts more of your payment toward paying back the principal. If the interest rate rises, on the other hand, the bank applies more and more of your payment to interest charges and less and less to paying off the principal. Conceivably, this could increase your debt: If the interest charge becomes higher than the total payment you are sending in each month, you get into what is called "negative amortization," actually increasing rather than paying down your loan. Let's look at an example.

Suppose you obtain an adjustable-rate mortgage for $45,000 for 30 years at 7.5-percent annual interest. Your monthly payment will be $315. In the second year, however, the interest rate rises to 8.5 percent. Now your payment should be $344, but you elect (and the bank allows you) to keep the payment at $315. Thus, when each monthly check comes in from you, the bank first takes its payment of interest, at 8.5 percent, then applies whatever is left over to reducing your principal. As long as the rate of interest stays at 8.5 percent (or goes even higher), you will be falling further and further behind in the amount that is being applied toward reducing your principal loan. For instance, with a payment of $315 at 7.5 percent, $281 is for interest payment and the balance of $34 goes toward paying off the principal. If you make the same payment at 8.5 percent, the amount due for interest will increase to $316 and nothing will go toward paying down the principal. If, on the other hand, the interest rate should fall to 6.5 percent, which would call for a monthly payment of $284, and you continue to send in your fixed payment of $315, the bank will apply less of your payment to interest and more to reducing your principal balance, and you will be paying down your loan at a faster rate.

The moral of all this is to try to find a bank that offers an adjustable-rate mortgage with infrequent adjustment and with a cap on increases in the interest rate or in monthly payments.

Some variations on the ARM that you should know about:

- *Graduated payment mortgage.* With this type of mortgage, the monthly payments are relatively low in the first few years. Then they rise until they are higher than conventional monthly mortgage payments would be. The idea is that payments are scheduled to increase at fixed intervals and by fixed amounts. The problem is that the payments in the early years might not be covering the interest, so you are not building any equity in your home unless property values are increasing generally.
- *Renegotiable-rate mortgage.* With this type, the interest rate comes up for renegotiation after a set period, usually one to five years, rather than when market factors, such as a change in the prime rate, force it to change. The new rate is determined, as is the adjustable rate, by the Federal Home Loan Bank Board.
- *Roll-over mortgage.* This is similar to the renegotiable-rate mortgage. The rate is set for three to five years. Then it is totally renegotiated, or "rolled over." In effect, the roll-over involves a series of short-term loans, with the entire loan coming due at the end of each period and then being replaced by another short-term loan. This goes on for a total of 25 or 30 years, as in a conventional mortgage.
- *Balloon mortgage.* For the first few years, this one is similar to the variable, or adjustable-rate mortgage, and you are paying it off like the conventional loan of 30 years. But at the end of a specified time, usually three to five years, you get hit with a "balloon" payment of the entire balance, which you pay by obtaining a new loan at the interest rates that then prevail. This type of loan is often used in second mortgages. If, on the second time around, when the balloon is due, you can borrow at lower interest rates than you were able to get the first time, you have the advantage. This is not a sure thing, however, and, in addition, it's possible you may be in an economic situation that makes borrowing difficult.
- *The assumable mortgage.* Sometimes you can assume the existing mortgage of the person who is selling the house. But you must come up with the difference between the asking price and the balance that is due on the mortgage. Suppose you are buying a $110,000 home on which the owner still owes $50,000 on the mortgage. If the owner's rate of interest is low, this could be an advantage for you, but now you will have to come up with $60,000. You may already have part of that amount as your planned down payment. To provide the missing difference, you could try to obtain a second mortgage. Or you might try making a deal with the bank that holds the previous owner's low-interest mortgage. They might be willing to make a "composite" loan—a new loan at a lower rate than is now prevailing, in order for them to retire the previous owner's loan, which has recently been giving them no profit margin at all.

Tip: Banks do negotiate. Banks do make deals. Banks do bend their own rules, if they see that you have a secure future. They will bend over backwards for a young doctor, or for someone who is going into a successful, closely held family business. When they know you are on a fast track, they anticipate future business and they will negotiate. They will not, however, bend government rules.

Don't expect them to. If you cannot get the loan you want and the amount you need, consider what is known as creative financing. Many lending institutions will handle second mortgages. Often a seller, especially if he or she is eager to close the deal, will finance part or all of the buyer's purchase price in a "take-back" mortgage (the seller will hold the mortgage). Many real estate developers offer special financing on new homes.

Mortgage companies are usually happy to add names to a mortgage—but they are seldom willing to take a name off. If you buy a home together and use both incomes to meet the qualifications for a mortgage, you can bump into problems later if you decide to split up. Simply signing away your ownership rights will not necessarily relieve you of the obligations under the original mortgage, and a bank is unlikely to release either of those who want out from their obligations under the note and mortgage unless the other partner takes out a note in his or her own name. In most cases, in fact, each party to a mortgage is jointly and severally liable. This means that each is liable for the entire debt. So, if one of you walks away, that means the other can be stuck with the entire obligation.

How much of a mortgage can you take on?

Say the monthly gross income of you and your partner together is $4,172. Of that, 28 percent, or $1,168, is the most you should spend per month on mortgage payment, taxes, and insurance. If you add car payments of $282 to that, your total monthly debt figure will come to $1,450, safely under $1,502, which is the 36-percent debt-to-income ratio considered acceptable by lenders.

> **MARKET DOWN, EQUITY ZERO**
>
> Look what can happen if the real estate market is down and you have little or no equity in the house. Alice and Ted bought a home in a city whose real estate values have since dropped considerably. They owned jointly. Now they have decided to split. Ted figured he would buy Alice out of her share. He took out a personal loan for $5,000 and paid it to Alice for her share of the equity. In exchange, he signed a release that held Alice harmless. But the bank wouldn't recognize the release, and Ted couldn't keep up with the mortgage payments. He filed for bankruptcy. The bank came looking for Alice, forcing her into bankruptcy. Now the bank has a house for sale.

Buying your home will probably be the largest and most important investment either of you will ever make. It is worth taking the time and trouble to check every aspect of your purchase, so you know you are making the best deal you can on the house and on the mortgage terms. Remember, too, that even if the price is high and the bank's interest rates are high, your home can be a valuable source of tax savings, capital growth, and protection against inflation. And if it works out right, owning a home often costs no more, or very little more, than renting.

How will you own your new home?

How your home is owned raises several issues related to taxes, estate planning, and human relationships. If you own the property as joint tenants in common, which is often the situation because of unequal ownership, you may risk future emotion-laden confrontations between a surviving partner and the heirs of a deceased partner. Types of ownership include:

1. *One owns all.* Here, one of you provides the entire down payment and owns the house outright. The other pays rent to the owner. The owner may leave the house to the partner, through a will.
2. *Equal ownership.* The down payment is split equally by the buyers, and they agree to share all costs (and eventual profits if the house is sold) equally.
3. *Unequal ownership.* One contributes more than the other for the down payment. This can be handled in any of several ways:
   a. Bob puts up three-fourths of the down payment. Tom provides one-fourth. They own the house as *joint tenants*, with Bob owning three-fourths and Tom one-fourth. Any future profit is divided in those percentages. *Important*: If the house is not owned equally, joint tenancy *with right of survivorship* may not be used.
   b. Bob puts up three-fourths of the down payment but wants Tom to own the house equally. Bob may make a gift of one-fourth of the house to Tom, but he will be liable for a gift tax. Or Bob may call the one-fourth amount a loan, and have Tom make monthly installments for a specified period. They should execute a promissory note.
   c. One buys the house and the other fixes it up. Tom is unable to come up with any of the down payment, but he is a great fixer-upper, and he is able to pay his share of the monthly expense. They agree that, if Bob puts up

$20,000, Tom will contribute $10,000 worth of materials and labor to improve the house. Tom's share will grow as he completes the renovated kitchen and makes other repairs. In this situation, it is important that they set an hourly rate for Tom's skills and keep accurate records of expenditures for materials and of Tom's time.

No matter which of these arrangements you make, it is extremely important that you write up contracts between you. In doing so, anticipate the "what ifs" and talk things through. Don't leave any doubt about what either of you *thought* was intended or *meant* to say.

Tax deductions and other savings

What are some of the tax savings you gain as homeowners? Here are ways you can take deductions from your income tax:

- *Mortgage interest.* The interest you pay to a lender on a mortgage loan is tax deductible, whether the mortgage is for a place that is for personal use (i.e., a place to live in), business use (i.e., a place in which to operate a business), or income-producing use (i.e., a place you have bought as an investment, to rent to others). The interest you pay may be claimed as an itemized deduction on Schedule A of Form 1040.

  Your monthly mortgage payments cover interest on the principal amount you owe, plus repayment of some of the principal. In addition, some banks pay your real estate taxes and homeowner's insurance for you and add those amounts to the total monthly payment, so you are paying one-twelfth of those costs each month. Most lending institutions provide you with a year-end statement that specifies how much you have paid during the year for each item.

  At the closing on your mortgage, you may have to pay some points. This is a one-time expense. Each point equals one percent of your mortgage ($450, for example, on a $45,000 mortgage). If points are considered to be prepaid interest, they are usually deductible on your income-tax return. If they are considered a service fee, they are not deductible, so this is a question to ask when you go shopping for your mortgage. If the points are in fact deductible, insist on paying for them with a separate check, so you have a record, rather than letting the bank automatically take them out of your loan.
- *Real property taxes.* These local taxes, imposed on all property owners, are deductible from your federal income tax. The money they bring in is, in most communities, the main revenue that pays for schools, roads, and municipal services such as police and fire departments and refuse collection.

  Note: Don't be surprised to find that taxes have a way of increasing as the value of property increases. Your city or town will reassess property every few years and increase taxes based on the new assessments. As mentioned earlier, this could happen soon after you move into your home, so before you buy find out what's going on in the locality where you are buying. Then, at least, you won't be surprised.

You can split deductions

Suppose you both want to have the advantage of a tax deduction. If you split the mortgage payments and real estate tax payments, you may each take the same percentage as deductions. That means that if you each pay half, you each get to deduct half of the total. If you split 60 to 40 or 75 to 25, etc., you follow the same proportion in your deduction. *Suggestion:* If you have a joint account to cover household expenses, make sure you contribute proportionate amounts. If you use separate accounts, each of you should make out a mortgage check and a real estate tax check in the same proportion as you plan to deduct.

What if you own your own home and want to give co-ownership to your companion? Legally married couples can transfer ownership without worrying about estate taxes. But you cannot do that. However, the IRS allows you two valuable exclusions. First, you may give away up to $10,000 each year without incurring gift taxes. And second, you may give as much as $600,000 once in your lifetime, also without paying estate taxes. So if you decide to use that one-time exclusion, you may give someone else a share in your home that is up to $610,000 in value without paying any taxes on the gift.

Another way around the gift tax is to sell a portion of your home to your companion. This is considered a taxable event, and you must report it on Form 2119: Sale of Your Home. *Warning*: Don't sell the share at a bargain rate well below its fair market value, or the deal may be ruled a gift as well as a sale, with tax consequences first on the sale price and second on the difference, which the IRS views as a gift to be taxed. The IRS has been known to step in after the death of one of the owners, demanding that the estate pay back taxes on the gift.

What about selling a house?

The federal income-tax regulations say if you are 55 or older you may claim a one-time capital-gain exclusion of $125,000 when selling the house you've been living in. If a married couple takes advantage of this exclusion and one of the couple later remarries, the exclusion may not be used again even if the new spouse has not already used her or his exclusion. *Note:* To qualify for this exclusion, the house must have been your principal residence for the last three out of five years.

Now, suppose you own the house together and the time to sell it comes. You must each file Form 2119. On it, you may each defer the tax on any profit by following the rollover-of-gain rules, and you may claim the one-time exclusion. You must divide the profits in the same ratio as your ownerships—usually half-and-half unless you originally set up some other proportions. What the IRS does not want you to do is take advantage of the sale to redistribute your assets without paying any taxes.

○ ○ ○

ONE REASON WHY JACK AND BOBBIE DON'T MARRY

When Jack sold his house and moved in with Bobbie, he took his one-time exclusion. If Bobbie sells her house, she may use her $125,000 exclusion. If she and Jack marry, however, she will lose it. She has lived in the house for so long that it has increased in market value many times over, and her capital gain will be substantial.

○ ○ ○

BOB AND TOM: RENT OR BUY?

Every weekend, Bob and Tom study the real estate section of the local newspaper. They also keep watch on mortgage rates. They know that home prices and mortgage rates have both come down in recent years—much to their advantage—but they want to be sure they can afford a house. So they are doing a lot of paperwork before they actually go out to look at houses.

They have been figuring out what it will cost them if they buy a house for $125,000 and take on a $112,500 mortgage. Here's how some of the figures come out: The average monthly total expenses of living in their apartment come to $703 ($8,436 per year). They expect the new house will cost $1,165 per month ($13,980 a year), or $462 more per month than they are paying now—assuming a 30-year fixed mortgage of $112,500 at 8.5 percent. That average will actually be less, however, on a yearly basis, because on one or both of their income-tax returns they will be able to deduct, from their gross incomes, their real estate taxes and the interest they will pay to the bank. The total annual federal tax savings will come to $3,108. Since they know that their rent will increase each year, they realize that over the years there will be less and less difference between renting and owning.

○ ○ ○

MAUREEN AND CINDY: WHO DEDUCTS?

While Maureen and Cindy were both working, they always sat down at tax time and figured out which one should take the mortgage interest and property taxes as itemized deductions. With Cindy's income almost twice that of Maureen's, it didn't take much figuring to realize that she should take the deductions while Maureen filed a simple 1040EZ form.

○ ○ ○

What happens if you split up? One can buy out the other, sell the property and divide the proceeds, or run the property as a business if both of you move out. You can rent it and split the income and the deductions. If one wants to stay in the house but does not have the finances to buy the other person's share, he or she should pay a fair rental value to the partner who is moving out.

○ ○ ○

JOYCE PAID HEAVILY WHEN SHE AND NANCY SPLIT

Joyce and Nancy bought a small house in a Chicago suburb for $80,000, with Joyce putting in her life's savings of $15,000 as a down payment. Her bank issued a mortgage in both their names.

To meet the monthly mortgage payments, Joyce agreed to cover 70 percent while Nancy paid 30 percent. Four years went by. Then they agreed to disagree. Nancy hired an attorney, forcing Joyce to hire her own lawyer.

The lawyers drew up an agreement. It included two major clauses: 1) Joyce was allowed to buy out Nancy's share over a 12-month period, and 2) Joyce accepted responsibility for meeting the monthly mortgage payments until she could refinance the mortgage in her own name. Meantime, Nancy continued as cosigner on the mortgage but moved out. Joyce paid heavily for not having insisted on an agreement in the beginning.

Three years passed before Joyce was in a position to refinance. A major obstacle during that time was the fact that the real estate market fell into a decline, making refinancing difficult.

○ ○ ○

Home sharing and shared housing

Two basic living arrangements help older or younger Americans to cope with the problem of finding or continuing suitable housing. Many older people turn to home sharing. Many younger people move into shared housing. The two terms sound alike, but they are not the same. Let's look at each.

1. *Home sharing.* Study after study has shown that, given a choice, most older Americans prefer by a huge

Worksheet XI:
YOUR HOME AS AN INVESTMENT

A home can be a valuable source of tax savings, inflation protection, and capital growth.

In many cases, the cost of buying a home isn't any higher than renting. Fill in the following information to determine the difference between owning and renting.

OWNING (Annual Costs)

Home Expenses:		**Income Tax Deductions:**	
Real Estate Taxes	$________	Real Estate Taxes	$________
Mortgage Interest	$________	Mortgage Interest	$________
Mortgage Principal	$________	**Subtotal II**	$________
Homeowner's Insurance	$________	**Your Income Tax Bracket:**	
Repairs	$________	State	________%
Utilities	$________	Federal	________%
Subtotal I	$________	**Subtotal III**	________%

- Multiply your income tax deductions (II) by your personal tax rate (III) to discover your total tax savings (IV).

  $________ × ________ = $________
  II III IV

- Subtract your total tax savings (IV) from your total home expenses (I) to find the cost of owning your home after taxes (this figure does not include the value of appreciation of your home).

  $________ – $________ = $________ **Total Cost of Owning Your Home**
  I IV V

RENTING (Annual Costs)

Rent	$________
Renter's Insurance	$________
Utilities	$________
	$________ **Total Cost of Renting**
	VI

- Subtract Total Cost of Renting (VI) From Total Cost of owning (V).

margin to "age in place"—staying within their homes or their familiar neighborhoods, with the services and support they need brought to them, rather than moving to some distant setting. In their minds, successful aging is achieved through self-determination and independence maintained in privacy.

In home sharing, a home owner (called a "provider" in the jargon of social workers and others) shares his or her home with another person. This is also called "match ups." Those who share the home find that they benefit by managing their limited or fixed incomes more effectively. How does it work financially? Either of two ways:

a. *Rent.* Some home owners rent one or more bedrooms to someone outside the family, including the use of the kitchen and other facilities—from washer and dryer to social life in the living room. The rental income gives the home owner cash for house repairs and maintenance. Before you do this, check with an accountant about the tax implications.

b. *Services.* Other home owners are willing to share the house in exchange for services. Having another person living with you on the premises and available to help with various facets of the daily routine can mean, if you are an aging home owner, the difference between maintaining an independent life and moving into some supportive housing and lifestyle.

Home sharing brings benefits not only to the people in the house; it offers favorable repercussions throughout the community, as a house and its setting are maintained in good condition rather than deteriorating (as so many homes of the elderly have been seen to do) to peeling paint, broken shutters, weed-filled lawns, and overgrown shrubbery—all of which depreciate the neighborhood and turn away prospective buyers.

○ ○ ○

JUDY AND FRED

Judy, an artist now in her eighties, has lived alone and in relative isolation in a barn long since converted to a studio. Her son lives some 300 miles away. She is determinedly independent, supporting herself on her Social Security benefits, her late husband's pension, and the interest and dividends from her portfolio. But after thinking over her situation, she found a fellow artist and photographer in his late forties who was recently divorced and needed a place to live. Fred teaches art in a local art school, where he also maintains his studio. He travels frequently on photography assignments. With him absent for a good part of the day, Judy has the solitude and independence she craves, saying, "I couldn't stand having someone underfoot all the time. But this is a 'touch base' situation, which we both like."

In effect, Fred provides some services. He does most of the marketing and some of the cooking, and he handles any small repairs needed around the house. None of his chores involves Judy's personal care. They both like the arrangement, and so does Judy's son, who is pleased that someone is living in the house, keeping an eye on his mother and ready to help if she gets sick or falls.

○ ○ ○

MARGE AND TOM

At age 45, Marge went back to school to get her long-postponed college degree, living on campus as a beloved "Grannie" (a job known to earlier generations as "house mother" in a women's dormitory) to help pay her way. Still, along with her sheepskin, she graduated with an $18,000 student loan to pay back. Before college, she had her own apartment. After college, she moved in with Tom, who is nearly 80 and needs daily care. For full room and board, plus $100 per week, she does the shopping, runs errands, and takes care of the household washing, cooking, and light cleaning. Tom realizes the price is cheap compared to what he would have to pay for 24-hour-a-day home care, which he would otherwise need.

○ ○ ○

Shared housing or group homes

Whatever your age, living in a shared residence can be a way of enhancing your quality of life, cutting down on expenses, and avoiding the isolation, loneliness and insecurity of living alone. It gives you a sense of community. And it can help you maintain your independence during your retirement years.

In effect, this is communal living in a private home or in a home sponsored by a local nonprofit group. For many younger people, shared housing is the only way they can make ends meet. They want to be on their own, yet they lack the financial resources to pay 100 percent of the rent for an entire house or apartment—especially in large cities, where rents are out of sight. If you are such a young person, you should be aware that by sharing independent housing, you can enjoy maximum autonomy in a setting that gives you privacy, independence, security, financial protection, and companionship with one or more housemates.

The house itself may be an older home that has been rehabilitated to meet the specific requirements of its residents. Or it may be a new home built for that purpose. Many such shared residences are sponsored by not-for-profit organizations that want to help provide housing that is affordable for older adults whose incomes are low or moderate. Or they want to help people who have specific disabilities.

In other homes, the sponsorship is simple and direct: People get together and rent or buy a residence with the intention of sharing it with others—usually unrelated people. A good example was set by the late Maggie Kuhn, who, as founder of the Gray Panthers, lobbied on behalf of older Americans. She lived in a multigenerational home (i.e., with residents of all ages) for many years.

In the simplest shared housing, two or more unrelated people pool their resources to share a dwelling. The resources are of three kinds: personal (the whole gamut of lifestyle, ranging from cooking to entertainment), financial (paying the rent and utilities), and physical (providing furniture and other furnishings). Usually each person has his or her private room but shares such common areas as living room, dining room, and kitchen.

In some more complex situations, the shared housing is jointly owned, so shared equity is being built up.

For information on home sharing, contact:

National Shared Housing Resource Center
321 East 25th Street
Baltimore, Maryland 21218
Phone (410) 235-4454

○ ○ ○

THE GOLDEN GIRLS AND GUYS

Marie, Annie, Bob, Ruth, and Frank live in a shared home that resulted from a partnership effort that brought together town, county, state, and federal governments. The town provided a building lot. The county donated the required survey and site plan as well as the time of two people: a housing consultant and the director of the county's Office of the Aging. The state's contribution was a grant for construction. And the federal government, through the Department of Housing and Urban Development (HUD), provided a Development Block Grant.

The house was designed and built for its specific use as a shared-living residence. Members of the board of Cooperative Housing Corporation who were well versed in the needs and limitations of older adults worked closely with the architect and builder. The modular construction was entirely on one floor.

While this shared-living residence lets each of its five residents have private time and space in his or her own room, with private bath, it also gives each the opportunity for companionship, meals with other people to chat with, recreational activities and family living. All find that having others around with whom they can do things helps to keep them active. They feel lucky because the financial side has been worked out for them so that no one person has to manage the collecting of rents or the payment of bills. And all agree that one of the best ideas in the house is the locked box containing the thermostat. It has eliminated all discussion or differences of opinion about the settings for heat and air conditioning.

○ ○ ○

JEANNE'S EXPERIENCE WITH TWO SHARED RESIDENCES

After Jeanne sold her big St. Louis house and bought a condo, she realized that she really didn't like living alone. She then turned over the money gained from selling the house only a year earlier and bought a house in which she could have others share. She kept one bedroom for herself as she found three others to share the other bedrooms. The four residents then shared the big living room, dining room, kitchen, and laundry room. She set up the kitchen so each person had the use of one shelf in the closet-size pantry cabinet, and she installed a large refrigerator-freezer that gave each the use of one shelf. The bathroom situation was not ideal, as she had a bathroom for herself but the other three had to share the house's second bathroom.

The occupants included one 65-year-old, divorced man who worked as a security guard, and a young woman who worked in the public library (only two blocks away) and who, like the security guard, stayed for over four years. The third room changed hands more often.

Jeanne set up a rent scale based on market value of the house, divided by the square footage of floor space of each bedroom plus one quarter of the total common space. The costs of heat and electricity, plus cleaning and paper supplies, were also factored in. Each resident provided his or her own telephone service.

Unlike the Golden people, Jeanne's group usually cook and dine on their own schedule, for all are working and keep various hours.

About 15 months ago, Jeanne bought another house. It was a rather run-down Victorian building but offered the attraction of seven bedrooms. A varied group moved in: an executive in his late fifties who is vice president of a large corporation and who travels all over the world; Ellen, a division manager of a giant out-of-state company for which she is spending close to a year in town, handling a major divestiture; Brian, a 23-year-old at a large general aviation airport outside St. Louis who is building up his flying time until he can qualify for an airline job; a 50-year-old service representative, who was widowed a couple of years ago; 28-year-old Sanchez, who is a registered pharmacist and is building experience and saving his money so he can buy out the older pharmacist-owner of the neighborhood drugstore; and Joe, who is in his late fifties and a widower who owns a small but busy welding business. Jeanne herself is age 53.

Jeanne's second home has two large refrigerators and one small one, so each person gets a full shelf. She furnished the entire house, from the kitchen's pots and pans to the dining room linens to the draperies and curtains. Keeping the decorating and furnishings unified avoided the problem of everyone bringing in a mix of odds and ends, which could make the place look unattractive if not rundown.

The big old house has four and a half baths. Jeanne put in a house-length second-story dormer so she could add the two full baths and enlarge two of the bedrooms. Altogether, she has restored the house to its original 1898 splendor and it fits in well with the other large old houses, all quite close together and now mostly converted into lawyers' and doctors' offices that complement each other on the street.

The residents come and go quite independently. Many travel on business, so they often go for weeks without seeing one another. Yet each enjoys the company of others, and the freedom to use all the shared facilities, when they are home. Real friendships have formed, and two or more get together for various activities beyond the house.

Jeanne insisted on a few basic rules, to which any resident must agree before moving in: no smoking, no loud music or TV before 9:00 A.M. or after 11:00 P.M. Friends are allowed to visit for dinner. Her fair-market rent scale is considerably less costly than a studio or one-bedroom apartment in the same area.

❍ ❍ ❍

Work out the finances beforehand

Whether you are getting into home sharing or shared housing, it is important to work out the financial details before you move in—not after. The economics cover more than rent, and more than money.

Make it clear which spaces in the house are to be shared and which are held private. Put down on paper exactly what is to be covered by the rent and by any other money that is to change hands. That includes paying for taxes, utilities, heat, telephone, insurance, and repairs and maintenance. Get together on all these questions:

- How much rent is to be paid? On what date? What is the penalty for late payment or nonpayment?
- Is there a security deposit? How much? On what basis will it be returned?
- How about services? Are you providing services in exchange for a reduction in rent? If so, what are the services? How frequently must you perform them?
- Who is to be responsible for maintaining the property—including lawn mowing, snow removal, garbage pickup, taking down storm windows, and putting up screens? Will you and/or others pay carrying charges to cover maintenance?

Think of money as a powder keg, ready to explode if touched off by any disagreement among people who are sharing a home or living in shared housing. By carefully working out, and committing to writing, all charges, services, and responsibilities, you will go a long way toward insuring the success of your arrangement. Some specific areas to negotiate are these:

- *Utilities.* Gas, electricity, water, heating fuel. Probably the easiest way to handle utilities is to total what they cost per month, divide that amount by the number of residents, and add that prorated amount to the rent payment.
- *Telephone.* One line for the entire house? Or a separate line, and number, for each person's room? If all are using the same line, you can split the monthly fee among the residents, then let each pay for his or her own long-distance or intrastate calls. Be ready for occasional haggling over the phone bill and, for the sake of world peace, keep it good-natured.
- *Unexpected expenses.* No house runs entirely according to plan. Unexpected repairs come up, usually at the most inconvenient moments. Plan for them. Put an agreement on paper that says how they are to be provided for. One way is to have each resident deposit a certain amount into a house fund, or common charges, each month. Keep such funds in an interest-bearing account. A little sensible forethought can determine who is to maintain the common rooms and how the repair or replacement of a toaster, microwave oven, or other appliances is to be paid for.
- *Food.* Unless you expect to have a resident diplomat always in the kitchen, get the food arrangement stated on paper, too. In some houses, the residents contribute a set dollar amount each month to a food fund, from which groceries are paid for to supply the common meals. In other houses, those sharing the premises have decided that each person will be responsible for getting his or her meals. If this is your plan, make sure you clearly designate storage and labeling. You need more storage space for such an individualized lifestyle. A third possibility combines the two systems: Staples are bought jointly, but each of you brings home what you want for your own meals.

Get down on paper your agreement on who does what about a bunch of financial matters:

- Who sees that the rent is paid? How about other common bills, such as utilities?
- Who is the collector who rounds up each resident's rent money and, if you have set up a common food fund, collects that, too?
- Who keeps the log on the telephone bill and collects from each phone user?
- Who's the master shopper who will make sure the household never runs out of light bulbs, vacuum-cleaner bags, cleaning supplies, dishwasher detergent, toilet tissue, paper towels, and who knows what else?
- What's the deal on service in exchange for housing? What is the dollar arrangement? What are the services to be provided? Is the rent reduced? Is the resident to live rent free? Free room and board? Free room and board plus some compensation? How much? How frequently?

CHAPTER TWELVE

EDUCATING KIDS: WHEN THEY GO TO COLLEGE, MUST YOU GO TO THE POORHOUSE?

"How much will it cost me, 15 years from now, to educate my child?"

"Just what is the 'kiddie tax'?"

"For my child's future, what types of investments should I consider?"

One of the most common errors parents make is their failure to plan for their children's educations. Whether you are responsible for a child from a previous marriage or for one adopted with your live-together, you must calculate future college expenses and figure out how you will meet them. You can predict future costs by factoring today's dollar costs, inflation, and the ages of your children.

Probably the tuition and other charges at a private college will add up to the largest purchase you will ever make—except for your home. Since 1980, college costs have been riding a skyrocket, with tuition increasing by a minimum of 6 percent each year—almost doubling the expense every 10 years. When you think about that grim fact, you will realize that if you wait until your child is in high school to start a fund for education, it is bound to be too little and too late.

Take a look at Exhibit 23. To find the factor by which inflation will increase college costs over the years, figure out how many years it will be until your child starts college. That will give you the rate of inflation to expect. For just one example: If one year in college costs $20,000 today and you want to know how much it will cost 10 years from now, multiply $10,000 by 1.80. Result? $36,000 only 10 years from now.

Scary, isn't it? It would be so easy to bury your head in the sand and hope the money for college will come

Exhibit 23
INFLATION FACTOR FOR FUTURE COLLEGE COSTS

YEARS TO START OF COLLEGE	FACTOR: RATE OF INFLATION (6%)	YEARS TO START OF COLLEGE	FACTOR: RATE OF INFLATION (6%)
1	1.06	10	1.80
2	1.12	11	1.91
3	1.19	12	2.02
4	1.26	13	2.14
5	1.34	14	2.27
6	1.42	15	2.41
7	1.51	16	2.55
8	1.60	17	2.70
9	1.70	18	2.87

Source: Fidelity Investments

out of thin air. Well, that's not going to happen. "But we'll get financial aid," say some people. The trouble is, you will find it hard to get enough. Federal grants cannot keep up with the increasing costs of higher education. And government funds for college grants and loans have been cut and cut again. The elimination of tax advantages for minors has also made it harder and more expensive to save for education.

Now that you have an idea of what it is going to cost to send your child to college, your challenge is to figure out how much you have to invest—each year—and the yield on investment needed to meet the goal. To determine the factor by which a 10-percent rate of return, compounded annually, increases your investment, look at the number of years until your child starts college and find the rate-of-return factor. See Worksheet XII to fill in your own numbers.

Next, divide the total cost of college by the rate-of-return factor to determine the amount you will need to invest each year.

Exhibit 24
INVESTMENT RETURN RATE FACTOR FOR FUTURE COLLEGE COSTS

YEARS TO START OF COLLEGE	FACTOR: RATE OF RETURN (10%)	YEARS TO START OF COLLEGE	FACTOR: RATE OF RETURN (10%)
1	1.00	10	15.94
2	2.10	11	18.53
3	3.31	12	21.38
4	4.64	13	24.52
5	6.10	14	27.98
6	7.71	15	31.77
7	9.49	16	35.95
8	11.43	17	40.55
9	13.58	18	45.60

Source: Fidelity Investments

The Tax Reform Act of 1986 eliminated certain tax advantages for minor children, creating instead what has become known as the "kiddie tax." The law says that, for children under 14, the first $600 of income is tax-free and the second $600 is taxed at the child's rate—for most children (i.e., those with typical incomes), 15 percent. If the investment income (i.e., what the IRS calls unearned income) is more than $1,300, however, it is taxed at the parent's rate, regardless of the source of that income. This means that, at a 9-percent return, slightly less than $13,000 can be held in an account before any of the investment, or unearned, income will be taxed at the parent's rate. Investment income for children over 14 is taxed at the child's rate.

If you have children under 14, think in terms of tax-deferred investments or fast-growing stocks. If you can defer taxation on returns on investments, it is likely that the funds will grow at higher after-tax rates. For an example of a tax-deferred savings vehicle, look at U.S. government Series EE bonds. If you hold them for more than five years, the interest is tax-deferred until you redeem them. The trick is to make sure that the bonds you buy will mature after your child reaches age 14.

Another tax-deferred investment is zero-coupon bonds. These bonds have been stripped of their interest coupons. The bonds may be corporate bonds, Treasury bonds, or municipal bonds. You receive no income while you hold them. The full amount is paid when the bond matures. The problem is that you must pay taxes yearly on the income earned, even though you do not receive the income directly. Municipal bond interest, however, is not taxable, so invest in municipal zero-coupon bonds. And remember to work it out so the bonds will mature when the first tuition bill is due.

Fast-growing stocks or mutual funds are another investment for the child under age 14. Here, you are buying into investments that have great growth potential over the years but currently do not pay much in dividends (see chapter 7). When your child reaches 14, these investments can be sold and the proceeds put into safe high-yielding investments.

Another tax-deferred investment to consider: life insurance—a whole, universal, or variable policy. In these, you invest in a policy and let the earnings accumulate. While they are accumulating, you pay no federal or state tax on the earnings. When your child turns 14, you can withdraw the accumulated earnings and invest the money in your child's name. Or, if you would rather not turn the funds over to your child, pay the tuition bills from the policy's tax-free earnings.

Think not only about what type of saving or investing you want to do. Think also about how you want the accounts set up. If you are a parent or grandparent, you may set up custodial accounts under the Uniform Gift to Minors Act (UGMA). As custodian, you are responsible for managing the funds until the child reaches majority—usually at age 18. Remember that, if the child is under 14, the account may earn up to $1,200 in interest tax-free. But think carefully: This type of account has one major drawback. Once the child reaches age 18, the money is his or hers. It may be spent on college, or on a flashy car, or on a trip around the world (if you have put enough in) without your say-so.

To keep control, consider setting up a trust under Section 2503(c) of the 1986 Tax Code. As the trustee, you hold complete control over the income and principal until the child reaches age 21. The trust pays income taxes at its own rate, thereby avoiding the age 14 "kiddie tax" rule. This means that the first $5,000 of income in the trust is taxed at the 15-percent rate. Higher amounts, however, are taxed at the 28-percent rate.

Some colleges and universities have been coming up with their own ideas to help parents foot the education bills. Some arrange for a parent to buy future tuition in one lump sum at a discounted cost—"pay now, attend later" or "tuition future" plans. The discounted cost is based on when the student will enter and what the college believes it can earn on your money between now and then. The interest is supposed to make up the difference between the current tuition and what it expects to charge in the future. One problem is that, if your child decides not to go to that college, you may be refunded only your original investment, with the college keeping all the earnings. If the school cannot earn enough return on the investment to meet future costs, it will have to come up with the shortfall. Spiraling costs of education and changes in interest rates have caused growing uncertainty about these plans. Many colleges, hoping to allow for a quicker response to changes in the financial markets, now set quarterly rather than annual contracts.

Many banks offer savings plans that are designed for saving for college. Here's one type of prepayment plan that may be used at any school: The bank sells certificates of deposit based on the average tuition rates at various groups of schools, and it guarantees that investment income will keep up with rising college costs. Because college costs have been increasing faster than inflation, the bank asks for an up-front premium. It issues a certificate of deposit. Such a CD usually has a $1,000 minimum, and may come in any maturity from one to 25 years.

Many state governments offer savings bonds that are a good investment toward college. These state-backed zero-coupon bonds are sold in lower-than-normal denominations. If you live in Connecticut, for example, you may buy $1,000 bonds, with interest exempt from

Worksheet XII:
EDUCATION FUNDING

What will college cost? To estimate how much college will cost, and how much is needed to invest to meet the target, complete the following worksheet.

	YOUR CHILD	JANE SMITH
1. Enter your child's age	______	6
2. Years to college; time to invest (18 minus child's age)	______	12
3. Annual college costs* a. Enter your own estimate or b. $7,000, public school c. $16,000, private school	______	$7,000
4. College Inflation Factors: According to the College Board, college costs are increasing 6% per year. Refer to Exhibit 15 for the inflation factor based on your time horizon.	______	2.02
5. Future annual cost of college Step 3 × Step 4	______	$14,140
6. Future total cost of college Step 5 × number of years of college	______	$56,560

*According to the College Board, these are approximate annual costs of public and private colleges for the 1993–94 school year.

How much should I invest?

	YOUR CHILD	JANE SMITH
7. Assumed rate of return (10%)** Take the number of years your child has until college, refer to Exhibit 16, and enter applicable return rate factor	______	21.38
8. Annual target amount to invest Divide Step 6 by Step 7	______	$2,645
9. Monthly amount to invest Divide Step 8 by 12	______	$220

**Assumed 10% pre-tax rate of return. This is the average rate of return of the S & P 500 for the 20 years ended 6/30/90. Source: Fidelity Investments

state and local income taxes. The bonds may be used for any purpose, not just for college savings.

Between now and the time when your children attend college, you can expect to see any number of changes in the tax laws. And new ways to invest are sure to come along for parents who are wise enough to be saving toward future college expenses. Keep an eye on what is happening in the world of saving for education. And when your child reaches high-school age, learn all there is to know about financial aid.

If you want to achieve the lowest cost of funding for education, make an immediate lump-sum transfer of money to your children at their youngest possible age. The younger they are, the less you have to put away, as the funds will have a longer period in which to grow. Most people, however, do not have money to set aside in one lump sum. The next-best thing is to save on a monthly basis (see Worksheet XII).

Putting money in an account in your child's name may seem like a good idea when the kids are young, but there's a catch. You do get the modest tax break that is accorded a child's investment, but it can save you only a few hundred dollars a year. Later on—the catch: You apply for student aid. You find out that most college admissions people who are determining who gets financial aid require that a student contribute as much as 35 percent of any assets held in his or her own name, while parents are expected to use only 5 to 10 percent of their assets for annual costs.

o o o

MAUREEN AND CINDY PLAN TO PUT MONEY ASIDE

Despite their tight budget, Maureen and Cindy are determined to put money aside for Joshua's and Sarah's educations. Cindy has already talked with a financial adviser even though she has not received her inheritance. She plans to set up an education fund for each child in an aggressive mutual fund, putting in $10,000 for each. The primary goal during the years while the kids are young is growth rather than income.

o o o

Suppose it is time for college but you have not saved for college

Where can the funds for your child's education come from if you have not saved?

Financial aid, in the form of scholarships, grants, and loans, is available to those who need it. Among the aids are Perkins loans, work-study programs, Supplemental Educational Opportunity Grants, and Pell grants. These and others are more readily available if you know how, when, and where to apply.

Start early. Don't wait until your child's senior year or you could miss out on financial aid that might be available. Find out all you can about financial aid. Start with your child's guidance counselor, the school library, and the public library. Be sure to check with all the colleges that your child is applying to. In most situations, financial aid is based on the income of the custodial parent. Some schools, however, look at the income-tax returns of both custodial and non-custodial parents.

If a college says you do not qualify for need-based grants and loans, you can borrow money from other sources—providing you pass a credit check. Usually you can get lower interest rates through a government loan than from a private lender such as a bank. Among the possibilities are:

- Stafford loans offered by the U.S. Department of Education. First- and second-year students may receive up to $2,625 annually; third- and fourth-year students, $5,500. The rate equals the 90-day Treasury bill plus 3.1 percentage points, adjusted annually with a cap of 8.25 percent. Repayment begins six months after the student leaves school, with the government covering the interest in the interim. The unsubsidized version of the Stafford loan is available to all families, whether or not they meet the Government's qualifications for aid. The terms are similar, except that borrowers may choose to either begin interest payments immediately or defer them until after graduation. If they are deferred, the interest will be added to the principal payment. The college will advise you on whether you are borrowing through a bank or through the financial-aid office.
- PLUS (Parent Loan for Undergraduate Students). This permits you to borrow the cost of tuition less the amount of financial aid your child is to receive from the school. You are not allowed to defer the interest payments until a later date. You do not have to demonstrate financial need. These are government-sponsored loans for parents of any income level. The college determines how you borrow the money—from a bank or elsewhere.

In addition to federally sponsored loans, there are private lenders. These private programs take many forms, from lines of credit to tuition budgeting plans to more conventional loans for both parents and students. You may find out about these through your child's guidance counselor or your public library. Remember that the loans they extend are considered personal loans, intended for families that do not qualify for federal aid. The interest you pay, therefore, is not tax deductible.

A change that occurred in 1993 has made it easier for middle income families to qualify for financial aid for education. Before then, the colleges counted the equity in your home as if it were a resource available to help pay college costs. They woke up on July 1, 1993, and realized how impractical that notion was. They then agreed to change the rule.

In fact, you might want to consider borrowing against the equity in your home. A home-equity loan is a line of credit secured by a mortgage on your property. You borrow as you need the funds, by simply writing a check. The interest rate is variable, usually based on the prime rate plus a margin. The margin and repayment schedule vary from state to state and from bank to bank. Most lending institutions have maximum annual percentage rates, and you are permitted to make interest-only payments, with the principal payment due at some time in the future. Repayment can, of course, become a problem if you must come up with a lump-sum payment at maturity. The chief advantage of the home-equity loan is that up to $100,000 of interest is tax deductible.

One more source of financial aid for college? Your retirement funds. Most 401(k) plans permit you to borrow up to one-half of your balance, up to a maximum of $50,000. The interest you pay is not tax deductible, and the loan must be repaid within five years. If you should lose your job, or quit it, while the loan is outstanding, you could be in trouble, because the debt is considered a distribution from the plan. That means the money is taxable as income to you and, if you are under age 55, subject to a 10-percent penalty for early withdrawal.

If you plan to use the equity in your home to help finance a college education, be sure to shop around. Compare rates, payback schedules, and fees. You will find considerable variation from bank to bank.

○ ○ ○

FORTUNATELY, CHRIS HAS EQUITY IN HER HOME

To finance the education of her son Tim, Chris has had to use the equity in her home, which is valued at $220,000. She is responsible for Tim's education, and she wants to send him to the school of his choice. Accepted by every school he applied to, he chose an Ivy League college that will cost at least $25,000 a year. Since her income as an administrative assistant is low, he will be able to get some grants and loans. One helpful factor: Tim has a kid brother. Most college financial-aid officers offer more help when they know that a sibling is coming along.

Chris has the house and its equity. Her partner, Randy, contributes by paying rent and picking up some of the living expenses. Luckily, she got a small amount of life insurance when her husband died. She is allowed to borrow 75 percent of the value of the house, less the outstanding first mortgage of $35,000:

Current market value	$220,000
times 75 percent	165,000
less mortgage	-35,000
equals amount Chris may borrow	$130,000

She was able to get an introductory rate of 1.5 percent under prime for one year, then an annual rate of 1.3 percent over prime thereafter—but not exceeding 17 percent. With this loan, she will pay interest only, with the principal due in full in 20 years.

○ ○ ○

CHAPTER THIRTEEN

INSURANCE: HOW MUCH IS ENOUGH?

Almost everybody has life insurance of one sort or another, yet few people seem to understand it completely or use it to its best advantage. Insurance companies add to the confusion by bombarding us with words and concepts that simply leave us baffled. The experts seem to be either super-salespeople who tell us only what they want us to hear, or dodos who have not managed to succeed in other lines of work.

The prime purpose of life insurance is to protect the income part of the Spending Plan. It exists to replace the income that stops if a breadwinner dies. But life insurance can also be used for a secondary purpose: to accumulate savings. *Important:* For live-togethers, life insurance is an easy way to provide for a partner without going through the complications of a will—you name the partner as the beneficiary of your life insurance policy.

The proceeds from life insurance are immediately available. This is money that does not have to go through probate. It cannot be questioned by relatives who might have disapproved of your living arrangements.

When you are buying the policy, you may be asked what the relationship is. You may have to state "business partners." This is true if you own any property together. In most instances, the owner of the policy and the insured person are one and the same. That makes it easy for you to name whomever you want as the beneficiary.

There are times, however, when the owner and the insured are different people. This is often the situation when you buy insurance for estate planning purposes (see chapter 14 on estate planning). Or it may be a factor if you are buying insurance to protect one or more partners in an actual business.

For your live-together partner to buy a policy on your life and be the owner of the policy may be more difficult. The insurance company will probably question whether there is an "insurable interest" in each other—meaning that the buyer of the insurance and the person insured must either be married or have a business relationship.

You and your live-together partner should also make sure you have life-insurance protection if you are raising children.

The key word in thinking about life insurance is *now*. Now is not 10 years ago, and it is not 10 years from today. Yet countless people carry life insurance that was right for them 10 years ago, or that will be right for them 10 years from now, but is dead wrong for them now. The fact is that your life insurance needs to be changed as your life changes, and at any given moment you may be overinsured or underinsured. It is important to recognize this and cope with it.

Fortunately, this does not mean that you have to revise your life insurance coverage every year. But if you go more than five years without a thorough review of your needs and coverage, you may be either wasting money on insurance or not buying enough.

The basic types of insurance

It seems as if each and every insurance company has its own variations on the different types of policies, so it is impossible to describe them all. But here are the basic types:

1. *Term insurance.* This is what its name implies: You buy life insurance for a specific term—usually one to 10 or more years. *Annual renewal term* is just that: You renew each year, with a higher premium. You can also get *level term* for 5, 10, or 15 years. Its premium will be higher, but will remain the same for whatever period you choose. When the term ends, your new rate will usually depend on the state of your health. If you are willing to take a medical exam, and if you pass it, your rate for the next term will be lower than if you choose not to "re-enter" (that's insurance-company jargon for taking the medical exam) because of some health problem. You will, however, be allowed to renew, but at a higher premium than if you took the exam and passed it.

The cost of term insurance is low. In fact, it is the cheapest form of insurance you can buy. It provides nothing but protection. That is, it pays off only if you die. At the end of the given term, you have nothing. But you have been protected during the term.

Why is the cost higher when you renew? Because you are now older and the likelihood of death increases as you get older. Usually by the age of 45 or 50, you will find the premium cost for term insurance rising rapidly, much faster than in earlier years. But by this age you should either not be buying term or buying less of it.

Term insurance is ideal for young people. It provides greater amounts of protection for less cost than whole or straight life insurance.

> *Important*: If you are buying term, be sure you get a policy that can be renewed without your having to pass another physical examination. Also be sure that it has a guaranteed rate and contains a clause that permits you to convert it into a whole policy without a physical exam. If your health changes, renewability and convertibility will become important. If you become a high risk, or uninsurable, and you do not have a guaranteed rate and renewability, you will find the cost prohibitive or the renewed coverage unobtainable.

2. *Whole or straight life insurance.* This gives you more than protection. It includes savings. The amount of the premium is determined by your age and state of health at the time when you buy the policy; it does not increase as long as the policy is in force. Therefore, the younger you are when you buy a whole or straight policy, the less it costs you.

During the first few years, the insurance company credits only a small amount to savings. Then, as time goes on, the savings build up. This amount is yours even if you cancel the policy. Or you can borrow from the insurance company the amount that is in savings, paying interest on it at a rate you will find stated in your policy. If you borrow against the policy, you continue to pay the premium, thus keeping the policy in force. If you die, however, the insurance company reduces the amount it pays your beneficiary by the amount you borrowed. For example, if you have a $25,000 policy but have borrowed $8,000 on it, the company will pay only $17,000.

This policy provision is a valuable right. It enables you to draw upon the cash value that has built up in your policy in order to meet financial needs.

3. *Universal life.* This variation of the whole life insurance policy provides a tax-deferred savings program. Its virtue is that it is flexible both in the benefits and in the investment potential it supplies. It permits you to vary your annual premium. Some years, you might put more money toward the policy, thus building up cash values more quickly. Other years, you might put in less, but with a resulting change in the death benefit.

If you buy a universal life policy and at some time elect to pay a lower annual premium, be certain that you always maintain enough accumulated cash value to cover monthly deductions that the company will make to pay for death protection and the expenses of maintaining the policy. If you skip too many premium payments or pay too little, such monthly charges can exhaust your cash value, making your policy worthless.

4. *Variable life insurance.* Here, a portion of the premium pays for insurance protection. The other portion is invested according to your wishes. It is worth noting that straight life and universal life policies earn interest from fixed-income investments. But in a variable life policy, your money can be invested in stocks, bonds, mutual funds, or zero coupon bonds. The insurance company manages the funds into which your investments are put, so your choice of investments is limited to those that the company offers. You may, however, switch from one to another. If you feel comfortable with investing, this type of policy may be for you.

5. *Single premium life.* In this one, you pay the premium once—a single lump sum, usually at least $5,000. The cash value buildup is tax-deferred. You are allowed

to borrow from the policy at any time, but all cash withdrawals are taxable. Many companies impose a "back-end load" charge if you make withdrawals during a certain time.

6. *Hybrids.* Some policies combine both term and whole life. As cash values accumulate each year, they pay for additional whole life protection, thus decreasing the amount of term coverage. Older people often use this type of policy in order to provide insurance for estate taxes. The premiums cost more than the traditional term but less than a whole life policy's.

Which to buy—term or whole life?

Many people today question which is better. They wonder if the savings aspect of whole life is worth it. Since it takes a number of years to build up a sizable cash value, the savings are eroded by inflation. What you must ask yourself is whether there are other ways to build up savings more quickly and with a greater return—i.e., interest or dividends paid on the amount saved. A key point to remember about whole life insurance is that the policy with the lowest premium may not be the best choice. Premiums are only one factor in building cash value. The other factors are investment results, interest-rate guarantees, fees and charges for mortality risk, commissions, and favorable borrowing rules.

If you expect to keep a term policy for some years, look at the total premiums for that length of time. Don't just look at the first year's cost, because term prices rise as you get older. Compare the cost per $1,000 of death benefits against other types of policy. Premiums will depend on your age, sex, health status, and amount of coverage you are buying.

Ask yourself: How much coverage do I really need *now*? For how long a period do I need it? How much can I afford? Am I being sold on a whole or straight life insurance policy when I need greater protection and could buy it for the same amount of money by taking a term policy? In other words, you must understand what your individual needs are, in terms of insurance coverage, at any given point in your life.

The only way to determine how much insurance you really need is to develop the numbers on Worksheet XIII. Also, refer back to your Spending Plan and Asset Evaluation worksheets. When you have worked out a sensible figure, buy no more insurance than you need.

Vitally important in filling in the worksheet: Remember that Social Security benefits are not available to a surviving partner as they are to a surviving spouse. And don't forget that pension benefits may not be available unless you have named your partner as a beneficiary. If you are the legal adoptive parent of a child under the age of 18, the child will receive Social Security benefits if you die, but the surviving partner who is left to take care of the child will not receive benefits. And the child's benefits will cease when he or she turns 18.

While insurance is on your mind, look at your Spending Plan. What income will be available for your partner if you die? Check for these sources:

- Partner's income, if he or she works or can return to work.
- Income from dividends and interest from investments (see your Asset Evaluation Worksheet).
- Benefits from a pension plan.
- Proceeds from insurance already in force or included in coverage at your place of employment. *Important*: In most employer-sponsored life insurance plans, you may name anyone you want as a beneficiary. If you do not specifically name your partner (or someone else) as the beneficiary, the proceeds from the life insurance policy will go into your estate.

Invested at a reasonable rate of interest, the proceeds from your life insurance policies should generate income that your beneficiary needs to fill the gap between other financial resources and financial needs.

Now turn to the expenses side of your Spending Plan. Which expenses will decrease if you die? Probably food, clothing, transportation, and life insurance premiums. In a typical family, it takes at least 75 percent of previous take-home pay to cover expenses and continue the lifestyle. An adjustment must also be made for inflation's effect on buying power. You can see how tough it would be to plan insurance needs accurately if you did not have the Spending Plan to give you a good picture of what it costs you to live.

In addition to replacing income, your life insurance should cover certain cash requirements that your beneficiary will be wise to pay off in the event of your death. Some you have already listed in the liabilities column on your Net Worth Statement. Be sure to include:

- Mortgages, installment loans, and all unpaid current bills and other debts.
- Education expenses. If you have children now at or near college age, you will have to calculate more closely than if they are younger. If they are indeed younger, and if an insurance policy had to pay off, the amount earmarked for college should be invested at a rate of return that keeps up with the ever-increasing costs of college.
- Final expenses. These unpleasantries include administration of your estate, probate costs, attor-

neys' and accountants' fees, appraisal fees, taxes, final unreimbursed medical expenses, and funeral expenses. Rule of thumb: Allow 2 to 5 percent of the total estate, plus at least $5,000 funeral expenses, to cover these.

With so many variables, you can see how the amount of insurance you need can change as life changes. So reevaluate your needs at least every five years. And always be sure to account for changes in inflation and taxes.

Financial fitness does not mean being overinsured. Careful planning can give you the amount of coverage you need, not the amount an agent wants to sell you. Your Net Worth Statement, Spending Plan, and Asset Evaluation Worksheets have helped you to learn which assets will produce income, which liabilities should be paid off with insurance, and what it will cost you to maintain your lifestyle.

How to handle the proceeds?

When an insured person dies, the insurance company may pay out the policy in any of several ways, known as settlement options. Some insurance policies specify the choice at the outset. This is an unfair method, however, because no one can know in advance, when the policy is created, what will best serve the beneficiary's needs later on. The intervening years can change too many things. So don't let anyone talk you into a decision on the choice of settlement options when you are buying a policy.

Nor does the decision have to be made immediately after the death of the insured person. The insurance company can hold the proceeds of the policy until the beneficiary makes the decision. If you are making such a decision, do not be rushed into it. And do not let anyone else make it for you. Here are the options:

1. *Lump sum.* This means you get a check immediately for the full amount of the policy, less any amount that may have been borrowed out from cash surrender values. If you have alternate investments, and if you are knowledgeable about investing (or have good advice and are willing to learn), this is a good option. If interest rates are currently high, the lump-sum settlement offers many advantages, for you should be able to get a better return on investment than the insurance company provides.
2. *Interest only.* This means the insurance company holds the principal amount but pays you the interest it is earning. This is a good holding position while you decide what to do with the proceeds.
3. *Fixed installments.* At stated intervals, you receive a check for a fixed amount—until the money is all used up. The company also pays interest on the remaining balance it is holding during the process.
4. *Fixed period.* The company agrees to pay you the proceeds, plus accrued interest, over a certain period. The size of each check depends on the length of time that the proceeds are spread over. In effect, you are buying an annuity.

What about life insurance for a stay-at-home partner?

Traditionally, life insurance has been sold to cover the major breadwinner. But with changing roles come changing attitudes.

The caregiver, who might be a stay-at-home or have a job, whether full- or part-time, probably needs some life insurance. If there are children who are still young, insurance should be provided that can replace his or her income and cover the added burden of child care. If there is a group policy at the workplace, it probably would cover cash requirements but would not replace income. Few people ever think of a homemaker as providing services to the family that would otherwise cost dollars and cents.

IMPORTANT TIPS ON INSURANCE OPTIONS

- If you choose the fixed installment or fixed period option, make sure you have the right to change your mind and withdraw the entire sum at any later date.
- If you choose an annuity, check out what is available from your insurance company versus other annuity contracts. Get the highest monthly income possible for each $1,000 you invest.
- Paying off the mortgage may not be the best thing to do, even if you have enough proceeds from the insurance policy to do so. The money you will use to pay it off might be invested at higher rates of interest. If the mortgage has been established for a long time, monthly payments are probably small, with little left to pay, and the rate of interest is probably low. So take a good, close look at the mortgage situation and use the money the best way.

Worksheet XIII:
HOW MUCH LIFE INSURANCE?

A. ANNUAL FAMILY LIVING COSTS ______________

B. SOURCES OF INCOME AVAILABLE

- Partner's Income ______________
- Children's Social Security Benefits ______________
- Income from Income-Producing Assets (from Budget form) ______________
- Income from Proceeds of Existing Life Insurance Policies (use an assumed rate of interest)
  6%—multiply amount of insurance by .06
  8%—multiply amount of insurance by .08
  10%—multiply amount of insurance by .10
  ______________ × .08 = ______________
- Other Sources of Income ______________

TOTAL SOURCES OF INCOME ______________

C. ADDITIONAL ANNUAL INCOME NEEDED (Subtract B from A) ______________

D. NUMBER OF YEARS NEEDED ______________

E. AMOUNT OF MONEY TO MAKE UP SHORTAGE

- Multiply Additional Income Needed (line C) times the number of years needed
  ______________ × ______________ ______________
- Inflation Adjustment above total times inflation times number of years
  ______________ × ______________ × ______________ ______________

F. ADDITIONAL CASH REQUIREMENTS

Final Expenses ______________
Education for Children ______________
Liabilities (including Mortgage) ______________ ______________

G. INSURANCE NEEDS (E PLUS F) ______________

○ ○ ○

MAUREEN NEEDS LIFE INSURANCE

She has a full-time job at home: cooking, cleaning, and taking care of Joshua and Sarah. All of this must be maintained to keep the family going, and these services will have to be paid for if she is not there. Cindy will need funds to provide for child care, something that Maureen has been doing for the last two years.

○ ○ ○

In addition, the expenses of a major illness and of a funeral should be thought about—but seldom are.

When you think about how much insurance is needed, think both present and future needs. Immediate needs include the funeral and settling of the estate. Future needs include housekeeping and child care for a number of years. You have to do some calculations. Figure the monthly cost in dollars, multiply by 12 months, and then by the number of years before the children will be on their own.

Many people find themselves left with a small business after a business partner dies. Family and business life may have been intertwined, and probably the business is the largest asset that live-togethers possess together. And, by the same token, often a small business is the largest asset that is left to one or more strictly business partners when one of them dies.

Life insurance is the key to protecting the business asset. It insures the stability and continuation of the business if a partner or major shareholder dies. It can provide the funds for the surviving members of the business to purchase the share that was owned by the partner who died, saving the surviving partner or partners from the possible nightmare of trying to take up where the deceased partner left off, and also saving the survivors from the possible embarrassment of not having enough money to buy out someone who is willed a share of the ownership.

How much insurance is needed? Enough to equal the partner's or shareholder's interest in the business. This should be formalized in a buy-sell agreement between (or among) the partners. In the case of a business owned by a single individual, life insurance can provide a beneficiary with money to live on while the business is liquidated—again, saving the beneficiary from the complications of taking over a business that he or she may not understand or want to be in.

o o o

WHAT IF CINDY DIED NOW . . .

How would Maureen be left, with Sarah and Joshua to take care of? She would have the income from the savings and money-market fund money she and Cindy put away. At work, Cindy was able to buy five and a half times her salary in life insurance at only $11 per month. That will pay out at about $350,000. Maureen has been named as beneficiary. They have each purchased an additional $100,000, naming each other as beneficiaries. As Cindy's natural child, Joshua would receive Social Security benefits, but Sarah and Maureen would not. Sarah would be eligible, however, if and when Cindy could adopt her—a matter that is pending.

o o o

Disability insurance

What happens if you are disabled by an accident or an illness? The odds of being disabled before you reach 65 are greater than the odds of dying before then. If you are disabled, the chances are high that your income will drop and your medical bills will soar. Not only would that be no fun, it would be disastrous. So whether you are male or female, if you are a breadwinner you must have disability insurance that insures a monthly income. Use Worksheet IV to calculate how much disability insurance you need. And bear in mind that most gays and lesbians have seen friends use up all their financial resources on medical and disability costs related to AIDS.

Social Security provides disability insurance for those who become severely disabled before they reach 65, but the coverage is limited. It will pay if you have a physical or mental condition so severe that it prevents you from working, and if it is expected to last, or has lasted, for at least 12 months, or if it is expected to result in death. To be eligible, you must be fully insured under Social Security regulations. You have to wait five months after your disability begins before Social Security starts to pay, and the amount it pays is the same as the amount you would start to get upon your retirement at age 65. *Note:* Seven out of 10 disability claims under Social Security are rejected.

Disability insurance as a fringe benefit

Many employers provide disability insurance, usually using either of two types of plan:

1. *Short-term.* This provides modest benefits for a short period. It usually pays weekly, based on your earnings, but with a maximum that is quite low. The waiting period before it starts to pay is anywhere from seven to 21 days. Some plans pay out for as few as 13 weeks, while others may pay for as long as 52 weeks.
2. *Long-term.* Designed to take care of more serious disabilities, most long-term plans provide a certain percentage of your earnings—usually 50 to 60 percent of your base salary. The maximum monthly payment may vary from $1,500 to $2,000 or more. You may have to go through a waiting period as long as three to six months, but payments may continue for any number of years (five, 10, or 20) or until you reach age 65.

If all this seems like a wide variety of benefits and conditions, it's because there are almost as many different disability policies as there are employers, so you have to check out what your company is offering and hope it is one of the better plans. Wondering why everything seems to stop at age 65? It's because that is when Social Security and Medicare take over. Since these two government programs are so universal, and since most people have traditionally retired at 65, the insurance companies just don't bother to work out actuarial tables or develop premium rates for employee group insurance after 65. However, any number of insurance companies do offer individual policies. Many advertise that they will pay a certain flat amount daily, from the first day of hospitalization, unrelated to any medical bills or hospital costs. Such policies—in effect, simple disability policies—are carried by many people who are over 65.

○ ○ ○

CINDY'S DISABILITY PLAN . . .

It covers 60 percent of her salary, up to a maximum of $3,000 a month. If she has to call upon it, it starts payments after a six-month waiting period and pays until age 65. Since her base salary is $45,000, or $3,750 per month, she could receive up to $2,250 per month (60 percent of her $3,750).

○ ○ ○

Coordination of benefits

One more wrinkle: In many disability policies, you will find a coordination-of-benefits provision. This prescribes how other disability income benefits payable to the disabled person will affect the benefits paid by the group plan. That means that if Worker's Compensation, Social Security, or any other policies are paying, the group policy on a long-term plan may not pay as much as it otherwise would.

Your group disability policy terminates, of course, if you leave your job for any reason, and when you reach 65. Probably your group policy will contain a "conversion clause" that guarantees your right to convert it to an individual policy within 30 days.

Importance of individual policy

Since Social Security and group plans do not usually pay as much as you really need if you are disabled, a supplementary disability policy is important. Its premium cost will be based on your age, condition of health, and income. Since policies can vary widely, be sure you know what you are buying. And be prepared to discover that the underwriting rules for a disability policy are tougher today than for a life insurance policy.

Certain features will affect your coverage, including:

- *Maximum benefit period.* This is the length of time during which the company will pay. Usually it is expressed in weeks, months, or years. Many insurers are now discontinuing lifetime benefits, which were once common on top-of-the-line policies.
- *Perils insured against.* This may state accident only or accident and illness. Be sure you get coverage for both. Some companies loudly advertise their bargain rates but cover accident only—something you don't realize until you read the policy carefully.
- *Elimination period.* This is the time that must elapse before the company starts to pay. Usually it is 30, 60, 90, or 120 days after your disability began.
- *Definition of disability.* This states the conditions under which you will be considered disabled for the purpose of collecting benefits. Some plans require only that your disability prevent you from performing your regular occupation. Others will pay benefits only if you cannot perform in *any* gainful employment.
- *Non-cancelable.* It used to be that just about all policies were non-cancelable, meaning that the insurance company could not cancel the policy, raise the premium, or change the benefits during the life of the policy. Many insurers have decided to charge higher premiums if they lock in the price or to drop the locked-in premium altogether. In new policies, the premium may rise if the state insurance department finds that expenses on a particular class of business are not covered by the premiums.

If you are buying any disability policy, make sure:

1. The period covered makes sense. It may be as short as one year, or continue until you reach age 65, or cover your entire lifetime. The longer the coverage, the higher the premium.
2. The policy is guaranteed renewable.
3. You know when benefits start. The longer the elimination period before they start, the lower your premium.
4. A future income option is added to the policy. This will allow you to buy additional coverage as your income increases, without presenting any evidence of medical insurability.
5. You get residual benefits. Often, a person who has been disabled can return to work on a part-time basis. Some policies provide for partial benefits that supplement part-time earnings after a total disability.

How much disability insurance do you need—and can you afford?

Go back to your worksheets, especially Spending Plan and Asset Evaluation. Review what it costs you to live and what sources of income you would have if you were disabled. Look over your current expenses, and take

Worksheet XIV:
HOW MUCH DISABILITY INSURANCE?

A. ANNUAL FAMILY EXPENSES (Budget form) ____________

B. SOURCES OF INCOME

- Spouse's Income ____________
- Social Security Benefits (if eligible) ____________
- Disability Benefits from Work ____________
- Income from Income-Producing Assets (Assets Evaluation form) ____________
- Other Income ____________

TOTAL SOURCES OF INCOME ____________

C. ADDITIONAL ANNUAL INCOME NEEDED (Subtract B from A) ____________

D. MONTHLY BENEFIT NEEDED ____________

into account the fact that expenses will be more than likely to rise if you become disabled. They will go up like a rocket if you run into special medical provisions and care. And don't forget to consider the effect of inflation on your purchasing power.

Health insurance

In recent years, medical costs have skyrocketed. Yet few people really know how much medical coverage they have or are entitled to, let alone how to file claims. When a major illness hits, they are staggered by the bills.

But we are becoming more aware. Since 1992, the health-care debate has alerted us to the fact that millions of people face financial disaster if a major illness strikes, and other millions have no health insurance whatever.

Company-sponsored plans have given millions of Americans and their families access to health care. Many plans are generous, and traditionally they have required the employee to make only a small contribution. But corporate budgets have become strained by spiralling medical costs, and many companies now insist that their employees take higher deductibles, pay for a larger percentage of the premiums, and accept the fact that certain things are no longer covered.

One thing that is not covered—and has never been covered—in most corporate plans is benefits for a live-together partner. If you and your partner are both covered by employer-sponsored insurance, you have no problem. But if one of you does not have a plan provided by your employer, and if you cannot qualify for your partner's plan because of your unmarried status, you are up against serious discrimination.

Things are changing. But slowly. At least 60 major companies and municipalities now offer health benefits to domestic partners. Most of them are large enough to self-insure, so they don't have to debate policies set by insurance companies—they make their own policies. Among these are Microsoft, Massachusetts Institute of Technology, Princeton University, Levi Strauss, Ben & Jerry's, the City of New York, and Apple Computer.

The fact that opposite-sex couples are covered if they are married seems to have influenced some companies to stop and think, with the result that they not only

APPLE VERSUS A TEXAS COUNTY

Apple Computer caused quite a stir. Attracted by promised tax breaks, it was about to move into a county in Texas. But county officials didn't like the fact that Apple provided health benefits to domestic partners, so they decided that Apple couldn't have the tax breaks. Apple announced that it would not move in after all. The county officially reversed its position.

extend coverage to unmarried domestic partners of the opposite sex but to same-sex partners as well. To get such coverage, you usually must sign a statement that attests to your commitment to the relationship, and you must show proof, such as a shared budget or joint ownership of property, of your financial interdependence.

The federal government treats coverage for domestic partners differently from other health insurance. It says domestic partners must pay federal income tax on the amount the employer pays toward the insurance premium. It does not make married couples treat that premium as income. Under COBRA (Consolidated Omnibus Budget Reconciliation Act) legislation, the government also requires employers to extend benefits to partners. COBRA provides extended coverage if an employee leaves work, coverage to a married spouse (i.e., a widow or widower) for 36 months after a death, and coverage to a divorced spouse for 18 months after the divorce.

○ ○ ○

HOW COBRA HELPED CINDY AND MAUREEN

When Maureen left her job to stay home and take care of Joshua, she took the COBRA benefits for the 18-month maximum. As luck would have it, the university where Cindy works started coverage for same-sex partners on the day Maureen's COBRA expired.

○ ○ ○

It is essential to understand the various types of coverage, especially if you are covered by a group plan at your place of work. You should then pick out what is best for you. Cost may be a major consideration, but you should get the best available for the amount you can afford to pay.

The purpose of health insurance is to protect you from high medical costs, including hospital bills, physicians' fees, and prescription drugs. The types of coverage include:

1. *Basic hospitalization.* This is provided by private insurance companies and the various Blue Cross companies nationwide. Usually the policy pays all or part of your hospital bills, including semi-private room, food, X-rays, laboratory tests, operating-room fees, and prescription drugs. The coverage in most cases is limited to a specific number of days during any one period, with a waiting period between confinements. The better the coverage, the more you pay.

2. *Basic surgical and medical expense.* Again, private companies provide these policies, while Blue Shield companies (usually associated with Blue Cross) are best known. Fees for doctors, whether surgeons or other physicians, are paid separately from hospital fees. Usually the insurance company sets a schedule of certain fees that it is willing to pay for certain operations. If your surgeon charges more than that fee, you must pay the difference. Obviously, again, the better the insurance coverage, the more it costs.

> *Note*: Often, basic hospitalization is combined with basic medical-surgical coverage. Everyone should have at least this basic coverage.

3. *Major medical.* This type of policy starts where basic hospitalization and basic medical/surgical insurance leave off. It covers the big expenses that are above the maximum of those policies. Usually a major-medical policy covers extensive hospitalization, surgery, other doctors' fees, private-duty nursing, home medical care, diagnostic work, therapies, medical devices, and rehabilitation. Major-medical policies contain a deductible feature, so the patient pays a certain amount —usually from $100 to $1,000—before the insurance company pays anything. (Often, the deductible is annual: With each new year, you pay the first $100 or so of claims yourself before the insurance company starts to pay your claims.) Once you have gone beyond the deductible amount, most major-medical policies pay 80 to 85 percent of each claim you file. You must pay the balance yourself. But at a still higher level, the insurance company takes over and pays 100 percent of all legitimate claims (this is called a "stop-loss limit"). Some policies put no limit on the maximum amount of claims they will pay. Others limit you to $250,000 or $500,000. Most policies set a lifetime maximum. For example:

> Suppose you are covered by a major-medical plan that has an annual deductible of $100 and a stop-loss limit of $2,000. If you have a claim for $1,800, you will have to pay $440 out of your own pocket:

Total claim	$1,800
Less deductible	- 100
	$1,700
Insurance company pays	
80 percent	-1,360
You pay 20 percent	$ 340
Plus deductible	+ 100
Total you pay	$ 440

> The amount you pay above the deductible is called coinsurance. In the example above, once your out-of-pocket expenses (i.e., the deductible plus all coinsurance amounts during any given year) reach $2,000, the insurance company will

pay 100 percent of all your claims for the remainder of the year.

How can you cut down on the cost of a major medical policy? Two ways: 1) Increase your deductible. Many people today accept a deductible of $1,000. 2) Ask for a higher stop-loss limit. Either step means that you increase the risk you are willing to take.

Many people prefer not to increase the risk. They pay a higher premium, rather than cutting it down, so they won't have to worry that out-of-pocket expenses, if a major illness occurs, might send them to the bank to borrow money.

4. *Medicare.* This national health insurance covers everyone age 65 or older who pays Social Security taxes or is eligible for Social Security or Railroad Retirement benefits. It is also available to those under 65 who are disabled or who have chronic kidney disease. Medicare is divided into parts. Part A is free of charge. It pays for hospital stays and care in a skilled nursing home as part of after-hospital care. Part B covers physicians' fees and outpatient services at a hospital, as well as certain medical services and supplies. It costs a small monthly fee, and pays for 80 percent of reasonable medical costs—which often means that it pays considerably less than the actual cost. Part B does not pay for eyeglasses, dentistry, prescription drugs, private nursing, custodial nursing-home care, treatment in a foreign country, or routine physical examinations.

If you decide not to take Social Security benefits at 65, it is important to register for Medicare. You have to do so within a rather strict timeline or risk a delay in starting your coverage. Jack delayed taking his Social Security benefits until age 70, but fortunately had been advised to sign up for Medicare, so he was covered. Among the regulations are these:

- If you apply up to three months before your 65th birthday, your coverage will begin as soon as you reach 65.
- If you enroll in the month in which you turn 65, your coverage will begin on the first day of the following month.
- If you enroll within the next three months after that, you must wait for two months after the date you enroll before coverage starts. In the meantime, Medicare will not cover any of your Part B claims.
- If you miss the latter deadline, you must wait until the next general enrollment period—January 1 to March 1 each year—to sign up. Say your 65th birthday is in April and you do not apply by the end of July. You may not enroll until the following January, and your coverage will not begin until the July after that.

Obviously, senior citizens can run into high out-of-pocket medical expenses. If you are moving into what the doctors euphemistically call "the mature years," you must carry some supplemental policy in addition to Medicare, in order to pay for items not covered by Medicare and for expenses that go beyond what Medicare is willing to pay. Your retirement nest egg can be wiped out by medical costs that Medicare does not cover. Anyone over 65 must carefully consider additional coverage.

5. *Medigap.* This additional coverage is called medigap insurance because its purpose is to bridge the gap between your medical bills and the amount that Medicare is willing to pay, which is usually less than the total bill from your doctor, hospital, or laboratory. Gaps occur because Medicare includes a deductible clause, just as your automobile insurance does, to help you pay a lower premium, and because your doctor is charging more than Medicare thinks the particular treatment should cost. The largest gap comes in the area of physicians' excess fees, as Medicare likes to call it. The excess is the amount above that approved by Medicare. You are responsible for such excess charges, up to a payment limit that the government sets.

Medicare sets up what it considers the allowable charge for every conceivable treatment. However, there is a problem. Medicare is national, but there is no standard rate nationally. Medicare's allowable charges, it has been found, vary from one part of the country to another. Medicare tells you how much the excess is, but until now it has not made any attempt to limit the fees of doctors who charge more than it is willing to pay.

When should you buy medigap insurance? In the first six months after you begin coverage under Medicare Part B. During that time, insurance companies are required by law to sell you the policy you want, so the timing becomes particularly important if you have a health problem that may put you in a high-risk category.

Altogether, 10 different standard medigap plans have been created, labeled A through J. They are sold as "medigap supplements." Each state decides on which of the plans may be sold to its residents, so you may not find all 10 plans available where you live. But wherever they are sold, all A plans are alike in the coverage they provide. So are all Bs, all Cs, and so on right down the line. That includes the look of the policy, what words it uses, and what those words mean. The only differences are the cost of the coverage among insurers and the efficiency with which they resolve claims.

What about Medicare and medigap if you are still working past age 65? Your employer will coordinate its health-insurance program with Medicare. In many companies, upon your retirement the health plan turns into a medigap plan, so you don't have to buy your own medigap insurance. You must, however, enroll in Medicare Part B in order to get basic coverage. Other companies tell you to buy your own medigap policy, but they provide the money for the premiums.

6. *Health maintenance organizations (HMOs).* While they offer prepayment plans that provide medical protection, HMOs do not supply health insurance as such. Most corporations now offer HMOs as an alternative to the traditional medical plan, and the number of HMOs is steadily increasing.

The HMO is organized as a nonprofit cooperative. For a fixed fee per month, it provides medical care for a member, based on the premise that it is cheaper to prevent illness than to cure it. Since the premiums of members constitute its only source of income, the HMO must hold down costs. Preventive medicine is one way to do so.

The HMO owns and operates hospitals and clinics and hires doctors, nurses, and medical technicians. It pays annual salaries to its professional staffs. This means that the doctors do not charge patient-by-patient or treatment-by-treatment in the traditional way. If you belong to an HMO, your premium covers nearly all medical expenses and you are entitled to care in one place, 24 hours a day, seven days a week. One disadvantage, however, is that usually you may not choose your own doctor. Rather, you must go to a doctor who belongs to the HMO. Before you make any decision about joining an HMO, find out how near the service is to you and talk with some of its members.

7. *Preferred provider organizations (PPOs).* These are networks of doctors. They provide discounted care to members of a sponsoring organization, such as an employer or a union. If you are a patient of a particular doctor, you pay a smaller copayment at the time of service—usually, $10 or 10 percent of the total charge. If you go to a doctor who is not on the list, your share of the bill jumps.

8. *Long-term nursing-home coverage.* Years of savings can be wiped out by a long-term stay in a nursing home or by lengthy custodial care at home. Worried by that well-known fact, many elderly people are buying insurance to pay for long-term care. But watch out: Such a policy almost never pays all the costs of living in a nursing home or having someone come in and take care of you. The premium on these policies is based on three factors: your age when you buy the policy, the elimination period (i.e., how soon after you enter a nursing home does the policy begin to pay?), and the benefits you receive.

Usually, a long-term policy pays a set dollar amount per day for care. But be realistic: A $50-a-day benefit will cover only a small portion of the daily cost of a nursing home. Note also that the benefits period can vary from one year to a lifetime and that most policies have a three-year maximum.

Some things to look for in health insurance

- *Combination plans.* Many insurance companies offer plans that combine basic hospitalization and medical and surgical benefits with a major-medical plan. Often you can get a lower deductible through such a package deal.
- *Items not covered.* Check for such benefits as cosmetic surgery, eyeglasses and routine examinations for glasses, regular physical, and psychiatric care. If covered, the last is usually under a special limitation.
- *Guaranteed renewable and non-cancelable policies.* Some companies reserve the right to cancel at any time. This could be disastrous if, when they cancel, you are uninsurable or have an illness that existed before the cancellation. For anyone who is HIV-positive or has developed AIDS, for instance, this could be disastrous. If you have a non-cancelable policy, that means your insurer cannot cancel it during the length of time it is stated to cover. Nor can your premiums be increased during this period. Usually, when the stated period has ended—and it may be as short as one year—the company must renew if the policyholder wants to renew. It may, however, increase the premium.
- *Alternatives.* Shop around and make some comparisons. Everyone should have major-medical insurance. A major illness or accident can bring on economic chaos. If you are eligible for group medical insurance, take advantage of it. If not, compare several plans. Note the various features—i.e., costs and benefits—of each. Consider accepting a larger deductible in order to pay a smaller premium. See if an HMO is near you. Often, an HMO offers group coverage to an individual who is not otherwise eligible to be in a group medical plan. If you are self-employed, think about joining an organization for self-employed people or a professional organization or union that provides coverage to its members. To keep premiums low, many such organizations offer large deductibles—up to $2,000.

Property, casualty, and homeowner's insurance

If you had a severe fire in your home, or a hurricane or flood roared through your town, or thieves took your TV set and computer and CD player and silver and priceless antiques, could you make repairs and buy replacements out of your financial assets? Few of us could. That is why property and casualty insurance is imperative.

Most of us understand the basic idea of the coverage: If a fire or theft, flood or wind damage occurs, we will be reimbursed for the loss. But few of us really understand what will be covered by the insurance company and what we must take care of ourselves.

Homeowner's policies, as they are called, usually cover:

1. Fire insurance on the house.
2. Extended coverage for damage to the house by such things as wind, hail, falling objects, smoke, and motor vehicles.
3. Allowance for additional living expenses if you have to live in a motel or rented house while repairs are made.
4. Allowance for personal property lost because of fire, theft, or mysterious disappearance. This covers such items as clothing, books, cameras, personal computers, and household furnishings.
5. Liability. This covers claims based on any injuries suffered by others and caused by your property. Classic example: The mail carrier is bitten by your dog or slips on the ice on your sidewalk. The coverage includes payments for medical expenses.

You should keep several key points about homeowner's insurance in mind:

- The policy always specifies an address and provides protection at that address. Most policies, however, also cover losses while your possessions are in storage or at the cleaner's or when you are traveling.
- Items stolen from your children while they are at camp or away at school or college *may* be covered. Look closely at what the policy says about college dorms; most policies do not stretch all the way to a dormitory or, even less likely, to an apartment near a college campus. If your student son or daughter is living off campus in a rented apartment, better get insurance on the CD player, the computer, the camera, the guitar, and the walk-around headset.
- Most policies limit the amount they will pay to the actual cash value of the property stolen or destroyed. The insurance company takes into account the age of the article and depreciates for each year you have owned it. (This is another area where your records come in handy: if the suit lost in the dry cleaner's fire was new only six months ago, you will have a way to prove it.) Since actual cash value may be substantially lower than what it will cost you to replace an item, especially considering the way property has appreciated in recent years, this insurance policy can be costly to you. However, you can get a replacement endorsement added to your policy by paying a higher premium. If a major loss occurs, you will consider the money well spent.
- The typical standard homeowner's policy limits the amount the company will pay for a loss of personal property. Usually the limit is 50 percent of the total amount that the building is insured for. The loss is also limited to that caused by a fire, windstorm, or other specific peril listed in the policy. If you have a valuable collection of art, jewelry, silver, antique furniture, or other similar objects, you will be wise to ask for a "personal property floater schedule." It broadens the policy's coverage, but it can be expensive. By having appraisals made, the insurance company sets a cash value on each item you list on the schedule. If you add this coverage, remember to reevaluate these items at least every couple of years, as the value of collectibles rises with inflation. (The trend can go the other way, too, of course; remember what happened to the price of silver between 1979 and 1981? It shot up dramatically, then fell right back.) Also update the schedule regularly to delete any items you no longer possess. Usually this type of coverage has a deductible amount to help keep down the premium cost.

  Important: Your record-keeping, including inventory of items, receipts for purchases, and photographs, is vital if you are carrying a personal property floater on your homeowner's policy.

- Homeowners are not the only ones who need coverage. If you are renting, you need both personal property and liability coverage just as much as if you were the owner. A person who falls and is injured can sue the tenant as well as the landlord.

Just how much insurance should you carry on your home? This depends mainly on the value of the house and its contents. With inflation and the resulting appreciation of homes over recent years, you cannot just let your homeowner's policy sit year after year without updating it. In fact, most of the insurance companies and their agents add an increment yearly for that upward spiral and simply bill you for the increase. The question, really, is whether that automatic increase is enough. Have you brought collectibles into the house? Do you need appraisals of certain valuables so you can take out a personal property floater? Since the floater is relatively expensive, do you want to insure only those items that would be really difficult to replace, such as heirlooms? Are you keeping smaller items in a safe deposit box and handling the risk that way? All these are questions that you should consider—and act upon.

Open an umbrella over your head

Liability insurance covers you against a claim by a person bitten by your dog or injured on your icy sidewalk. It does not cover you in a situation where a repairman, cleaning woman, gardener, or painter is injured while working in your home. They should be covered by Worker's Compensation. Never just assume, however, that a repairman or housepainter or other contractor has his or her own insurance. Ask to see proof.

How much liability insurance should you carry? Usually the range for an "umbrella" policy is between $25,000 and $300,000. With the number of liability claims and the size of the settlements moving through our legal system today, it is not a bad idea to increase your coverage to as high as $1 million if you have a fairly substantial income and assets. People who are suing are usually advised by their lawyers to try for as much as they can and to dig the well where the water is.

Automobile insurance

In most states, the law requires this. If you drive one inch without it, you are courting financial disaster.

If you own a car jointly, you get only one insurance policy. You may have to shop around for it, because there have been cases where insurance was refused on a jointly-owned vehicle. If you each own cars, you should have no trouble getting insurance individually. Two separate policies will be written, but each may list the owner as the primary driver and the partner as a secondary driver.

A married couple who own two cars qualify for a discount on the coverage for the second car. You and your live-together partner do not qualify for that. To get the discount on the second car, one of you must own both cars and insure them on a single policy. But note: Some companies treat live-togethers the same way they treat married couples. Find an insurance broker who will find them.

Four things you should understand about auto insurance:

1. *Liability coverage.* This protects you, the owner of the car, from claims that may result from the injury or death of another person, as well as from damage to property. The other person may be a pedestrian or a passenger or driver of another vehicle. The situation itself may be of any kind; the newspapers regularly report crazy happenings involving vehicles that no one could have anticipated. The property may be another vehicle or any kind of stationary object.

   The liability part of the policy is written in figures that look like this: $100,000/$300,000–$25,000. What does it mean? The first two figures mean that the insurance company will pay up to $100,000 for bodily injuries to any one person and up to $300,000 for injuries to two or more persons in any one accident. The $25,000 means they will pay that maximum for property damage.
2. *Collision.* This pays for damage to your car caused by a collision with another vehicle, or with any other object, whether it is stationary or moving. To cut down the premium cost, it carries a deductible, usually $100 or more, so you pay for minor repairs yourself. Usually the company pays for the cost of repairs above the deductible amount or pays the actual cash value of the car, less the deductibility, if you total the car. When buying a policy, you can usually choose how much of a deductible you want to risk. The higher the deductible, the lower your premium, of course.
3. *Comprehensive.* Many things, in addition to other vehicles, can damage your car. This part of the insurance covers loss due to fire, theft, wind, hail, and falling objects. Again, a deductibility clause may reduce your premium.
4. *Medical payments.* All passengers injured while in your car are covered by this section. It also covers the members of your family while they are riding in any other vehicle.

When you are buying auto insurance, or reviewing what you have, keep these important points in mind:

- Like all other insurance, policies must be reviewed and updated regularly. Nothing stays the same.
- Premium rates vary according to where you live, and according to the amount of risk you are willing to handle yourself by taking higher deductibility. Rates in big cities are usually higher than in small towns and rural areas, presumably because the heavier the traffic, the more likely an accident.
- Unless you simply cannot afford it, your liability coverage should be the maximum possible. If you have substantial assets, you should have substantial liability coverage.

- As your car gets older, its value depreciates. Watch its cash value. If you keep a car for several years, there comes a time when you may consider dropping collision coverage altogether because the annual premiums approach the replacement value of the car.
- Shop around. Auto insurance is high-priced stuff, but there are many insurance companies competing for your business. Your best approach is to work with an independent broker to get the best coverage for the lowest premium.

To summarize, ask yourselves

Whether you are reviewing life, health, disability, property and casualty, or automobile insurance or considering it for the first time, ask yourselves some basic questions:

What if? What if this, what if that? What risks do I take? What things could possibly happen?

Which of those risks must I assume myself, and which can I pay an insurance company to take over? That, in turn, will determine what kinds of policies and coverage you need.

How much will it cost? Shop around. Get several quotes, or bids, from various brokers and companies. Make your decision based on coverage, service, and cost.

From time to time, ask yourselves this question: Are we carrying enough insurance, or too much, for our situation right now? Nothing is more important than reevaluating and updating your policies every so often—certainly every couple of years.

CHAPTER FOURTEEN

ESTATE PLANNING: MAKING SURE YOUR ASSETS GO WHERE YOU WANT

Estate planning sounds like something for the wealthy to do. But it is not just for those who have accumulated large sums of money or vast holdings of property of one sort or another. Estate planning is necessary and important for anyone who expects to leave anything—money, investments, real estate, or personal property—to anyone.

This is one of those important areas for live-togethers. If walls could speak, more than one courtroom would testify to the squabbling it has seen among parents, siblings, and children from previous marriages—no two of whom agree over the settling of a given estate—when a live-together tries to make a claim without a will to support it.

Your estate is everything you own at the time of your death. The actual dollar value is not the key issue. Rather, what counts is that you set up a way to pass on some (if not all) of what you have created or accumulated to those whom you love and whom you expect to survive you.

By following the advice and instructions in this book, you are already well on your way to estate planning, because:

- You have your papers and records in order.
- You know how much your assets add up to.
- You know who owns what.
- You understand income and expenses.
- You know how much your pension benefits amount to.

A four-part process

Think of estate planning as a four-part process: 1) Drawing up a living will and a health power of attorney that determine what you want to happen if you are so ill or incapacitated that you cannot make your own decisions; 2) Drawing up a will that clearly states and legally establishes what you want to happen to all your property; 3) Minimizing federal estate taxes; and 4) Establishing living or testamentary trusts.

Four parts, yes. But think of it as all the same process, for your living will and estate plan should be done at the same time. And in the process you plan simultaneously for the disposition of your assets to those whom you want to get them and for the reduction (or avoidance) of taxes and other expenses that could shrink your estate.

Your living will and health power of attorney

It's no fun to think about what might happen if you were out of it—so seriously ill from any disease, or so badly injured in an accident, that you could not make your own decisions about your medical treatment or your finances. But it is vitally important that you think about it. Whom do you want to have the authority to act for you if you cannot act for yourself?

More than one live-together has been forced to stand back and watch while a doctor was instructed by the family of his or her partner in ways that the live-together knows the partner would not have wanted. Partners sometimes find themselves barred from visits in a hospital's intensive-care unit. Hospital staff people and doctors are in the habit of looking to a patient's immediate family for the authority to act. Furthermore, many medical people—especially in "teaching" hospitals, with their nursing and medical students, interns, and young resident physicians—are eager to demonstrate the wonders of life-support systems.

You can head off such troubles by preparing simple legal documents that specify how your health care and your finances are to be managed. You should have two different documents. One is the health power of attorney. It gives someone else the authority to make medical decisions for you if you are unable to do so. That person is not usually a doctor. Rather, it is a friend, a relative, or your live-together partner. The other document is your living will. It is directed to the medical profession and tells doctors, nurses, and hospital staff what treatments you want or don't want, usually in the last stages of life.

1. *Health power of attorney.* A power of attorney is a formal document that gives a person the legal authority to act for another person. A health power of attorney restricts that authority to medical matters. It empowers the person you designate to hire and fire medical personnel, to make decisions about such matters as surgery on your behalf, and to visit you in the hospital even when visiting rights are limited to immediate family. It allows your designee to act on your behalf just as a legal spouse would. In using a health power of attorney, you are doing much the same thing you do when you create a living will. *Important:* Be sure to name an alternate designee.

2. *The living will.* This is a statement directly from you to the medical profession. Your right to make such a statement is now recognized by law in many states. The law in such states includes suggested forms for you to use in declaring your living will, and usually you are permitted to add your own personalized directions.

Within the approved legal form, you may, for example, declare that, in the event you are in a terminal condition as a result of illness or injury and you are not capable of participating in decisions about your treatment, you do not want your life to be prolonged by the use of any artificial life-support systems. You may want to consider, for example, listing particular treatments to be withheld or withdrawn—such as surgery, antibiotics, mechanical assistance in breathing, or cardiopulmonary resuscitation.

Some people know they don't want to be fed artificially if their medical condition is considered terminal. Some want to emphasize that it is their desire to be kept comfortable and free of pain even if it shortens their lives. Some want to name a proxy—a person who can be trusted to make decisions they would make for themselves if they could.

Your living will must be signed by you in the presence of two witnesses. Usually no restrictions are imposed as to who may serve as witnesses, as long as they are not minors.

In some states, statutes have been enacted that protect doctors and medical staff people from liability suits for withdrawing life support from a dying patient in accordance with the patient's declared wishes, if the physician has informed the patient's next of kin or legal guardian and obtained that person's consent.

Important: Talk with your family and your physician, so they understand and support your wishes about terminal care. Give your doctor a copy of your living will to put in your permanent medical records. If you change doctors, remember to give your new doctor a copy. Give copies to family members, too, or to anyone else who might someday have to make decisions about treatment for you. It's a good idea to have your lawyer keep a copy in your file. If you are pretty sure which hospital you are most likely to land in, should an emergency occur, file a copy there, too—or even in a hospice facility. Keep the original copy at home and easily available with your personal papers—*not* in your safe deposit box.

Your living will stays in effect until you revoke it. But you can always supersede it if you have reason (or need) to.

For more information, and to get a copy of the declaration form that is authorized in the state where you live, write to:

Society for the Right to Die
250 West 57 Street
New York, New York 10107

Financial durable power of attorney

Often, someone who is struggling through a medical crisis is incapable of handling his or her financial affairs. Bills must be paid, incoming checks deposited, tax forms filed, insurance claims filed, stocks sold, and other financial matters handled. You can use a durable power of attorney to authorize another person to handle money matters for you, and you can limit that person's authority in any reasonable way, as well as make any specific directions you want.

Probably the most important aspect of setting up a durable power of attorney is your decision on whom to appoint as attorney-in-fact (that's the legalese that lawyers and bankers like to use). Actually, you will be smart to name more than one person, so you have an alternate available.

❍ ❍ ❍

EVAN'S AND BOB'S DURABLE POWERS OF ATTORNEY

Evan and Bob have decided to give each other durable powers of attorney. This means that either one can handle the affairs of the other, starting the moment they sign them. If either becomes incapacitated, the other can then handle any needed financial transactions. The powers of attorney will stay in effect as long as both are alive and well or until, for any reason, they decide to revoke either one or both.

❍ ❍ ❍

LIMITING EACH OTHER'S POWERS OF ATTORNEY

After careful thought and discussion, Bobbie and Jack decided to set limits on transactions either could handle. They made sure the powers of attorney enable either one to take care of all their bank accounts, but they agreed that neither could use his or her power of attorney to sell real estate, the home that Bobbie owns, or any stocks or bonds.

The Golden Guys and Gals have been careful about this matter. Each resident in their shared home must not only have a health examination, or physical, before moving in, but each must have signed a health power of attorney and a living will. With their families living nearby, each has named a family member to have the power of attorney. And each is aware that he or she is to take copies of both documents along on any visit to the hospital—via ambulance or private car.

❍ ❍ ❍

Key points about your power of attorney

Almost any financial institution will accept your power of attorney, as long as it is properly filled in, signed and dated by you, and witnessed by two people and notarized. If the person you are appointing as attorney-in-fact is to be allowed to handle real estate transactions, you must formally record it (in most states) in the recorder's office of the county where you live.

> *Important*: Make sure that the person whom you appoint as attorney-in-fact keeps your power of attorney in an absolutely safe place.

Why you should have a will providing for your live-together

If you die without leaving a will, you will be said to have died *intestate*. If that is the case, the state in which you lived immediately before your death will decide who gets your property. What the state decides may not be what you had in mind, but only those you leave behind will know that—if, indeed, you told them. More likely than not, the state will not agree with the ideas you had. The possibilities of inequities are considerable.

What intestate succession laws are designed to do is pass property only to blood relatives or to a legal spouse. It is impossible, in fact, in most states, to disinherit a legal spouse. If one of an unmarried couple dies without a will or other legal protection for the survivor, that survivor has no way of inheriting anything. So it is important that you find and use some means to see that your property is transferred, legally and actually, to your partner. You can use any or all of several ways to do that: a will, living trust, testamentary trust, joint tenancy designation, or pay-on-death account. And you can name your live-together as beneficiary on retirement accounts and insurance policies.

Do both of you need wills?

Absolutely. Your will accomplishes a number of things. If you are a parent, it lets you name a personal guardian for a child. It appoints the person you want as your executor, in charge of supervising the distribution of your estate. If you leave no will, the state names a guardian and appoints an executor. Your will may also direct how your body is to be handled, what kind of funeral you want, and who is to take responsibility for such arrangements.

Each of you undoubtedly has property of your own, from such personal property as jewelry or heirlooms to stocks or bonds. You will want to pass such items on to your partner or a child or grandchild. Many live-togethers own property left to them by their late spouses. Some have sizable estates. In most cases, live-togethers want to provide for each other as well as for the children of earlier marriages. One typical arrangement, carefully set forth in a will, provides that a surviving partner may have the life use of a house owned by a partner who died. But when the second partner dies, the ownership passes to the children of the original owner—i.e., the first partner.

Maybe you think you don't need a will. Lawyers and judges are always busy settling the affairs of people who thought that. A live-together contract is not a substitute for a written will. Such a contract usually defines how a couple owns property while both partners are living. Most states enforce *written* live-together contracts that cover real property. But if your partner leaves a will that contradicts a written live-together contract, you can be left with nothing.

An oral or implied contract is even more flimsy. Many states will enforce it—if you can prove it existed. To do so, you, the surviving partner, would have to sue the heirs who inherited the property and prove either that the oral or implied contract did exist or that an equitable remedy should govern. This could be a tough one to win—costing lots of time, a fortune in legal fees, and the stress of some nasty law-office and courtroom battles. In short, no will means big risk. Get yours drawn as soon as you can.

Writing your will

Your will has only one purpose: to make certain that your property goes where you want it to go after you die. Check your list of assets (see chapter 4). Insurance policies, company benefits, household furnishings, investments, your home—you probably own more than you thought you did.

Drawing a will is the process of making decisions, committing them to paper, and making sure that the paper becomes a legal document that is indisputable. You want to have absolute confidence that no one can argue with your will. When you have it completed properly, you can be satisfied that it conserves and distributes your estate *the way you want it done.*

Get professional help. That means a lawyer. A good lawyer will know your state's laws and will know how to head off problems. Is there any chance that some family member or other relative might challenge your will? Your lawyer will take action to prove that you are competent and not under undue influence when you sign your will, and will make sure it is witnessed properly.

You can take some steps that will help save your lawyer's time and thus save you money. One is to write your own first draft, or at least a statement covering what you want the will to accomplish. Your lawyer can then review and adapt your draft. In most law offices today, however, standard "boilerplate" wording is waiting in the computer, ready for your name and other specific details to be slugged in quickly and easily.

When you go to see your lawyer, be ready with:

- A list of your assets (from your Net Worth Statement, chapter 4).
- The name of your executor. This should be a friend or relative whom you trust. This person will be fully responsible for seeing your will through probate and making sure your estate is disposed of in accordance with your will. Your executor should live nearby. It won't hurt to name two executors—maybe your live-together and some family member, such as an adult child from an earlier marriage. If your executor dies or becomes incapacitated, it will be important to revise your will to name someone else. In such an event, do not delay: if you should die without replacing your executor, the state will name the replacement.
- The name of a guardian for minor children. A guardian is obliged to provide proper care and to manage any money left to the children. Legal parents of a minor child are entitled to custody of that child. If there are two legal parents—for instance, the divorced parents of the child—each is entitled to custody. If one dies, the other automatically gains sole custody. But adoption is much more difficult for same-sex couples. In the District of Columbia and in several states, the child of one member of a same-sex couple may be adopted by the other. But this is by no means common. Therefore, it is important to name a guardian. Furthermore, the live-togethers should sign an agreement that states that the natural parent and the live-together are both considered responsible for the child, with all the rights of legal parenting.

○ ○ ○

CINDY'S AND MAUREEN'S SECOND-PARENT ADOPTIONS

Cindy and Maureen each have a biological child. They are working with a lawyer to "cross-adopt," so that the children will have the protection of a legal parent on each side. This gives the children—Joshua and Sarah—the advantages of automatic inheritance rights, Social Security benefits, and health benefits provided by the employer of *either* parent. Meanwhile, pending the adoptions, Cindy and Maureen have named each other as guardians in their wills.

○ ○ ○

In most cases, only one of the couple—the biological parent or the sole adoptive parent—has custody rights. In a will, only the legal parent may name a personal guardian for a minor child. However, if there is only one legal parent, that parent may direct—but is not allowed to mandate—who is to have custody of the child if that legal parent dies. The final decision is made by a judge, who uses the standard of the child's "best interest."

- Usually, among gay and lesbian couples, a parent names her or his partner as the guardian. But if the parent does not, and then he or she dies, the surviving partner will probably have to win a court battle to gain custody.
- What if the person whom you want to name as guardian just doesn't have good financial sense? You can name one person to care for the child and another to handle the money. But make sure the two people know each other and get along well, because they are going to have to work together.

  Before you complete your will and sign it, be sure to check with your proposed guardian to see that she or he is willing to be named. Otherwise, there could be some embarrassment or even resentment.
- Decide who is to get what. Make careful notes on just how you want your estate distributed, including any specific instructions on particular items.
- Ask your lawyer to keep the signed original copy of each of your wills (yours and your partner's) in his or her office safe. Keep photocopies in your files at home. Don't put them in a safe deposit box, for they must be accessible the first moment they are needed.
- Review your will regularly—at least every five years. Why? Because a child may have been adopted, a beneficiary may have died, an executor may have died or moved far away, you may have moved to another state where estate laws are different, you may have seen a major change in your financial circumstances, new laws affecting estates may have been passed in your state—there are countless reasons.

Is yours a taxable estate or a probate estate?

Your estate may be either probate or taxable—or both. Ask your lawyer about how your estate relates to each.

1. *Probate estate*. The function of probate court is to authorize and supervise the payment of funeral expenses, taxes, and debts owed by a person who has died, and to authorize payment for administering the estate (an executor is usually paid for handling an estate). The court then sees that any remaining property is distributed to the beneficiaries named in the will or to others who may be entitled to it.

The executor acts under the probate court's supervision and scrutiny. If you die without leaving a will, the probate court, acting on behalf of the state, will name an administrator.

Probate procedure to be followed by your executor includes:

a. Applying for probate of the will, which is filed with the court. A probate judge reviews it, declares it valid (presumably), and certifies approval of the executor named in the will.
b. Posting of a bond by the executor, unless your will waives the requirement. The amount of the bond depends on the size of your estate. It protects the estate from the possibility of an executor absconding with funds.
c. Making an inventory of all assets that you owned in your name alone. This helps determine whether your estate is solvent. Assets must not only be inventoried, they must be evaluated by reputable appraisers who can judge the value of real estate and such collectibles as jewelry, coins, or antique furniture. Your up-to-date Net Worth Statement can be a big help in this process.
d. Advertising for claims against the estate. What your executor does not want is the headache of having someone show up with a claim on your estate after the probate process has been completed. So it is important to publish a notice, usually in local or area newspapers, specifying that all claims must be submitted within a stated period or by a specific deadline, after which they will not be honored.
e. Paying all recent and outstanding bills, such as funeral or medical expenses.
f. Filing state and federal tax forms and paying required taxes.
g. Accounting for the remaining estate and distributing it to those named in the will.

How long does all this take? Anywhere from nine months to two or three years, depending on how complex your will is, how large your estate is, and how many beneficiaries you have named (many a lawyer has spent months on end tracking down distant relatives in faraway places). Some priorities have to be watched, too: state law sets certain time limits. The inventory, for example, must usually be completed within a specific period.

When your will is probated, it becomes a matter of public record. That is one reason why many people prefer to dispose of their estates by setting up trusts, which are not made public.

2. *Taxable estate*. You probably have some assets that will be part of your taxable estate but that do not have to go through probate. These include any assets that name a beneficiary: retirement accounts, insurance policies, even simple pay-on-death bank accounts. It will also include joint tenancy with right of survivorship, whether real estate or anything else. Ask your lawyer to explain what happens to a taxable estate where you live, for federal estate and gift tax laws change frequently and state laws vary greatly.

Jointly held property

Property that is held jointly is exempt from probate. It passes immediately, and automatically, to the survivor. And it has other advantages:

- It is easy to set up.
- It assures a live-together, who has no protection if there is no will, of an inheritance.
- It can prohibit ancillary probate (i.e., a second probate, in another state). This can be valuable, for instance, if you own a vacation home in another state. Make sure the place is jointly held, so your executor avoids probate costs.
- Depending on the laws in your state, your creditors may not be able to seize jointly held property, unless your live-together has assumed liability.

Jointly held property has its *disadvantages*, too. Keep these in mind:

- Property cannot be sold without the signatures of both parties. If you and your partner split, or if one of you is absent or incapacitated and has not given a power-of-attorney to the other, a stalemate occurs.
- A joint bank account can be cleaned out by either partner.
- Because property passes immediately to the surviving partner without going through a will, neither partner has any power to make a predisposition. Whoever becomes the survivor has the entire say.
- Gift taxes may be imposed.
- A bank can freeze the account pending settlement of all claims on the estate, preventing the survivor from using the money in the meantime.

Trusts: living or testamentary

One of the best advantages of living or testamentary trusts is that they are difficult to contest. If you are concerned that someone who expected to be your heir may jeopardize your estate, you may find a trust to be a most valuable device.

If you set up a trust during your lifetime, it is called a living or inter-vivos trust. If your will sets up a trust to be created after your death, it is called a testamentary trust. Each has its good points, depending on what you want to accomplish.

1. *The living trust*. This is also called a revocable living trust, which means that you can revoke it if you wish. You keep full control over any assets you place in the trust while you are alive, putting funds in, taking funds out, changing the terms if and when you need to. You gain privacy, as a trust does not pass through probate and become part of a public record.

Eventually, all assets in the trust will be included in your taxable estate. Meantime, the trust gives you an orderly way to manage those assets. If you name a successor trustee in the trust papers you set up, and if you later become physically or mentally unable to manage your assets, your successor trustee is authorized to manage them. When you die, the successor trustee transfers the trust property to your beneficiary without going through any court proceedings. Incidentally, your successor trustee is permitted to be a beneficiary.

How do you set up a trust? You must change the title to your assets so the trust has title. This will cost you some legal fees, and taking care of the bothersome details can be a nuisance, but—depending on your particular circumstances—it can be well worth the trouble.

> *Important*: Setting up a living trust does not free you from making a will, because you will continue to accumulate assets and you must provide instructions about them. What you do is state in your will that any property you own in your own name at the time when you die is to "pour over" into your trust.

What about taxes? If you establish a revocable living trust and are its sole beneficiary, you and the trust are considered to be a single taxable entity. On your income tax return, you report the income from the trust. The trust is not required to file a separate tax return.

○ ○ ○

FORTUNATELY, JAMES ESTABLISHED A TRUST

Living in San Francisco, Frank and James were thousands of miles away from James's family in Boston. Setting up a trust, James had named Frank as successor trustee. During James's long and devastating illness, Frank was able to take care of all the needed check-writing and keep up with the medical bills. But he took all the checks to James to sign, up until a few days before James died. This gave James the satisfaction of feeling that he was still able to take care of his own finances. Upon James's death, Frank was the beneficiary of what was left in the trust.

○ ○ ○

2. *The testamentary trust.* Your will establishes this trust. In fact, it can establish as many testamentary trusts as you think are needed, if you have the assets to support them. Nothing takes effect until you die. The advantage that you gain during your lifetime is that you know that after your death your assets will be managed in the way you want them to be managed.

3. *The charitable remainder trust.* This type of trust allows you to provide for yourself, a beneficiary, and a charity—all at the same time. You donate property to a trust. Income from the trust is paid in the form of an annuity to any beneficiary, which may or may not include yourself. The balance of the trust goes to the charity at the end of the specified term.

You receive a charitable deduction on your current tax return, that is equal to the present value of the charity's interest in your property. A charitable remainder can be used to avoid capital gains taxes on the sale of appreciated assets, such as stocks, bonds, and real estate. The trust can sell the appreciated asset and avoid the capital gains tax that you would have to pay if you sold it. Any appreciation in trust assets remains outside your estate for tax purposes.

What you are doing is providing income for yourself and your live-together at the same time you are receiving a tax benefit. In the end, the charity profits from your generosity by receiving the assets. This type of trust would be almost impossible to contest.

Retirement assets remaining at death.

Death before your required beginning date If the retirement assets are payable to your estate, all the money has to be paid to the estate by December 31 of the fifth anniversary of the date of death. This is called a five-year distribution rule. For instance, if you are 65 years old and die on July 1, 1996, the estate must receive the entire distribution by December 31 of 2001. The assets remaining in the retirement account continue to grow on a tax-deferred basis during this five-year period. Significant tax planning can be done during this period.

However, if you have named a beneficiary of your retirement accounts, the IRS allows two options for withdrawals:

1. The five-year distribution rule requires that withdrawals begin no later than December 31 of the fifth year following the year of your death.

2. The life expectancy rule allows payments to your beneficiary to be spread over his or her life but not beyond that. If your beneficiary elects the life expectancy option, he or she must make a *written* election no later than December 31 in the year following your death.

Your plan might be more restrictive than the IRS rules—providing only one option. If both options are available and your beneficiary fails to make a written election, the five-year rule applies. It is also possible that your plan limits the distribution to a 20-year period, even though your beneficiary's life expectancy is 40 years.

Death after required distribution date. If you die after distributions have begun, the method of distribution will depend on two factors: 1) whether you were using the recalculation method or the term-certain method, and 2) who is to receive the proceeds—a named beneficiary, a trust, or your estate. Using the recalculation method, your life expectancy is reduced to zero in the year following your death. The term-certain method survives death.

The recalculation method. Suppose you are over 70½ and you have started taking distributions from an IRA or 401(k) account using the recalculation method. Then suppose you die. If retirement assets are payable to a revocable trust, they will immediately be subject to income tax. Why? Because such a trust has a life expectancy of zero. Nor should you name your estate as beneficiary of your retirement assets, for it too has a life expectancy of zero. The retirement assets immediately become subject to income and estate taxes.

If withdrawals have been based on two lives, the beneficiary must use a single life expectancy at the death of the owner. Suppose you were 70½ when you started distributions and your partner was 55 at the time. And suppose you died after three years. Since the beneficiary was 55 years old when you began distributions, he or she would use a life expectancy of 28.6 years. Subtracting three years, the distribution of the remaining funds would be made over 25.6 years.

The term-certain method. With the term-certain method, however, the payouts to a beneficiary continue at the same pace as before.

HOW PAUL HANDLED HIS DISTRIBUTIONS

Paul, age 70½ named his 62-year-old partner, Bernard, as his designated beneficiary. He elected to make withdrawals on two lives, using a period of 24.9 years over which to receive required distributions. Paul died when he was 76. Starting in the calendar year following Paul's death, Bernard received minimum distributions from Paul's IRA.

The required minimum distribution was made over a 17.9-year term-certain period, based on the fact that Paul had elected the 24.9-year period and seven years of the term-certain period had elapsed. The balance that Bernard may use is 17.9 years.

If Paul, instead, had used the recalculation method, Bernard's withdrawals would have been based on Bernard's single life expectancy. At the time when minimum distributions were started, Bernard was 62 years old, with a life expectancy of 22.5 years. Since Paul lived for seven calendar years (i.e., age 70½ to age 76), Bernard's minimum distribution would have been determined by subtracting seven from 22.5 (Bernard's single life expectancy) so the distributions would be spread over 15.5 years, meaning he would have to take more out of the IRA each year than Paul had been taking out. Also the distributions would be taken out over a shorter period of time than with the term-certain method—15.5 years versus 17.9 years.

Upon the death of the beneficiary, any money that is left is paid to the estate over the remaining period, thus prolonging the tax-deferred growth.

WHAT HAPPENS TO PAUL'S IRA ACCOUNT AFTER BERNARD'S DEATH?

Assume that Bernard dies after receiving required minimum distributions from Paul's IRA over a five-year period. The required minimum distributions would be made to Bernard's estate over 12.9 years.

Initial term-certain period elected by Paul	24.9 years
Less: Years used by Paul	(7.0) years
Years used by Bernard	(5.0) years
Balance of term-certain period	12.9 years

If Bernard's executor does not want to keep Bernard's estate open for 12.9 years, he can accelerate the distributions from Paul's IRA to Bernard's estate or assign the rights to the future payments from Paul's IRA to the beneficiaries of Bernard's estate.

What if you have several beneficiaries?

If you die before the required date of distribution (April 1 of the year following the year when you reach age 70½), your beneficiaries can choose the five-year rule or the life expectancy rule. It is important to remind your beneficiaries that they must elect by a certain date. If more than one person is selected as a designated beneficiary, the period over which the required minimum distribution must be made to all of them is determined by the shortest life expectancy of any one of them. If, for example, you select as beneficiaries your 65-year-old partner with a life expectancy of 20 years and your son from your previous marriage, your son's required minimum distributions will be based upon a life expectancy of 20 years.

One way to avoid this situation is to establish two different accounts—one naming your partner as beneficiary and the other naming your son. Instead of having to use a life expectancy of 20 years, your 35-year-old son can use his own life expectancy of 47.3 years. The required annual minimum distributions will be substantially less, the balance in the account will continue to grow for a longer period on a tax-deferred basis, and conflict between a live-together and a child from a previous marriage can be avoided.

If you have already started to receive required minimum distributions using the term-certain method of distribution, the IRA accounts can be separated before your required date of distribution (April 1 of the year after you turn 70½) and each beneficiary can use his or her own life expectancy.

> *Note*: Beware the IRS. If you haven't planned carefully, income taxes and estate taxes can decimate your retirement accounts. Tax deferral is great but the IRS wants its share—if not while you are alive, then after your death. Plan ahead.

Estate taxes

Taxes are imposed on estates by the federal government and by many state governments. Let's look at each.

1. *Federal estate taxes*. When you die, the feds want to know the net worth of your taxable estate. If you leave total property worth less than $600,000, no tax is due. Above that, the tax rate begins at 37 percent and rises to a maximum of 55 percent on an estate with net worth greater than $3,000,000.

A key factor is the marital deduction. It protects a surviving spouse from having to pay any federal estate tax, as it exempts from taxation *all* property left to the spouse who survives. The marital deduction has become controversial because it is not available to people who are living together. It is one of the reasons why gay and lesbian couples want to be allowed to marry legally.

Certain items are deductible when calculating federal estate taxes: the expenses of a final illness, funeral costs, probate fees, certain debts, and any bequests made to tax-exempt charitable organizations.

What is not exempt? Your taxable estate will include all property that you owned legally at the time of death, any property that you have transferred but continue to control (e.g., property you have placed in a living trust), and property held in joint tenancy. The fact is that the total value of jointly held property—even though it stays out of probate—will be included in your taxable estate unless your surviving joint tenant can prove that he or she contributed in its purchase. If there is such proof, the tax on your estate will be reduced in proportion to your surviving joint tenant's share of ownership. Better keep good records.

2. *State inheritance taxes*. Many states impose estate taxes (some states call them death, estate, or succession taxes). And many discriminate against beneficiaries of wills who are not legal family members by imposing higher taxes on them. In fact, numbers of states use a sliding scale, providing classes of death tax exemptions that vary according to the legal relationship of the beneficiary to the deceased. The largest exemption goes to the surviving spouse, the next largest to children (whether natural or adopted), and smaller exemptions to such family members as surviving parents and brothers and sisters. In some states, a small exemption is allowed when property is left to a person who is not a member of the deceased's family—such as a live-together partner. The state where you legally reside at the time of your death is the state that gets the taxes.

Avoiding estate taxes

If all your reckoning shows that your estate is likely to have to pay some taxes, you can reduce that burden by several methods:

1. *Make tax-free gifts*. The law allows you to give as much as $10,000 a year to each of as many people as you want to, without having to file a gift-tax return. The recipient does not have to declare the money as income or pay income tax on it. If you give more than $10,000 to any one person, you must file a gift-tax return and the amount that exceeds $10,000 will be applied against the unified estate and gift tax.

Exhibit 25
UNIFIED FEDERAL ESTATE AND GIFT TAX RATE SCHEDULE

Column A	Column B	Column C	Column D
Total net taxable estate over	but not over	Tax on amount in Column A	Rate of tax on excess over amount in Column A (percent)
$0	$10,000	$0	18%
10,000	20,000	1,800	20
20,000	40,000	3,800	22
40,000	60,000	8,200	24
60,000	80,000	13,000	26
80,000	100,000	18,200	28
100,000	150,000	23,800	30
150,000	250,000	38,800	32
250,000	500,000	70,800	34
500,000	750,000	155,800	37
750,000	1,000,000	248,300	39
1,000,000	1,250,000	345,800	41
1,250,000	1,500,000	448,300	43
1,500,000	2,000,000	555,800	45
2,000,000	2,500,000	780,800	49
2,500,000	3,000,000	1,025,800	53
3,000,000	infinity	1,290,800	55

○ ○ ○

JACK'S ESTATE

To reduce his estate, because of a loss of certain estate-planning techniques that are not available to singles, Jack has been giving $10,000 annually to his children. Before taking minimum distributions from his $600,000 IRA, he has divided it into three separate, but equal, accounts—naming one of his three children as beneficiary of each account. He has specified the term-certain method of distribution. Upon his death, the life expectancy for each account will be figured separately. Conflicts among Jack's siblings can be avoided by separating the accounts, especially since their investment philosophies differ significantly.

○ ○ ○

The federal government has unified estate taxes and gift taxes. That means the same rates and the same dollar exemptions apply to each. But there is also a unified credit. For example, if Dick gives Dave $100,000 this year, the first $10,000 is exempt from any gift tax. But the remaining $90,000 is subject to taxation. Dick must use his unified credit against the tax owed on the $90,000 gift. The result is that he owes no gift tax now, but at his death only $510,000 of his estate (assuming that he makes no more gifts) can avoid estate taxes. Over time, if you have the money to give, you can give substantial amounts in this way—to your live-together, your children from an earlier marriage, or anyone else.

2. *Give life insurance.* Under federal law, the proceeds from a life insurance policy will not be included in your taxable estate if you do not own the policy. If you do already own a policy, you may transfer ownership to someone else at least three years before your death. If you owned it more recently, it will be included in your estate.

Warning: Before you transfer ownership of a life insurance policy, think it over carefully. The new owner can name the policy's beneficiaries (or change any you have named), borrow against the policy, select payment options, make premium payments, or surrender, convert, or cancel the policy. Furthermore, the gift of a life insurance policy is irrevocable. Once you do it, that's it. If you and the person you give it to should split, you cannot get the policy back.

An insurance policy can be owned, however, by someone other than the insured (usually, the owner and the insured are the same person). Such ownership can be in either of two ways:

First, someone who has what the insurance people call an "insurable interest" can take out and pay for insurance on another person's life. "Insurable interest" means that the buyer of the insurance and the person insured must either be married or have a business relationship. Some insurance companies are willing to let unmarried partners (i.e., live-togethers) buy insurance on each other. You might want to list each other, if one of you is buying a policy on the other's life, as "engaged," but don't claim to be married if you are not—that's falsifying information on your application form, a sure guarantee of trouble some time later. If you are a lesbian or gay couple, you can state truthfully that you are business partners if you own anything together.

Adult children from an earlier marriage can, of course, own a policy on your life. But if you want your live-together to get the proceeds, you have no control. Your children can change the beneficiary.

Second, even if you do not have an insurable interest, you can buy a policy and transfer its ownership to another person. The usual way to do this is to make it a gift to the new owner, who then becomes responsible for paying the premiums. Why go through this? Making someone else the owner keeps the proceeds from the policy out of your taxable estate.

3. *Create an irrevocable life insurance trust.* You set up a trust that owns the insurance policy. This keeps the proceeds out of your taxable estate. To pay the premiums, the trust uses funds that you have given it. Jack has done this in order to help pay federal estate taxes, as his estate will amount to more than $600,000.

○ ○ ○

JACK PRESERVES HIS ESTATE

Jack wants to take care of Bobbie, yet protect his estate for his kids and help pay federal estate taxes. The first thing he did, long before he met Bobbie, was establish a life insurance trust. Because much of his assets are in real estate and the federal taxes are due within nine months of death, the cash will provide his children the needed liquidity to pay the taxes. In addition, when he moved in with Bobbie, he gave her the money to buy an insurance policy on his life. He continues to give her money to pay the premium every year. The proceeds from both the trust and the policy will not be counted in his estate because he does not own them.

○ ○ ○

4. *Set up trusts.* You can minimize estate taxes by establishing an irrevocable living trust. But you give up control over assets that you may need in the future. And irrevocable is just that—you can't get it back. That fact excludes it from your estate, because you have relinquished all ownership rights and control of that particular property.

Exhibit 26

SIX WAYS TO TRANSFER YOUR PROPERTY

Method	What it does	Advantage	Disadvantage
Naming a beneficiary to insurance and retirement accounts	Transfer property after you die	• Easy to set up • Avoids probate	
Will	Transfer property after you die	• Only way to name a guardian for minor children • Can name specific beneficiaries	• Time and expense of probate • Can be contested
Joint tenancy	Surviving joint tenant takes title after you die	• Easy to set up • Avoids probate • Difficult to contest	• Does not avoid estate taxes
Living trust	Allows you to pass property directly to your beneficiaries	• Avoids probate • Allows you to control the property while you are still alive • Privacy • Difficult to contest	• Attorney's fees • Time and expense of retitling assets to go into trust • Management fees
Testamentary trust	Set up at your death. Funded by your estate. Names someone to manage the assets	• Protects inheritance for your beneficiaries, either children from a previous marriage or your partner • Difficult to contest	• Assets go through probate • Management fees
Life insurance trust	An irrevocable trust to hold life insurance	• Proceeds do not become part of your taxable estate • Difficult to contest	• Must be done three years before death if transferring existing policies • Can't have any ownership interest in policy • Can't name self or immediate family member as trustee

The bottom line is simple and obvious: If you know you are going to leave a substantial estate, see a lawyer who specializes in estate planning. If you have a substantial amount in retirement funds, consult with an attorney who is very knowledgeable in pension distributions.

CHAPTER FIFTEEN

EVALUATING YOUR ASSETS: ARE THEY FINANCIALLY FIT?

Probably each of you has come into the relationship with some assets—maybe a house, retirement plan, savings accounts, collectibles, stocks, and bonds. In the time you've been living together, you have probably acquired some assets together. Even if you have kept all assets separate, it is important now to evaluate them in two ways: first, in light of your own individual current needs and future objectives, and second, in view of the needs of the two of you together. The first—a look at your needs as an individual—should take precedence over the second for a very simple and practical reason: because the second—your joint needs—brings with it the possibility of problems if your relationship breaks up. If you are both in your forties, for instance, you may need more income together to maintain your lifestyle. But one of you may have a child or children whose educations have not been completed, so that you have a current need to help provide that education.

How often should you evaluate your assets? At least every two years, more frequently if your family situation, lifestyle, or the assets themselves are undergoing change.

What aspect of assets is the most important? The income they produce. Some assets, of course, are not income producing, but the idea of holding *any* asset is that eventually, on the day when you sell it, you will get back more than it cost you.

A popular term today is "asset allocation." This is Wall Street jargon's way of referring to how you line up assets and select investments in a portfolio to meet your current and future objectives. How, for example, will you allocate your assets among cash, stock equities, bonds, real estate, commodities, collectibles, etc.? The allocation you devise creates a picture: The portfolio that seeks income and safety of principal is a picture quite different from the one that seeks rapid growth.

At various stages of your life, varying needs dictate what you want assets to do for you. Sometimes income from wages or salary is enough to meet your needs. Sometimes it is not. If you have children in college, for example, or if you are in retirement, income from salary or from a pension may not be enough. Income from assets will then be extremely valuable.

Three ways to look at assets

Think of three things as you look at your assets: first, the assets themselves; second, your insurance program; and third, your retirement program. If you see that your assets are large, you can let your insurance plans and retirement program remain relatively small. If, on the other hand, you have rather small assets, it will be imperative to have insurance and retirement programs that are relatively large.

If you are young, you probably have few or very little income-producing assets. The two of you are working, producing two salaries, and, it is likely, spending as much as you can on non-income-producing assets such as your house and home furnishings and some collectibles. If so, this is the time to buy life insurance, while you can get the lower rates available to young people. You will start to build cash surrender values that will become important future assets.

If and when you make a commitment to a first home, your net worth picture changes dramatically. From this point on, you are likely to be putting the purchase of furniture and other household possessions ahead of buying personal possessions. Probably you will be piling up considerably more debt than you have in the past. Yet it is important at just this time to plan for assets that will help pay for your early retirement—15 or 20 years from now. As your income rises, you should keep an eye on your life insurance and the cash values it is building, to make sure it keeps pace. This is also the time to buy investments for growth. Later, as retirement time nears, you can realign them to produce more income.

Not many parents are able to pay college expenses out of their salaries. Income-producing assets, built up over several years, can help. In fact, one of life's pleasant surprises is the discovery, after devoting 15 or 20 years to developing assets that do produce income, that you do not have to go out and borrow at high interest rates to meet tuition payments.

When the nest empties

This is another time of change. From the day when you are relieved of education costs until you retire, you can again invest for growth and appreciation, building up your assets as your expenses drop. Living expenses should again be covered easily by salary, with some money left over to build up assets.

Now you can invest for capital appreciation, a stockpile that you will be able to convert to actual income in your retirement years. Credit-card debt and other such obligations should be kept as low as possible.

At this time, your Net Worth Statement will tell you how much your assets total, and your Spending Plan sheets will show what it costs you to maintain them.

Is it a sin to sell off assets? No. You bought them with your own money. You can do as you please with them. That is true even of a major asset such as your home. Think objectively about intangibles, too—such as insurance policies. When your dependents are no longer dependent on you, it is likely that you don't need the same high coverage you were smart to buy when they were kids in grade school.

Your Assets Evaluation Worksheet

Use this sheet to analyze your income-producing and non-income-producing assets. (Refer back to Exhibit 9 and 10 in chapter 7.)

Income-producing assets include your savings and checking accounts, etc., as you've listed them on your Net Worth Statement (page 26). You should be aware that, once you acquire them, these cost you nothing to own or maintain, except for broker's fees or commission. Fill in the annual income from the "sources of income" section of your Spending Plan. You can get yields from your record-keeping sheets.

Non-income-producing assets are your real estate, personal property, and other long-term assets—including fine art, antiques, stamp and coin collections, etc. Here you do incur some annual costs: taxes, utilities, insurance, and maintenance on the house; insurance on such personal property as an automobile or a boat. You should be tracking these costs on the fixed-expenses side of your Spending Plan.

What is net sale value? That's the amount you would receive if you sold a particular asset. Example: the market value of your home, less such selling costs as a realtor's commission, attorney's fees, and so on. When you sell collectibles, too, you may run into paying some fees.

Analyzing assets in retirement

When you contemplate retirement, it is time to make your money work hard for you. Now you will find that your Asset Evaluation Worksheets really prove their worth. They not only sum up the acquisitions you have made, over perhaps as long as 40 years. They also raise a number of questions, helping you to look carefully at each and every asset and think objectively about it. The basic question, always, is this: Should you exchange your assets, whether income-producing or non-income-producing, for something that can produce additional income or give you some other benefit?

When you are retirement age, it is not always easy to change your way of thinking about money matters. If you have invested in such safe institutions as passbook savings for 30 or 40 years, you may not find it easy to put your money into a money-market fund. And it is so easy to resist change.

Worksheet XV:
ASSETS EVALUATION

INCOME-PRODUCING ASSETS CURRENT ASSETS	NET SALE VALUE	ANNUAL INCOME (From Budget)	% YIELD (Income ÷ Market Value)	ANNUAL COST OF OWNERSHIP (From Budget)
Checking Accounts				
Savings Accounts				
Credit Union Accounts				
Money Market Funds				
Certificates of Deposit				
Treasury Bills				
Treasury Notes				
Securities				
Stocks				
Bonds				
Mutual Funds				
Total				
NON-INCOME-PRODUCING				
Personal Residence				
Recreational Property				
Cash Value Life Insurance				
Business Interests				
Home Furnishings				
Automobiles				
Jewelry				
Antiques—Fine Art				
Coin Collection				
Stamp Collection				
Total				

But the practical reality is that it makes sense to take hard-earned dollars out of some low-income-producing account and make them work harder for you. In fact, it is a must.

You don't have to look far to find the way to create a better lifestyle. Just look at your assets. What do they offer? Can you induce those that now produce income to produce more? Are you keeping too much cash in a checking account where it earns no interest? Can't you force yourself to move all extra money over into a savings account, and then transfer cash into checking only when you must use it?

How about the savings account—are you keeping too much in an account that yields the lowest interest?

Why not buy a certificate of deposit, or move into a money-market fund that produces greater income? By all means, keep your money where it is reasonably available if you need it, but do some research to find the highest interest rates without tying it up for long periods.

Then, look at any stocks and bonds you bought years ago. Are they low-income investments? Are you holding onto low-interest bonds? Many people do, for no good reason. Safe-deposit boxes often contain long-forgotten Series EE bonds. And there are those folks who think they shouldn't sell certain stocks because they bought them at such low prices years ago, and if they sell them now they will have to pay taxes on them. But the fact that you must pay taxes is never a good reason for not selling—if it is time to sell.

More income from assets

How can you make your assets produce more income? Let us count the ways.

1. *Stocks.* Let's assume you own stocks that originally cost you $10,000. And suppose these stocks have been yielding 5 percent annually. Now suppose you sell them for $25,000. At 5 percent, the yield would be $1,250. And the difference between your buying price and your selling price is a taxable capital gain of $15,000.

When you make that sale, if you are paying tax at 23 percent, you will have $21,570 ready to reinvest after taxes. And if you put that money into investments that pay 8 percent, your income will be $1,725. That's $476 more than you were getting before.

2. *Bonds.* Here's another reason why paying taxes should not keep you from selling stocks or bonds. Suppose you are one of the many people who bought a bond when interest rates were low. It may now be worth less on the open market than when you bought it. That means you can take a loss if you sell it before maturity.

Let's say you bought a corporate bond for $10,000 but it is now worth only $7,500 on the market. You've lost $2,500. But you can apply that loss to your $15,000 gain from selling stocks, so your total taxable gain is reduced to $12,500. Remember, however, that live-togethers are not allowed to file joint tax returns. If a married spouse has a loss while his or her mate has a gain, the loss may offset the gain. Not so with live-togethers.

3. *Non-income-producing assets.* What about assets that are not producing income? What are your choices with them? Is there a way to invest for more income? How can you turn an asset that costs a lot to own into an asset that produces income? Check out the following:

> **SUPPOSE YOU BOUGHT A CONDO . . .**
>
> Here's a possible scenario. You sell the current house for $80,000 and buy a small condominium for $50,000. You invest the $30,000 difference at 8 percent, so it produces $2,400 a year in income. And, since the condo is sure to cost less than your house did to maintain, you pick up some nice savings on expenses.
>
> Or: You sell the house for $80,000 and invest the entire $80,000 at 8 percent, producing an income of $6,400 a year. That can pay rent of $533 every month. If you rent for less, you have more income.

a. *Your home.* This is probably your largest investment. It also carries the heaviest expenses: fuel, taxes, insurance, maintenance. Are you and your live-together fed up with emptying the gutters and trying to knock out the crabgrass? Wondering whether the roof can go another winter without reshingling? Rattling around inside more room than you need nowadays? Keeping too much money tied up in this non-income-producing asset?

You might sell the house and invest in another that's smaller, giving you leftover money to invest in other ways. Or, if the cost as about the same, you would still gain because you'd have lower upkeep on a newer, smaller house.

You might sell and try a mobile home—if you live where they are suitable and popular.

You might sell and invest the money, using the income to pay rent.

One caution on selling your house. You will face certain selling expenses: Realtor's commission, lawyer's closing fees, moving expenses (moving is not cheap; the cost depends on how much you move how far), plus a miscellany of expenses ranging from carpeting and draperies to landscaping. Be sure to plan a contingency amount (at least 10 percent of the total of all these other expenses) for the unforeseen.

If you are considering a major geographic move to an area you don't know, try a shakedown cruise. Get familiar with the place under its worst conditions: Florida or Arizona in midsummer, the Carolinas' coast in August, mile-high Denver in February. See how you like it.

Then think about taxes. Get the tax forms of any state you are serious about moving to. The state's department of taxation, in its capital, will send them. Fill out a set as if you were a resident, so you see just what taxes you must pay if you live there.

You don't want two different states trying to tax you. So as soon as you actually move, be sure to register to vote, change your auto registration and driver's licenses to your new state, and open local bank accounts. Update your will to include the new address. If you are keeping a home in your former state—such as a vacation home—establish records that make it clear that your primary residence is now in the new state.

New residence? New questions

Any move to an unfamiliar state is sure to raise some important questions:

- Does it tax Social Security benefits?
- What about capital gains, dividends, or interest? Suppose you are moving to where capital gains are taxed more heavily than in the state you are leaving. In that case, *before* the move, get rid of any assets that you plan to sell anyway. Got municipal bonds? If they are tax-free where you now live, they may be taxed where you are going. Check it out.
- Next—pension taxes. Chances are, if you are now getting monthly payments, the pension company is not withholding income taxes. But state law probably considers your pension money as taxable income. Lump-sum distributions are a particular headache. Get good advice from your accountant or lawyer.
- Don't forget estate taxes. They vary from no tax in some states to heavy inheritance taxes in others. A major determining factor in many states is the status of heirs—offspring or spouse?
- What are the *latest* tax laws where you're going? States, like the federal government, are always changing tax laws. So do some research, or check in with a competent accountant in your target area, to see not only what has changed lately but what is likely to change in the near future.

○ ○ ○

WHEN LOUISE AND FRED MOVED TO FLORIDA

Louise was a 57-year-old widow left with a home in a New Jersey suburb. She could receive reduced Social Security benefits at age 60, or full benefits at 65. Fred's wife died soon after he retired at 63. Both couples had been longtime friends and had worked together on many activities at their church, beginning way back when their children were in Sunday school. Soon Louise and Fred were, as she put it, "just like high-school kids—going steady." They agreed to sell their homes, each taking the $125,000 capital-gains allowance, and move to Florida, where they would face no state income tax and property taxes would be lower than almost anywhere else, and the general cost of living would be lower. They pooled the gains they had on their houses after taxes and bought a comfortable home—smaller than either had sold, but big enough for grandchildren's visits. They did not marry, for Louise would lose her late husband's Social Security benefits if she married before she was 60. She even figured that her benefits as a widow would be greater than as Fred's wife. They counted on that money to provide them airfare to visit their children and grandchildren, who, they were sure, could not manage to make trips to Florida frequently enough to keep doting grandparents happy.

○ ○ ○

b. *Recreational property.* The cottage at the lake or shore, the ski hut or condo in New England or northern Michigan—are you using it as much as you once did? Is its expense justifiable? Probably it's a chore to rent it, and, if you do rent it, you have to take care of its maintenance by remote control, which is an extra burden. Then there's the insurance. And the property taxes. So maybe you're not getting enough out of it and it's time to sell it so you can reinvest the proceeds to produce some real income.

c. *Cash value life insurance.* Do you really need this insurance at this time in your life or lives? Is it paid up? Or are you still writing checks for premiums? Every policy has a table of guaranteed values, remember. Check yours. For example, for a $10,000 policy bought at age 35, the following are some of the options available at age 65:

1. Cancel the policy. On your $10,000 policy, the cash surrender value is $5,504. If the beneficiary is your live-together, that person would lose $4,496 ($10,000 minus $5,584). But by surrendering the policy, you save $230 annually. You invest the $5,504 at 8 percent, producing $440 a year. Add that to the premium saving of $230, and you have $670 per year that you do not now have.

2. Borrow on the policy. Suppose you borrow the full amount of the cash value: $5,504. This will leave $4,496 of insurance in force. You must still pay the $230 premium, however, and you will have to pay interest—probably $275 a year—to borrow the $5,504. That means that, with paying the interest and the premium, your

income from the investment will be reduced to $229—an expensive way to keep $4,496 of insurance in force.

3. Take out a reduced paid-up policy. The $10,000 will probably provide about $7,860 in paid-up insurance—a significantly smaller policy, and you save only the $230 annual premium.

4. Use cash value to buy a term policy. See the policy's table of guaranteed values. It tells you the length of the term you can get for the cash value, in years, months, and days. $10,000 of cash value at age 65 might buy 16 years and 147 days of term coverage. If you should live longer than that, however, the policy would have expired and you would be without further coverage.

5. Buy an annuity. Your policy probably also states how large an annuity you can get for each $1,000 of cash value. If you want an annuity, start shopping around. You do not have to buy it from your present insurance company. Rather, you may cash in the policy and take the money to a company that gives you more per $1,000. Go make your best deal.

d. *Collectibles.* Are you still getting the same satisfactions from these that you once did? Holding them for children who may or may not have the same interest? Paying for insurance coverage on them? Cleaning, dusting, polishing them regularly? And getting no income from your fine art, books, coins and stamps, period antique furniture, silverware and gold pieces, and vintage cars? Maybe it's time to let go and pare down.

Talk to each other. Does your partner want some of your collectibles? Do you have grown offspring who want some? If the value of an item or a collection is sentimental and emotional rather than intrinsic and remunerative, find out now who wants it. And don't be shocked to learn that many young people are not interested in polishing the sterling silver or preserving the antiques. And, in the final analysis, remember that only you can make the judgment on whether to hold on to them or cash them in and put the money into income-producing investments.

If you decide to sell, do your homework. Get appraisals. Don't be surprised that silver and gold may not be paying as much as they did a few years ago, but bear in mind that in any liquidation you have to deal in terms of today's prices.

○ ○ ○

LOUISE AND FRED IN FLORIDA—WITH POSSESSIONS IN NEW JERSEY

When Louise and Fred moved to Florida, they put Louise's heirloom silver (handed down from her grandmother) in a vault in New Jersey because they didn't really have room for it and her two sons had wives who already

Exhibit 27
DIPPING INTO YOUR NEST EGG
(Based on an interest rate of 7% per year compounded quarterly)

STARTING WITH A LUMP SUM OF . . .	. . . YOU CAN WITHDRAW THIS MUCH EACH MONTH FOR THE STATED NUMBER OF YEARS, REDUCING THE NEST EGG TO ZERO					. . . OR YOU CAN WITHDRAW THIS MUCH EACH MONTH AND ALWAYS HAVE THE ORIGINAL NEST EGG INTACT.
	10 YRS.	15 YRS.	20 YRS.	25 YRS.	30 YRS.	
$ 10,000	$ 116	$ 89	$68	$ 70	$ 66	$ 59
15,000	174	134	116	106	99	88
20,000	232	179	155	141	133	118
25,000	290	224	193	176	166	142
30,000	348	269	232	212	199	179
40,000	464	359	310	282	266	237
50,000	580	448	386	352	332	285
60,000	696	538	464	424	398	360
80,000	928	718	620	564	532	467
100,000	1,160	896	772	704	668	585

had full complements of silverware. Louise couldn't bear to sell it. The dilemma hangs over them: Whether to authorize someone in New Jersey to get the silver out and put it up for sale, or have it sent to Florida and somehow cope with it, or leave it up to the executor of Louise's will to liquidate it and add the proceeds to her estate. Fred says it's Louise's decision to make. Meantime, he and Louise keep house using the silverware he and his late wife received as wedding presents nearly 40 years ago.

❍ ❍ ❍

Why not invade principal?

Many a retiree remembers vividly the cautious advice of his or her grandparents: Never touch principal—you can live off income from investments, but don't invade your principal amount. That advice is all right in theory, but what is really important is to protect your quality of life. If, for example, you spend just 3 percent of your capital each year, it would take you 33 years to use up a given amount even if the remaining balance were not earning annual interest.

Some people have the fixed idea that they should not invade principal because they should leave it for their children, grandchildren, nieces, and nephews. But there is, in most cases, no reason to lay that guilt trip on yourself, especially if it reduces your quality of life. You did the work. You earned it. The principal is yours.

As you review your assets and ponder all these factors, check out your life expectancy on the insurance charts. For the average man of 68, it is 12 years. Suppose you make that 24 years, just double what the insurance experts predict. Then suppose you decide to use a certain percentage of your total capital each year for 24 years. Thinking that way could help you fight inflation's inevitable drain on your retirement income and improve your standard of living in the years ahead.

A final word

You are the only one who knows your needs. Your live-together partner knows them, but not as well as you do. So do the paperwork. Talk to dependable advisers and to blood relatives—if their advice can be helpful, but not if they are blood relatives who want to bleed or manipulate you. Find advisers who understand your point of view.

APPENDIXES

LIFE EXPECTANCY TABLES

TABLE I
(Single Life Expectancy)*

AGE	DIVISOR	AGE	DIVISOR
35	47.3	73	13.9
36	46.4	74	13.2
37	45.4	75	12.5
38	44.4	76	11.9
39	43.5	77	11.2
40	42.5	78	10.6
41	41.5	79	10.0
42	40.6	80	9.5
43	39.6	81	8.9
44	38.7	82	8.4
45	37.7	83	7.9
46	36.8	84	7.4
47	35.9	85	6.9
48	34.9	86	6.5
49	34.0	87	6.1
50	33.1	88	5.7
51	32.2	89	5.3
52	31.3	90	5.0
53	30.4	91	4.7
54	29.5	92	4.4
55	28.6	93	4.1
56	27.7	94	3.9
57	26.8	95	3.7
58	25.9	96	3.4
59	25.0	97	3.2
60	24.2	98	3.0
61	23.3	99	2.8
62	22.5	100	2.7
63	21.6	101	2.5
64	20.8	102	2.3
65	20.0	103	2.1
66	19.2	104	1.9
67	18.4	105	1.8
68	17.6	106	1.6
69	16.8	107	1.4
70	16.0	108	1.3
71	15.3	109	1.1
72	14.6	110	1.0

* Table I does not provide for IRA owners younger than 35 years of age. For additional life expectancy tables, see Publication 939.

TABLE II
(Joint Life and Last Survivor Expectancy)*

AGES	35	36	37	38	39	40	41	42	43	44
35	54.0	53.5	53.0	52.6	52.2	51.8	51.4	51.1	50.8	50.5
36	53.5	53.0	52.5	52.0	51.6	51.2	50.8	50.4	50.1	49.8
37	53.0	52.5	52.0	51.5	51.0	50.6	50.2	49.8	49.5	49.1
38	52.6	52.0	51.5	51.0	50.5	50.0	49.6	49.2	48.8	48.5
39	52.2	51.6	51.0	50.5	50.0	49.5	49.1	48.6	48.2	47.8
40	51.8	51.2	50.6	50.0	49.5	49.0	48.5	48.1	47.6	47.2
41	51.4	50.8	50.2	49.6	49.1	48.5	48.0	47.5	47.1	46.7
42	51.1	50.4	49.8	49.2	48.6	48.1	47.5	47.0	46.6	46.1
43	50.8	50.1	49.5	48.8	48.2	47.6	47.1	46.6	46.0	45.6
44	50.5	49.8	49.1	48.5	47.8	47.2	46.7	46.1	45.6	45.1
45	50.2	49.5	48.8	48.1	47.5	46.9	46.3	45.7	45.1	44.6
46	50.0	49.2	48.5	47.8	47.2	46.5	45.9	45.3	44.7	44.1
47	49.7	49.0	48.3	47.5	46.8	46.2	45.5	44.9	44.3	43.7
48	49.5	48.8	48.0	47.3	46.6	45.9	45.2	44.5	43.9	43.3
49	49.3	48.5	47.8	47.0	46.3	45.6	44.9	44.2	43.6	42.9
50	49.2	48.4	47.6	46.8	46.0	45.3	44.6	43.9	43.2	42.6
51	49.0	48.2	47.4	46.6	45.8	45.1	44.3	43.6	42.9	42.2
52	48.8	48.0	47.2	46.4	45.6	44.8	44.1	43.3	42.6	41.9
53	48.7	47.9	47.0	46.2	45.4	44.6	43.9	43.1	42.4	41.7
54	48.6	47.7	46.9	46.0	45.2	44.4	43.6	42.9	42.1	41.4
55	48.5	47.6	46.7	45.9	45.1	44.2	43.4	42.7	41.9	41.2
56	48.3	47.5	46.6	45.8	44.9	44.1	43.3	42.5	41.7	40.9
57	48.3	47.4	46.5	45.6	44.8	43.9	43.1	42.3	41.5	40.7
58	48.2	47.3	46.4	45.5	44.7	43.8	43.0	42.1	41.3	40.5
59	48.1	47.2	46.3	45.4	44.5	43.7	42.8	42.0	41.2	40.4
60	48.0	47.1	46.2	45.3	44.4	43.6	42.7	41.9	41.0	40.2
61	47.9	47.0	46.1	45.2	44.3	43.5	42.6	41.7	40.9	40.0
62	47.9	47.0	46.0	45.1	44.2	43.4	42.5	41.6	40.8	39.9
63	47.8	46.9	46.0	45.1	44.2	43.3	42.4	41.5	40.6	39.8
64	47.8	46.8	45.9	45.0	44.1	43.2	42.3	41.4	40.5	39.7
65	47.7	46.8	45.9	44.9	44.0	43.1	42.2	41.3	40.4	39.6
66	47.7	46.7	45.8	44.9	44.0	43.1	42.2	41.3	40.4	39.5
67	47.6	46.7	45.8	44.8	43.9	43.0	42.1	41.2	40.3	39.4
68	47.6	46.7	45.7	44.8	43.9	42.9	42.0	41.1	40.2	39.3
69	47.6	46.6	45.7	44.8	43.8	42.9	42.0	41.1	40.2	39.3
70	47.5	46.6	45.7	44.7	43.8	42.9	41.9	41.0	40.1	39.2
71	47.5	46.6	45.6	44.7	43.8	42.8	41.9	41.0	40.1	39.1
72	47.5	46.6	45.6	44.7	43.7	42.8	41.9	40.9	40.0	39.1
73	47.5	46.5	45.6	44.6	43.7	42.8	41.8	40.9	40.0	39.0
74	47.5	46.5	45.6	44.6	43.7	42.7	41.8	40.9	39.9	39.0
75	47.4	46.5	45.5	44.6	43.6	42.7	41.8	40.8	39.9	39.0
76	47.4	46.5	45.5	44.6	43.6	42.7	41.7	40.8	39.9	38.9
77	47.4	46.5	45.5	44.6	43.6	42.7	41.7	40.8	39.8	38.9
78	47.4	46.4	45.5	44.5	43.6	42.6	41.7	40.7	39.8	38.9
79	47.4	46.4	45.5	44.5	43.6	42.6	41.7	40.7	39.8	38.9
80	47.4	46.4	45.5	44.5	43.6	42.6	41.7	40.7	39.8	38.8
81	47.4	46.4	45.5	44.5	43.5	42.6	41.6	40.7	39.8	38.8
82	47.4	46.4	45.4	44.5	43.5	42.6	41.6	40.7	39.7	38.8
83	47.4	46.4	45.4	44.5	43.5	42.6	41.6	40.7	39.7	38.8
84	47.4	46.4	45.4	44.5	43.5	42.6	41.6	40.7	39.7	38.8
85	47.4	46.4	45.4	44.5	43.5	42.6	41.6	40.7	39.7	38.8
86	47.3	46.4	45.4	44.5	43.5	42.5	41.6	40.6	39.7	38.8
87	47.3	46.4	45.4	44.5	43.5	42.5	41.6	40.6	39.7	38.7
88	47.3	46.4	45.4	44.5	43.5	42.5	41.6	40.6	39.7	38.7
89	47.3	46.4	45.4	44.4	43.5	42.5	41.6	40.6	39.7	38.7
90	47.3	46.4	45.4	44.4	43.5	42.5	41.6	40.6	39.7	38.7
91	47.3	46.4	45.4	44.4	43.5	42.5	41.6	40.6	39.7	38.7
92	47.3	46.4	45.4	44.4	43.5	42.5	41.6	40.6	39.7	38.7

* Table II does not provide for IRA owners or survivors younger than 35 years of age. For additional life expectancy tables, see IRS Publication 939.

TABLE II (continued)
(Joint Life and Last Survivor Expectancy)

AGES	45	46	47	48	49	50	51	52	53	54
45	44.1	43.6	43.2	42.7	42.3	42.0	41.6	41.3	41.0	40.7
46	43.6	43.1	42.6	42.2	41.8	41.4	41.0	40.6	40.3	40.0
47	43.2	42.6	42.1	41.7	41.2	40.8	40.4	40.0	39.7	39.3
48	42.7	42.2	41.7	41.2	40.7	40.2	39.8	39.4	39.0	38.7
49	42.3	41.8	41.2	40.7	40.2	39.7	39.3	38.8	38.4	38.1
50	42.0	41.4	40.8	40.2	39.7	39.2	38.7	38.3	37.9	37.5
51	41.6	41.0	40.4	39.8	39.3	38.7	38.2	37.8	37.3	36.9
52	41.3	40.6	40.0	39.4	38.8	38.3	37.8	37.3	36.8	36.4
53	41.0	40.3	39.7	39.0	38.4	37.9	37.3	36.8	36.3	35.8
54	40.7	40.0	39.3	38.7	38.1	37.5	36.9	36.4	35.8	35.3
55	40.4	39.7	39.0	38.4	37.7	37.1	36.5	35.9	35.4	34.9
56	40.2	39.5	38.7	38.1	37.4	36.8	36.1	35.6	35.0	34.4
57	40.0	39.2	38.5	37.8	37.1	36.4	35.8	35.2	34.6	34.0
58	39.7	39.0	38.2	37.5	36.8	36.1	35.5	34.8	34.2	33.6
59	39.6	38.8	38.0	37.3	36.6	35.9	35.2	34.5	33.9	33.3
60	39.4	38.6	37.8	37.1	36.3	35.6	34.9	34.2	33.6	32.9
61	39.2	38.4	37.6	36.9	36.1	35.4	34.6	33.9	33.3	32.6
62	39.1	38.3	37.5	36.7	35.9	35.1	34.4	33.7	33.0	32.3
63	38.9	38.1	37.3	36.5	35.7	34.9	34.2	33.5	32.7	32.0
64	38.8	38.0	37.2	36.3	35.5	34.8	34.0	33.2	32.5	31.8
65	38.7	37.9	37.0	36.2	35.4	34.6	33.8	33.0	32.3	31.6
66	38.6	37.8	36.9	36.1	35.2	34.4	33.6	32.9	32.1	31.4
67	38.5	37.7	36.8	36.0	35.1	34.3	33.5	32.7	31.9	31.2
68	38.4	37.6	36.7	35.8	35.0	34.2	33.4	32.5	31.8	31.0
69	38.4	37.5	36.6	35.7	34.9	34.1	33.2	32.4	31.6	30.8
70	38.3	37.4	36.5	35.7	34.8	34.0	33.1	32.3	31.5	30.7
71	38.2	37.3	36.5	35.6	34.7	33.9	33.0	32.2	31.4	30.5
72	38.2	37.3	36.4	35.5	34.6	33.8	32.9	32.1	31.2	30.4
73	38.1	37.2	36.3	35.4	34.6	33.7	32.8	32.0	31.1	30.3
74	38.1	37.2	36.3	35.4	34.5	33.6	32.8	31.9	31.1	30.2
75	38.1	37.1	36.2	35.3	34.5	33.6	32.7	31.8	31.0	30.1
76	38.0	37.1	36.2	35.3	34.4	33.5	32.6	31.8	30.9	30.1
77	38.0	37.1	36.2	35.3	34.4	33.5	32.6	31.7	30.8	30.0
78	38.0	37.0	36.1	35.2	34.3	33.4	32.5	31.7	30.8	29.9
79	37.9	37.0	36.1	35.2	34.3	33.4	32.5	31.6	30.7	29.9
80	37.9	37.0	36.1	35.2	34.2	33.4	32.5	31.6	30.7	29.8
81	37.9	37.0	36.0	35.1	34.2	33.3	32.4	31.5	30.7	29.8
82	37.9	36.9	36.0	35.1	34.2	33.3	32.4	31.5	30.6	29.7
83	37.9	36.9	36.0	35.1	34.2	33.3	32.4	31.5	30.6	29.7
84	37.8	36.9	36.0	35.1	34.2	33.2	32.3	31.4	30.6	29.7
85	37.8	36.9	36.0	35.1	34.1	33.2	32.3	31.4	30.5	29.6
86	37.8	36.9	36.0	35.0	34.1	33.2	32.3	31.4	30.5	29.6
87	37.8	36.9	35.9	35.0	34.1	33.2	32.3	31.4	30.5	29.6
88	37.8	36.9	35.9	35.0	34.1	33.2	32.3	31.4	30.5	29.6
89	37.8	36.9	35.9	35.0	34.1	33.2	32.3	31.4	30.5	29.6
90	37.8	36.9	35.9	35.0	34.1	33.2	32.3	31.3	30.5	29.6
91	37.8	36.8	35.9	35.0	34.1	33.2	32.2	31.3	30.4	29.5
92	37.8	36.8	35.9	35.0	34.1	33.2	32.2	31.3	30.4	29.5

TABLE II (continued)
(Joint Life and Last Survivor Expectancy)

AGES	55	56	57	58	59	60	61	62	63	64	65	66	67	68	69	70	71	72	73	74
55	34.4	33.9	33.5	33.1	32.7	32.3	32.0	31.7	31.4	31.1										
56	33.9	33.4	33.0	32.5	32.1	31.7	31.4	31.0	30.7	30.4										
57	33.5	33.0	32.5	32.0	31.6	31.2	30.8	30.4	30.1	29.8										
58	33.1	32.5	32.0	31.5	31.1	30.6	30.2	29.9	29.5	29.2										
59	32.7	32.1	31.6	31.1	30.6	30.1	29.7	29.3	28.9	28.6										
60	32.3	31.7	31.2	30.6	30.1	29.7	29.2	28.8	28.4	28.0										
61	32.0	31.4	30.8	30.2	29.7	29.2	28.7	28.3	27.8	27.4										
62	31.7	31.0	30.4	29.9	29.3	28.8	28.3	27.8	27.3	26.9										
63	31.4	30.7	30.1	29.5	28.9	28.4	27.8	27.3	26.9	26.4										
64	31.1	30.4	29.8	29.2	28.6	28.0	27.4	26.9	26.4	25.9										
65	30.9	30.2	29.5	28.9	28.2	27.6	27.1	26.5	26.0	25.5	25.0	24.6	24.2	23.8	23.4	23.1	22.8	22.5	22.2	22.0
66	30.6	29.9	29.2	28.6	27.9	27.3	26.7	26.1	25.6	25.1	24.6	24.1	23.7	23.3	22.9	22.5	22.2	21.9	21.6	21.4
67	30.4	29.7	29.0	28.3	27.6	27.0	26.4	25.8	25.2	24.7	24.2	23.7	23.2	22.8	22.4	22.0	21.7	21.3	21.0	20.8
68	30.2	29.5	28.8	28.1	27.4	26.7	26.1	25.5	24.9	24.3	23.8	23.3	22.8	22.3	21.9	21.5	21.2	20.8	20.5	20.2
69	30.1	29.3	28.6	27.8	27.1	26.5	25.8	25.2	24.6	24.0	23.4	22.9	22.4	21.9	21.5	21.1	20.7	20.3	20.0	19.6
70	29.9	29.1	28.4	27.6	26.9	26.2	25.6	24.9	24.3	23.7	23.1	22.5	22.0	21.5	21.1	20.6	20.2	19.8	19.4	19.1
71	29.7	29.0	28.2	27.5	26.7	26.0	25.3	24.7	24.0	23.4	22.8	22.2	21.7	21.2	20.7	20.2	19.8	19.4	19.0	18.6
72	29.6	28.8	28.1	27.3	26.5	25.8	25.1	24.4	23.8	23.1	22.5	21.9	21.3	20.8	20.3	19.8	19.4	18.9	18.5	18.2
73	29.5	28.7	27.9	27.1	26.4	25.6	24.9	24.2	23.5	22.9	22.2	21.6	21.0	20.5	20.0	19.4	19.0	18.5	18.1	17.7
74	29.4	28.6	27.8	27.0	26.2	25.5	24.7	24.0	23.3	22.7	22.0	21.4	20.8	20.2	19.6	19.1	18.6	18.2	17.7	17.3
75	29.3	28.5	27.7	26.9	26.1	25.3	24.6	23.8	23.1	22.4	21.8	21.1	20.5	19.9	19.3	18.8	18.3	17.8	17.3	16.9
76	29.2	28.4	27.6	26.8	26.0	25.2	24.4	23.7	23.0	22.3	21.6	20.9	20.3	19.7	19.1	18.5	18.0	17.5	17.0	16.5
77	29.1	28.3	27.5	26.7	25.9	25.1	24.3	23.6	22.8	22.1	21.4	20.7	20.1	19.4	18.8	18.3	17.7	17.2	16.7	16.2
78	29.1	28.2	27.4	26.6	25.8	25.0	24.2	23.4	22.7	21.9	21.2	20.5	19.9	19.2	18.6	18.0	17.5	16.9	16.4	15.9
79	29.0	28.2	27.3	26.5	25.7	24.9	24.1	23.3	22.6	21.8	21.1	20.4	19.7	19.0	18.4	17.8	17.2	16.7	16.1	15.6
80	29.0	28.1	27.3	26.4	25.6	24.8	24.0	23.2	22.4	21.7	21.0	20.2	19.5	18.9	18.2	17.6	17.0	16.4	15.9	15.4
81	28.9	28.1	27.2	26.4	25.5	24.7	23.9	23.1	22.3	21.6	20.8	20.1	19.4	18.7	18.1	17.4	16.8	16.2	15.7	15.1
82	28.9	28.0	27.2	26.3	25.5	24.6	23.8	23.0	22.3	21.5	20.7	20.0	19.3	18.6	17.9	17.3	16.6	16.0	15.5	14.9
83	28.8	28.0	27.1	26.3	25.4	24.6	23.8	23.0	22.2	21.4	20.6	19.9	19.2	18.5	17.8	17.1	16.5	15.9	15.3	14.7
84	28.8	27.9	27.1	26.2	25.4	24.5	23.7	22.9	22.1	21.3	20.5	19.8	19.1	18.4	17.7	17.0	16.3	15.7	15.1	14.5
85	28.8	27.9	27.0	26.2	25.3	24.5	23.7	22.8	22.0	21.3	20.5	19.7	19.0	18.3	17.6	16.9	16.2	15.6	15.0	14.4
86	28.7	27.9	27.0	26.1	25.3	24.5	23.6	22.8	22.0	21.2	20.4	19.6	18.9	18.2	17.5	16.8	16.1	15.5	14.8	14.2
87	28.7	27.8	27.0	26.1	25.3	24.4	23.6	22.8	21.9	21.1	20.4	19.6	18.8	18.1	17.4	16.7	16.0	15.4	14.7	14.1
88	28.7	27.8	27.0	26.1	25.2	24.4	23.5	22.7	21.9	21.1	20.3	19.5	18.8	18.0	17.3	16.6	15.9	15.3	14.6	14.0
89	28.7	27.8	26.9	26.1	25.2	24.4	23.5	22.7	21.9	21.1	20.3	19.5	18.7	18.0	17.2	16.5	15.8	15.2	14.5	13.9
90	28.7	27.8	26.9	26.1	25.2	24.3	23.5	22.7	21.8	21.0	20.2	19.4	18.7	17.9	17.2	16.5	15.8	15.1	14.5	13.8
91	28.7	27.8	26.9	26.0	25.2	24.3	23.5	22.6	21.8	21.0	20.2	19.4	18.6	17.9	17.1	16.4	15.7	15.0	14.4	13.7
92	28.6	27.8	26.9	26.0	25.2	24.3	23.5	22.6	21.8	21.0	20.2	19.4	18.6	17.8	17.1	16.4	15.7	15.0	14.3	13.7
93	28.6	27.8	26.9	26.0	25.1	24.3	23.4	22.6	21.8	20.9	20.1	19.3	18.6	17.8	17.1	16.3	15.6	14.9	14.3	13.6
94	28.6	27.7	26.9	26.0	25.1	24.3	23.4	22.6	21.7	20.9	20.1	19.3	18.5	17.8	17.0	16.3	15.6	14.9	14.2	13.6
95	28.6	27.7	26.9	26.0	25.1	24.3	23.4	22.6	21.7	20.9	20.1	19.3	18.5	17.8	17.0	16.3	15.6	14.9	14.2	13.5
96	28.6	27.7	26.9	26.0	25.1	24.2	23.4	22.6	21.7	20.9	20.1	19.3	18.5	17.7	17.0	16.2	15.5	14.8	14.2	13.5
97	28.6	27.7	26.8	26.0	25.1	24.2	23.4	22.5	21.7	20.9	20.1	19.3	18.5	17.7	17.0	16.2	15.5	14.8	14.1	13.5
98	28.6	27.7	26.8	26.0	25.1	24.2	23.4	22.5	21.7	20.9	20.1	19.3	18.5	17.7	16.9	16.2	15.5	14.8	14.1	13.4
99	28.6	27.7	26.8	26.0	25.1	24.2	23.4	22.5	21.7	20.9	20.0	19.2	18.5	17.7	16.9	16.2	15.5	14.7	14.1	13.4
100	28.6	27.7	26.8	26.0	25.1	24.2	23.4	22.5	21.7	20.8	20.0	19.2	18.4	17.7	16.9	16.2	15.4	14.7	14.0	13.4
101	28.6	27.7	26.8	25.9	25.1	24.2	23.4	22.5	21.7	20.8	20.0	19.2	18.4	17.7	16.9	16.1	15.4	14.7	14.0	13.3
102	28.6	27.7	26.8	25.9	25.1	24.2	23.3	22.5	21.7	20.8	20.0	19.2	18.4	17.6	16.9	16.1	15.4	14.7	14.0	13.3
103	28.6	27.7	26.8	25.9	25.1	24.2	23.3	22.5	21.7	20.8	20.0	19.2	18.4	17.6	16.9	16.1	15.4	14.7	14.0	13.3
104	28.6	27.7	26.8	25.9	25.1	24.2	23.3	22.5	21.6	20.8	20.0	19.2	18.4	17.6	16.9	16.1	15.4	14.7	14.0	13.3
105	28.6	27.7	26.8	25.9	25.1	24.2	23.3	22.5	21.6	20.8	20.0	19.2	18.4	17.6	16.8	16.1	15.4	14.6	13.9	13.3
106	28.6	27.7	26.8	25.9	25.1	24.2	23.3	22.5	21.6	20.8	20.0	19.2	18.4	17.6	16.8	16.1	15.3	14.6	13.9	13.3
107	28.6	27.7	26.8	25.9	25.1	24.2	23.3	22.5	21.6	20.8	20.0	19.2	18.4	17.6	16.8	16.1	15.3	14.6	13.9	13.2
108	28.6	27.7	26.8	25.9	25.1	24.2	23.3	22.5	21.6	20.8	20.0	19.2	18.4	17.6	16.8	16.1	15.3	14.6	13.9	13.2
109	28.6	27.7	26.8	25.9	25.1	24.2	23.3	22.5	21.6	20.8	20.0	19.2	18.4	17.6	16.8	16.1	15.3	14.6	13.9	13.2
110	28.6	27.7	26.8	25.9	25.1	24.2	23.3	22.5	21.6	20.8	20.0	19.2	18.4	17.6	16.8	16.1	15.3	14.6	13.9	13.2
111	28.6	27.7	26.8	25.9	25.0	24.2	23.3	22.5	21.6	20.8	20.0	19.2	18.4	17.6	16.8	16.0	15.3	14.6	13.9	13.2
112	28.6	27.7	26.8	25.9	25.0	24.2	23.3	22.5	21.6	20.8	20.0	19.2	18.4	17.6	16.8	16.0	15.3	14.6	13.9	13.2
113	28.6	27.7	26.8	25.9	25.0	24.2	23.3	22.5	21.6	20.8	20.0	19.2	18.4	17.6	16.8	16.0	15.3	14.6	13.9	13.2
114	28.6	27.7	26.8	25.9	25.0	24.2	23.3	22.5	21.6	20.8	20.0	19.2	18.4	17.6	16.8	16.0	15.3	14.6	13.9	13.2
115	28.6	27.7	26.8	25.9	25.0	24.2	23.3	22.5	21.6	20.8	20.0	19.2	18.4	17.6	16.8	16.0	15.3	14.6	13.9	13.2

TABLE II (continued)
(Joint Life and Last Survivor Expectancy)

AGES	75	76	77	78	79	80	81	82	83	84	85	86	87	88	89	90	91	92	93	94
75	16.5	16.1	15.8	15.4	15.1	14.9	14.6	14.4	14.2	14.0										
76	16.1	15.7	15.4	15.0	14.7	14.4	14.1	13.9	13.7	13.5										
77	15.8	15.4	15.0	14.6	14.3	14.0	13.7	13.4	13.2	13.0										
78	15.4	15.0	14.6	14.2	13.9	13.5	13.2	13.0	12.7	12.5										
79	15.1	14.7	14.3	13.9	13.5	13.2	12.8	12.5	12.3	12.0										
80	14.9	14.4	14.0	13.5	13.2	12.8	12.5	12.2	11.9	11.6										
81	14.6	14.1	13.7	13.2	12.8	12.5	12.1	11.8	11.5	11.2										
82	14.4	13.9	13.4	13.0	12.5	12.2	11.8	11.5	11.1	10.9										
83	14.2	13.7	13.2	12.7	12.3	11.9	11.5	11.1	10.8	10.5										
84	14.0	13.5	13.0	12.5	12.0	11.6	11.2	10.9	10.5	10.2										
85	13.8	13.3	12.8	12.3	11.8	11.4	11.0	10.6	10.2	9.9	9.6	9.3	9.1	8.9	8.7	8.5	8.3	8.2	8.0	7.9
86	13.7	13.1	12.6	12.1	11.6	11.2	10.8	10.4	10.0	9.7	9.3	9.1	8.8	8.6	8.3	8.2	8.0	7.8	7.7	7.6
87	13.5	13.0	12.4	11.9	11.4	11.0	10.6	10.1	9.8	9.4	9.1	8.8	8.5	8.3	8.1	7.9	7.7	7.5	7.4	7.2
88	13.4	12.8	12.3	11.8	11.3	10.8	10.4	10.0	9.6	9.2	8.9	8.6	8.3	8.0	7.8	7.6	7.4	7.2	7.1	6.9
89	13.3	12.7	12.2	11.6	11.1	10.7	10.2	9.8	9.4	9.0	8.7	8.3	8.1	7.8	7.5	7.3	7.1	6.9	6.8	6.6
90	13.2	12.6	12.1	11.5	11.0	10.5	10.1	9.6	9.2	8.8	8.5	8.2	7.9	7.6	7.3	7.1	6.9	6.7	6.5	6.4
91	13.1	12.5	12.0	11.4	10.9	10.4	9.9	9.5	9.1	8.7	8.3	8.0	7.7	7.4	7.1	6.9	6.7	6.5	6.3	6.2
92	13.1	12.5	11.9	11.3	10.8	10.3	9.8	9.4	8.9	8.5	8.2	7.8	7.5	7.2	6.9	6.7	6.5	6.3	6.1	5.9
93	13.0	12.4	11.8	11.3	10.7	10.2	9.7	9.3	8.8	8.4	8.0	7.7	7.4	7.1	6.8	6.5	6.3	6.1	5.9	5.8
94	12.9	12.3	11.7	11.2	10.6	10.1	9.6	9.2	8.7	8.3	7.9	7.6	7.2	6.9	6.6	6.4	6.2	5.9	5.8	5.6
95	12.9	12.3	11.7	11.1	10.6	10.1	9.6	9.1	8.6	8.2	7.8	7.5	7.1	6.8	6.5	6.3	6.0	5.8	5.6	5.4
96	12.9	12.2	11.6	11.1	10.5	10.0	9.5	9.0	8.5	8.1	7.7	7.3	7.0	6.7	6.4	6.1	5.9	5.7	5.5	5.3
97	12.8	12.2	11.6	11.0	10.5	9.9	9.4	8.9	8.5	8.0	7.6	7.3	6.9	6.6	6.3	6.0	5.8	5.5	5.3	5.1
98	12.8	12.2	11.5	11.0	10.4	9.9	9.4	8.9	8.4	8.0	7.6	7.2	6.8	6.5	6.2	5.9	5.6	5.4	5.2	5.0
99	12.7	12.1	11.5	10.9	10.4	9.8	9.3	8.8	8.3	7.9	7.5	7.1	6.7	6.4	6.1	5.8	5.5	5.3	5.1	4.9
100	12.7	12.1	11.5	10.9	10.3	9.8	9.2	8.7	8.3	7.8	7.4	7.0	6.6	6.3	6.0	5.7	5.4	5.2	5.0	4.8
101	12.7	12.1	11.4	10.8	10.3	9.7	9.2	8.7	8.2	7.8	7.3	6.9	6.6	6.2	5.9	5.6	5.3	5.1	4.9	4.7
102	12.7	12.0	11.4	10.8	10.2	9.7	9.2	8.7	8.2	7.7	7.3	6.9	6.5	6.2	5.8	5.5	5.3	5.0	4.8	4.6
103	12.6	12.0	11.4	10.8	10.2	9.7	9.1	8.6	8.1	7.7	7.2	6.8	6.4	6.1	5.8	5.5	5.2	4.9	4.7	4.5
104	12.6	12.0	11.4	10.8	10.2	9.6	9.1	8.6	8.1	7.6	7.2	6.8	6.4	6.0	5.7	5.4	5.1	4.8	4.6	4.4
105	12.6	12.0	11.3	10.7	10.2	9.6	9.1	8.5	8.0	7.6	7.1	6.7	6.3	6.0	5.6	5.3	5.0	4.8	4.5	4.3
106	12.6	11.9	11.3	10.7	10.1	9.6	9.0	8.5	8.0	7.5	7.1	6.7	6.3	5.9	5.6	5.3	5.0	4.7	4.5	4.2
107	12.6	11.9	11.3	10.7	10.1	9.6	9.0	8.5	8.0	7.5	7.1	6.6	6.2	5.9	5.5	5.2	4.9	4.6	4.4	4.2
108	12.6	11.9	11.3	10.7	10.1	9.5	9.0	8.5	8.0	7.5	7.0	6.6	6.2	5.8	5.5	5.2	4.9	4.6	4.3	4.1
109	12.6	11.9	11.3	10.7	10.1	9.5	9.0	8.4	7.9	7.5	7.0	6.6	6.2	5.8	5.5	5.1	4.8	4.5	4.3	4.1
110	12.6	11.9	11.3	10.7	10.1	9.5	9.0	8.4	7.9	7.4	7.0	6.6	6.2	5.8	5.4	5.1	4.8	4.5	4.3	4.0
111	12.5	11.9	11.3	10.7	10.1	9.5	8.9	8.4	7.9	7.4	7.0	6.5	6.1	5.7	5.4	5.1	4.8	4.5	4.2	4.0
112	12.5	11.9	11.3	10.6	10.1	9.5	8.9	8.4	7.9	7.4	7.0	6.5	6.1	5.7	5.4	5.0	4.7	4.4	4.2	3.9
113	12.5	11.9	11.2	10.6	10.0	9.5	8.9	8.4	7.9	7.4	6.9	6.5	6.1	5.7	5.4	5.0	4.7	4.4	4.2	3.9
114	12.5	11.9	11.2	10.6	10.0	9.5	8.9	8.4	7.9	7.4	6.9	6.5	6.1	5.7	5.3	5.0	4.7	4.4	4.1	3.9
115	12.5	11.9	11.2	10.6	10.0	9.5	8.9	8.4	7.9	7.4	6.9	6.5	6.1	5.7	5.3	5.0	4.7	4.4	4.1	3.9

TABLE FOR DETERMINING APPLICABLE DIVISOR FOR MDIB*

(Minimum Distribution Incidental Benefit)

Age	Applicable divisor	Age	Applicable divisor
70	26.2	93	8.8
71	25.3	94	8.3
72	24.4	95	7.8
73	23.5	96	7.3
74	22.7	97	6.9
75	21.8	98	6.5
76	20.9	99	6.1
77	20.1	100	5.7
78	19.2	101	5.3
79	18.4	102	5.0
80	17.6	103	4.7
81	16.8	104	4.4
82	16.0	105	4.1
83	15.3	106	3.8
84	14.5	107	3.6
85	13.8	108	3.3
86	13.1	109	3.1
87	12.4	110	2.8
88	11.8	111	2.6
89	11.1	112	2.4
90	10.5	113	2.2
91	9.9	114	2.0
92	9.4	115 and older	1.8

*Use this table if your beneficiary is someone other than your spouse.

INDEX

❍ ❍ ❍